Diesel Dawn

Ireland's contribution to the development of the DMU 1931–1967

Colm Flanagan

COLOURPOINT

About the Author

Colm Flanagan comes from Ballywalter in County Down and became interested in trains at seven years of age, as a result of a Christmas present of a Hornby Dublo train set! Later this interest widened to include public transport – his father was a UTA bus manager – but railways retained their 'top spot'. Colm is professionally involved in sound system design, recording and broadcasting. He has previously contributed articles on Irish railways for magazines such as *Backtrack* and *Modern Railways*.

6 5 4 3 2 1

Designed by Colourpoint Books
Printed by W & G Baird Ltd

ISBN 1 904242 08 1

Colourpoint Books
Unit D5, Ards Business Centre
Jubilee Road
Newtownards
County Down
Northern Ireland
BT23 4YH
Tel: 028 9182 0505
Fax: 028 9182 1900
E-mail: info@colourpoint.co.uk
Web-site: www.colourpoint.co.uk

Cover Pictures

Front

The Belfast to Bangor line of the UTA was the first significant railway in the UK to be wholly dieselised. A UTA MED train pulls away from Holywood station in 1957, made up of six vehicles in different variations of the UTA livery. At the rear is early power car No 12 in 'original' condition. Next to it is a trailer recently converted from a non-corridor carriage.
Colour-Rail

Rear

Upper: *After the winding up of the Great Northern Railway Board in 1958 and its division between CIE and the UTA, some of its pioneering railcars found little employment, being underpowered for main line work and with insufficient capacity for city/suburban work. By June 1961 the rural lines they worked had by now been mostly closed and so Ex-GNR C2 (nearest the camera) and C1 were stored out of use at Dundalk pending scrapping.*
JD Fitzgerald

Lower: *In 1957 the UTA began to produce its most hi-tech railcar type, the Multi Purpose Diesel, designed for main line services to Londonderry. A test train comprised of the first two MPD cars. 36 and 37, is seen at York Road in October 1957.*
WE Robertson, Colour-Rail

Contents

A UTA publicity photograph showing the fleet of new Multi-Engined Diesel trains at Queens Quay, Belfast, in April 1954 (see also page 89).

DJA Young collection

Introduction

Some years ago my interest in the Irish railway scene of the 1950s and 1960s was re-kindled by a conversation in which a friend from school days recalled the formation of the Coleraine Inst Railway Society. I was one of a 'triumvirate' (we learnt Latin in those days) – three schoolboys in the lower sixth form who felt that we wanted to spread our interest in railways – both real thing and model. At the time I was more interested in modelling the GWR in England (an interest which is now non-existent, I may add) and so the finer points of MPDs and MEDs, which I travelled on regularly in those days, passed me by. How much easier those chapters of this book would have been if I'd had a good camera and notebook with me on my journeys to and from York Road.

At that time we were interested in diesel railcars, despite my friend Russell Currie describing them in his book on the NCC, published in 1972, as "noisy, unreliable and evil smelling". I think that was on a particularly bad day – and Russell was never one to understate anything! We had even proposed the formation of a preservation society back in 1967, to preserve and run the pioneer NCC diesel railcars 1 and 4 on the then almost defunct Portrush branch. The 'North Atlantic Railway Preservation Society' – for so it was to be called – never got off the ground. Thankfully, No 1 has been (almost) preserved. But no representative of any of the other major railcar types in this book have been, although one or two trailers have been reconverted to steam haulage for RPSI specials, and one still exists, albeit in much altered form, at Downpatrick.

This is a shame. Part of the problem was blue asbestos (see chapter 8) which made preservation too expensive. However, without the AECs and BUTs of the GNR and the MEDs and MPDs of the UTA, I doubt if any railways in Northern Ireland would exist today, except possibly the Dublin line for inter-city traffic.

Lest we should be quick to judge some of these cars (the MPDs in particular) as failures, it is interesting to note that a recent state-of-the-art type of British DMU, introduced only four or five years ago, required re-engining of the entire class after less than three years!

Most railway enthusiasts turned their backs on the diesels too. Literally, in many cases. The articles of the time frequently contained phrases such as "the following train was a railcar and so of little interest". Russell's scathing comments on them in 1972 were not unique. But it does mean that data on comparative running, etc, is virtually impossible to find. Added to an official attitude which was usually disinterested (with a few honourable exceptions) and at worse downright obstructive, it is no wonder that most diesel units passed to the scrapyard unrecorded and unloved. I would have liked to include comparative runs and such like with different types of units, but this has proved impossible. Perhaps someone will one day come across a treasure trove of such material. Sadly, I have not.

So, today, the machines which are descendants of the railcars described in the following chapters hold sway over large sections of mainline railways in the British Isles, other than electrified lines. The 'Virgin Voyager' is in many respects a synthesis of the two strands in UTA railcar development – it has underfloor engines but electric drive. It is admittedly in a different league of performance and development from its '70' class and MPD forbears, and a far cry from its ancestor, GNR Railcar B! NIR is due to take delivery of a fleet of brand new underfloor-engined railcars next year.Even the Republic of Ireland, where locomotive-hauled mainline trains have held sway since the 1960s, may be seeing a change of policy that will see many more railcars there, even on main lines.

One final point should be noted. The role of the GNR and UTA in the development of the Modernisation Plan DMUs of British Railways has never been properly acknowledged. I believe it is time to put this right. A number of those I spoke to while writing this book, told of visits to and from works in England in the early 1950s. There were visits to places such as York Road by men from BR, both on the traffic side and the engineering side. It seems clear to me that the knowledge gained here was exported – one only has to compare the specifications of the 'Derby Lightweights' in particular, with those of the UTA Multi Engined Diesel railcars to discover that there are only a few significant mechanical differences.

This in turn means that large sections of the railways in Britain owe their continuing existence to those Irish pioneers, often starved of funding, who developed the multiple unit railcar on these shores. I believe we Irish enthusiasts should be proud of their story, which is worth telling in full. I hope I have done them all – named and anonymous - justice.

Colm Flanagan
Ballywalter
2003

Acknowledgements

Many people gave of their time and experiences to help me in the writing of this book; it wouldn't have been possible without them and any errors are my own!

Ian Sinclair put me in touch with photographers such as Richard Whitford and Derek Young, whose colour pictures have added so much to the book. As I have only a tiny photographic collection their help was essential! Charles Friel cheerfully allowed me to plunder his large black and white collection, including that of the late Dr EM Patterson, whose detailed pictures of UTA units proved invaluable. John Edgington and Colin Boocock helped also, as did Jonathan Allen, Martin Baumann and Desmond Coakham. Jim Hunter provided some photos and also lent me an original maker's plate of NCC railcar No 1.

My publisher, Norman Johnston, was able to access the Colour-Rail collection for early colour photographs and also found photographs of the British Railways units. In that particular connection I must mention Stuart McKay of the Railcar Association in the UK, whose detailed information on British Railway's first generation railcars, much of it available on their website www.railcar.co.uk, was of great value.

The Topley brothers, Joyce and Norman, were particularly helpful in regard to the GNR railcars, while Stan Myers provided some fascinating material on railcar development and drawings of the MPD cars. Other drawings came from a variety of sources although many have their origins in the UTA's drawings from the period.

Billy McCormick provided me with useful magazine material, as did Sean Martin of Ballymena who turned up an article on the introduction of the MPDs, which I had almost given up hope of obtaining. Frank Dunlop spent many hours with me explaining some of the operational aspects of the UTA's railcars.

My friend Edmund Calvert-Harrison lent me working documents relating to the NCC railcars and also some work he had done on MEDs and the like. Kay Coulthard, wife of the late John Coulthard, the last railway manager under the UTA, kindly gave me access to his papers. Walter Burke turned up some useful material on the early County Down diesel engines, and Ian Sinclair gave me access to interviews conducted with some now deceased railwaymen who had first hand knowledge of NCC and UTA railcar development.

I was able to make use of the facilities provided by the PRO(NI) and the Ulster Folk and Transport Museum. I consulted articles from many railway magazines, especially the IRRS Journal which contains the October 1965 article by LW Stafford, UTA development engineer at that time – 'base camp' for any student of UTA diesels, and also the Irish Railfans News, Railway Magazine, Trains Illustrated, and The Engineer.

The lists of individual railcar vehicles is, I hope, the fullest and most accurate yet published to date, and is the work largely of Norman Johnston and Martin Baumann, who have followed the torturous story of modifications and so on with great patience. Colin Holliday provided vital information for the CIÉ list and Michael Stevenson for the GNR, whilst Alan McFerran and Michael Pollard are due thanks for proof reading the final drafts.

1

The Irish narrow gauge 1931–51

If one could make use of a time machine, it might be an interesting experience to go back in time to 1925 for a run on the Castlederg & Victoria Bridge Tramway's latest technological marvel.

We would be sitting in a garden shed-like wooden vehicle as we progress erratically along the line, reaching the giddy speed of 30 mph (though not on the corners!), the smell of paraffin in our nostrils, the whole vehicle shuddering from the vibration of the solidly mounted Fordson tractor engine up front.

Would we ever imagine that the descendants of this rattling contraption would sweep along mainline tracks at 125 mph, providing their passengers with air-conditioned comfort, and a well stocked on-board shop? Probably not, yet there is a link which connects the CVBT mobile shed of 1925 with the Virgin Voyagers of today.

The idea of traction that would be cheaper and more versatile than the traditional steam locomotive hauling non-powered coaches had long exercised the minds of railway managements. Various weird machines had been placed on tracks all over Great Britain since the internal combustion engine, usually petrol powered, had made its appearance. Many of these were of course little more than adapted road vehicles, but these are not the main subject of this book, though their development continued on and off until the early 1980s.

Here in Northern Ireland one of the last railbuses to be built still operates on part of the old Belfast and County Down Railway, operated by the Downpatrick Railway Society. The petrol (or diesel) powered railbus was always going to be very much a 'niche' product – and it could be

argued that if traffic was so light as to make one of these machines sufficient, why not simply leave the bus on the road?

One brand of railway management in Ireland had more reason than most to greet the 'new' form of traction with alacrity. Narrow gauge lines in many cases had struggled to make ends meet from their inception. As far as can be ascertained, the first non-petrol-powered passenger railway vehicle to run in Ireland was the one described above, on the little-known Castlederg and Victoria Bridge Tramway, a 7¼ mile roadside-based line which linked the town of Castlederg to the GNR at Victoria Bridge station. It finally closed to traffic in 1933 as an early casualty of changing travel patterns and rural economics. The CVBT was a steam-powered operation, of course, but in

The Castlederg & Victoria Bridge paraffin railcar lying out of use in Castlederg yard in August 1930. The 20 bhp engine had been mounted on the metal frame protruding from the bodywork and was sold to a local sawmill. The railcar was sold to County Donegal in due course, and, with a new body, finished its railway career in 1959.

HC Casserley 7021

the 1920s it began to suffer badly from road competition. The company's own Locomotive Superintendent, a Mr Pollard, designed a railcar and had it built in the company's own workshops. He is reported to have been helped by a carpenter and a blacksmith, and in 1925 this unusual contraption was placed on the rails.

It was a utilitarian vehicle in the extreme; the body was oblong, with a long overhang over the four-wheel chassis at each end. The windows were small and set high in the sides – in fact the machine had a strong resemblance to a garden shed on wheels with the engine bonnet sticking out of one end! The unit contained 24 wooden seats and could be driven from either end. Power was provided by a Fordson 20-bhp engine which burned paraffin, and there was a four-speed forward and reverse gearbox which drove all four wheels via chain drive (this seems to have worked remarkably well). The railcar weighed ten tons and was reported to be capable of 30 mph on the level, though the 20-bhp motor struggled on some upgrades. It was unwise to try to take corners at this breakneck speed, however, and drivers were asked to drive it at a 'moderate' rate! Its main weakness seems to have been that the lubrication system found steep gradients hard to cope with. Oil often drained to one end of the crankcase resulting in the No 1 piston running dry!

Nevertheless the railcar remained in service for three years and covered 30,000 miles until Christmas 1928 when it was withdrawn. The engine was removed. The remains lay at the back of the locomotive works at Castlederg and it never ran again under CVBT ownership. However, it was bought by the County Donegal Railway in August 1934. It was fitted with a petrol engine and a new body, becoming that company's No 2. In 1944 the engine was removed and it finished its life as an unpowered trailer car.

The Castlederg and Victoria Bridge Tramway may therefore be considered for the honour of being the 'first specifically designed non-petrol railcar'! It was not a diesel in the technical sense of the term (see Appendix 3). The paraffin engine still required an electric ignition system to initiate combustion, although paraffin (or lamp oil) will run in a diesel, albeit for a limited period.

It was to be the application of the true diesel engine in a passenger carrying vehicle which was the path most railways in Ireland were to follow. One of the first enthusiasts for this form of traction was Henry Forbes, the energetic Manager of the County Donegal Railways Joint Committee. In 1906 the ailing County Donegal company had been jointly taken over by the Midland Railway and the GNRI. As road traffic increased during the 1920s, Forbes believed that to survive, the company must look to more economical forms of passenger traction for the widely scattered population of Donegal served by the railway.

There were a number of earlier efforts with petrol-driven railbuses, but in 1931 the Great Northern's works at Dundalk constructed, for the CDR, what became railcars 7 and 8. These were the first true diesel-engined railcars to operate in the British Isles. A 74 bhp Gardner engine was chosen, this also powering many of the company's bus fleet. Maximum speed was quoted as 43 mph – a figure typical of the pre-war railcar scene. The engine was mounted at the front under a long 'bonnet', and drove a four-wheel bogie under the rear passenger section. The bodywork was built by O'Dohertys, a firm of coach builders in Strabane, and could seat 32 people. Entry was by a front door opposite the driver's seat on one side, and a rear door on the other side. No 7 was first into service in June 1931, followed in November by No 8. Both were withdrawn in 1949.

Some miles south and east of County Donegal was the Clogher Valley Railway. This was a mainly roadside line which meandered through a number of towns in the southern part of Northern Ireland, between Maguiresbridge in County Fermanagh and Tynan in County Armagh, a distance by rail of some 37 miles.

Like so many other narrow gauge railways in the north of Ireland, the Clogher Valley hit disastrous financial troubles in the 1920s and a government enquiry decided to run this ailing concern by means of a committee of management set up by

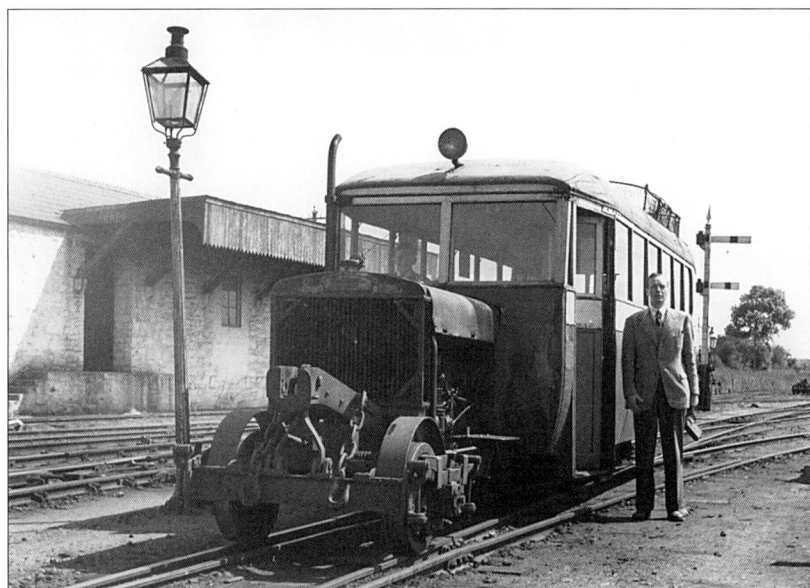

Tyrone and Fermanagh County Councils. They appointed Henry Forbes of the CDR as a representative and he set in train a number of innovations. The first was not a success: a Sentinel style steam tramway engine was ordered from Atkinson Walker but when it arrived it was found to be 'virtually useless'. Efforts to improve its performance came to nothing and the machine was finally left out of use at the locomotive shed at Aughnacloy. Fortunately the Clogher Valley had not actually purchased it, and the builders went out of business in the interim. It was sold to the CDR in 1932 and we will meet this machine again later.

The second experiment in cost cutting was to prove much more successful. Indeed, it might be seen as an early version of the multi-purpose diesel concept pursued by the UTA some 25 years later. Forbes had been involved with the first diesel railcars on the Donegal Railway and he commissioned a new design using this form of traction. The power unit of this new railcar was designed and built by the firm of Walkers of Wigan (who were to feature significantly in many other early railcar projects). In 1932 the firm delivered a traction unit, based on the Gardner 6L$_2$ 74-bhp engine, onto which was articulated a passenger body built by the GNR at Dundalk

works. In true cost-cutting fashion – we shall meet this theme in Irish railway life again and again – a bogie from a withdrawn coach was used to carry the rear of the passenger accommodation.

The new railcar was a much more sophisticated machine than its predecessors on the County Donegal. The power unit was mounted on its own bogie, with four coupled wheels driven from the engine. Immediately behind the driver's cab (which was of a design very similar to contemporary buses) were double entrance doors leading to a bus-like body seating 29, which had a further four-wheel bogie towards the rear. As the overhang at the rear was now much reduced, the riding qualities of the vehicle were substantially improved, and the bogie construction meant that sharp curves were less likely to cause derailments. Although the power unit had its own brakes, its braking power was limited and the railcar always ran with a brake van attached, to assist with braking and to convey luggage, light goods and parcels.

This unit, delivered in December 1932, proved most successful, so much so that a second one was proposed in 1933. However, funds proved to be a problem, and an ingenious solution was found. Instead of a full railcar, a second traction unit,

Clogher Valley Railway railcar No 1 was the first Irish product from Walkers of Wigan, who were instrumental in the development of the type which later dominated the County Donegal Railway. It was introduced in 1932 and was sold to the CDR on closure of the CVR in 1941.

Real Photographs X6527

A year later Walkers supplied a 'rail lorry' which used a similar power bogie to the railcar and was interchangeable with it. A number of CVR coaches were converted to electric lighting to run with the diesel units. The rail lorry unit was also sold to the Co Donegal although it never ran there in that form, being used as a spare unit for the Donegal's railcar fleet. In this undated photo, the lorry is on a passenger working, approaching Aughnacloy.

Real Photographs X6525

The ex Clogher Valley railcar as CDR No 10 at Stranorlar in April 1955. Seating just 29, it was the smallest of the CDR articulated railcars. It is now preserved at the Ulster Folk and Transport Museum.

Kelland collection 24141

identical to the first, was ordered and delivered in September 1933. This could be used a spare and brought into service when the first one was being serviced or had a breakdown. But having a spare unit doing nothing for any length of time was not an idea which found favour with the cash-strapped management of the CVR. So a removable wagon body was built which meant that the second unit could be used as a self-propelled goods vehicle. It was also found to have sufficient power to pull a coach and wagon or two, and so it was variously used as a spare passenger traction unit, self-propelled goods unit, or locomotive – not bad for a 74-bhp diesel engine!

Together the two diesel units made a great difference to the quality of service on the Clogher Valley and both worked until the line was closed in December 1941. They were both sold to the County Donegal Railway where the railcar become No 10 and worked until the closure of the line. It is now preserved in the Ulster Folk and Transport Museum at Cultra near Belfast, though it is thought that the actual power unit there may be the lorry one! The diesel 'lorry' did not run on the CDR as such but was used as a spare traction unit for the CDR railcars.

The economies of diesel operation were most attractive to the cash-starved managements of Ireland's smaller railways and prime in the field

was the County Donegal. Though the CVBT was the first in the field, the CDR undoubtedly led the way in the 1930s, so much so that, by the end of the World War Two, virtually the entire network was operated by diesel (and a few older petrol) railcars. The County Donegal was able to call on the expertise of both the LMS(NCC) and GNR, though the relationship with the latter's Dundalk works seemed to have been closer.

A series of railcars were to follow, beginning with No 12, produced in 1934. The articulated power unit was built again by Walkers of Wigan and was similar to that of the Clogher Valley machine with which Forbes had been impressed. The body was constructed in the GNR works at Dundalk, as were all future ones. However, the County Donegal unit was capable of carrying a significantly greater payload of 41 passengers. Others followed over the next six years, each similar in size and using the same engine, until No 16, the engine of which was an uprated Gardner 6LW of 102 bhp. The system of four coupled wheels was retained. The half-cab front changed with the arrival of No 15, which had a full width cab, although still with the protruding bonnet. One feature of these railcars was that they frequently ran with the bonnet wings open, to assist ventilation. Railcars 17 and 18, dating from 1939 and 1940 respectively, could hold two

County Donegal railcar No 12, location & date unknown. With this railcar the familiar layout of engine mounted on an articulated unit and the rear carried on a separate bogie, became the standard for all succeeding narrow gauge diesel railcars. No 12 survives, in working order at the Foyle Valley Railway Museum in Londonderry.

CP Friel collection

County Donegal Railway railcars 15 and 16 at Stranorlar in 1954. These were mechanically identical to the earlier railcars, but the cab was extended across the full width of the body, giving a more 'modern' appearance, though the engine still protruded. No 18, very similar in appearance, has been preserved in running order. Until recently it was at the Foyle Valley Museum but in early 2003 was moved to Fintown.

Photomatic 188

more passengers than the earlier units. No 18 has fortunately been preserved, as well as No 12.

The type reached its final development on the narrow gauge in 1950–1 with the delivery of the last two articulated railcars, again using the Gardner engine. Numbered 19 and 20, they looked much more 'modern', having totally enclosed engines, although they were mechanically the same as the earlier units. They were sold to the Isle of Man Railway on the closure of the County Donegal in 1959 and remain there still. There is some hope that a long restoration process will eventually lead to their running again.

These railcars proved a great success. Without them there is no doubt that the County Donegal would not have survived as long as it did. One (No 17) was destroyed in a collision with a steam train in 1949 – the driver of the railcar and two passengers were killed, in what was a relatively low-speed accident. If it happened today, it would undoubtedly have raised question marks over their crash worthiness – the lightweight construction needed to make the most of the available power meant that they did not have great structural integrity in the case of a severe collision. The braking ability of some of these railcars was always suspect – conversely, lack of adhesion under power sometimes led to them slipping badly under poor conditions. But this was considered a minor issue in an era where 'safety issues' were rarely allowed to stop innovation – and the railcars were statistically a much safer means of transport than the road buses they so resembled!

County Donegal Railway railcar No19 with three wagons at Strabane. This car and its sister, No 20, were the final development of the type. Both were sold to the Isle of Man Railway in 1960 and are still there, and being restored to working order. Walkers of Wigan built a number of similar machines for the West Clare Railway in 1952 and for the Victoria State Railways in Australia.

Author's collection

2 Railcars on the GNRI 1932–38

Whilst the narrow gauge railways in Northern Ireland may have led the way into diesel traction, it was not long before engineers and management on standard gauge lines also began to pursue experiments into diesel traction.

In Ireland, with its small, widely scattered population, and many meandering branch lines, economies in operation had long been thought desirable. Both the LMS(NCC) and GNR produced 'railbuses' – literally buses which ran on tracks. These are described in Chapter Four and in fact were mostly introduced after the prototype railcars described here. In the early 1930s both the GNR and NCC began planning 'proper' diesel trains which would have more capacity and be more flexible in operation – the railcar concept had arrived.

The Great Northern's first 'true' railcar appeared in July 1932. The design brief was for a bogie vehicle capable of 50 mph on the level, reducing to 40 mph if hauling a loaded wagon, or 35 mph if pulling two. The GNR called this machine 'A' and it was 40 feet long, with a driving cab at each end – unlike most of the narrow gauge railcars. 'A' was constructed to mainline standards. It had full-length frames, buffers, drawgear and railway-style seats. There was provision for 32 passengers seated in 2+2 configuration (two seats either side of the central passageway), all seats facing the same way. There were doors at either end of the passenger compartment and eight bus-like windows down each side. There was no guard's section as such, but at the engine end opposite the driver was a compartment which presumably could be used by him. A livery of Oxford blue and cream was adopted for this machine and all subsequent railcars, similar to that carried by the company's

bus fleet. A large red 'A' on each side identified it. Initially 'A' had a 6-cylinder AEC engine which developed 130 bhp, and there was a large AEC radiator at the engine end. The engine was mounted vertically on one bogie, driving both axles through a mechanical gearbox and fluid coupling, and the bogie wheel base was 6'6" with 3'5" wheels. The weight of railcar 'A' was 18¾ tons, giving a power/weight ratio (with original engine) of 6.9bhp/ton.

The idea behind railcar 'A' has been recently unearthed by research in the IRRS archives in Dublin, where drawings of a 'light diesel car' to seat 32 people formed part of a submission to the board of the GNR by the then chief engineer Glover. The latter believed that such a railcar could cover an ambitious daily routine, helping speed up steam expresses by operating as a stopping train on the main line, as well as filling in on other lines. Railcar 'A', as finally turned out a year later, bore a strong resemblance to the subject of these plans, though longer, heavier

GNR Diesel Railcar 'A'. It was introduced in 1932 and seated 32 passengers, with a top speed of 50 mph. 'A' proved to be very long lived; it was not withdrawn from passenger service until 1964, and then mainly because of accident damage.

CP Friel collection

GNR diesel electric railcar 'B' at Scarva. It had a much shorter working life than its sister 'A'. The shortcomings of the electric drive motors led to its withdrawal in 1949 but the body and underframe were used as a hauled coach for a time.

Real Photographs X124

and with greater seating capacity.

A few months later a second railcar – 'B' – appeared. On the surface this seemed a repeat of 'A', apart from being two feet longer, but there was a significant mechanical difference because 'B' used a revolutionary form of drive – diesel-electric. A 120-bhp Gleniffer engine and a Tilling Stevens generator drove an electric motor which powered one axle of the leading bogie. This arrangement made it heavier – 'B' weighed

21 tons. It was also two feet longer and the power bogie had a 8'0" wheelbase. 'B' was one of the first railcars in the British Isles to use diesel-electric drive (but see page 39) and was thus the ancestor of diesel trains such as the 'Hastings' type on British Railways, and the later Blue Pullmans, HSTs and even Virgin Voyagers! A year later, in June 1933, Harland and Wolff's 'D1', the first diesel-electric locomotive in the British Isles, made its inaugural run on the Belfast and County Down Railway.

Railcars 'A' and 'B' both went into service in the Portadown area and were regularly on the Scarva branch. Seating was later altered to 3+2 with front seats facing forwards and the rear ones backwards: This gave 'A' 50 seats (later reduced to 48 – as seen on page 16) and 'B' 40 seats. Some years later 'A' received a 102-bhp Gardner 6LW engine, a type being used with great success on the narrow gauge. At the same time the AEC radiator was removed and new roof mounted ones fitted, and steps were added for use at level crossings.

This rebuilt railcar became 101 under the UTA after 1958. It was based at Londonderry and used on locals to Strabane and Omagh. In the summer of 1962 it was re-engined and re-painted into UTA Brunswick green livery. It had been destined

Continued on Page 18.

For many years both 'A' and 'B' worked on the Scarva Banbridge branch line; here 'A' waits for passengers from a connecting service at the Banbridge end of the line. By now the original AEC engine had been replaced by a Gardner diesel similar to those in use on the Co. Donegal, and steps fitted for use at level crossing stops.

J Pollock collection

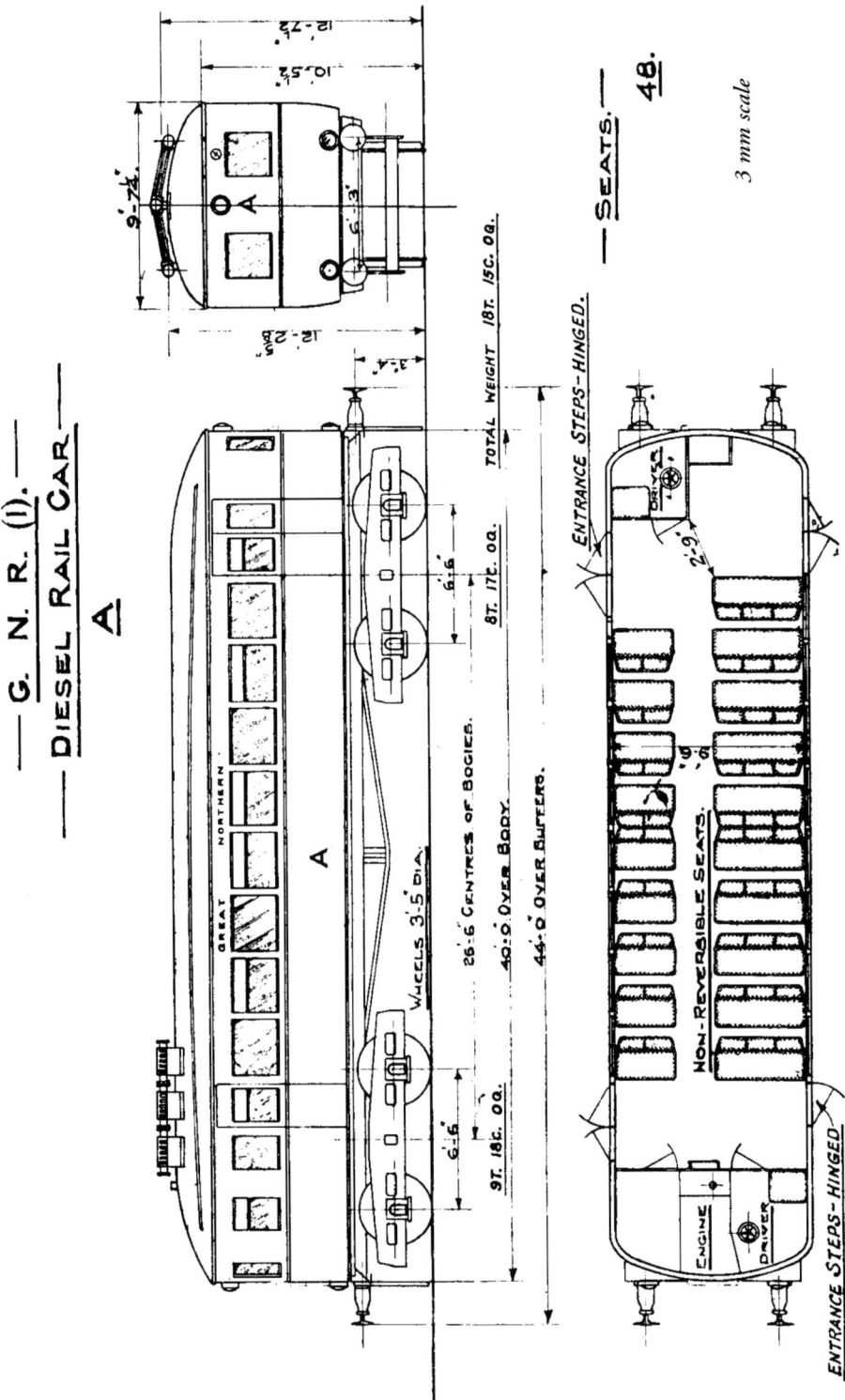

G. N. R. (I).

DIESEL RAIL CAR

A

SEATS. **48.**

3 mm scale

GNRI railcar 'A' with 3+2 seating after modification to Gardner engine in 1940.
The addition of a double door on one side probably led to the seating being reduced from 50 to 48.

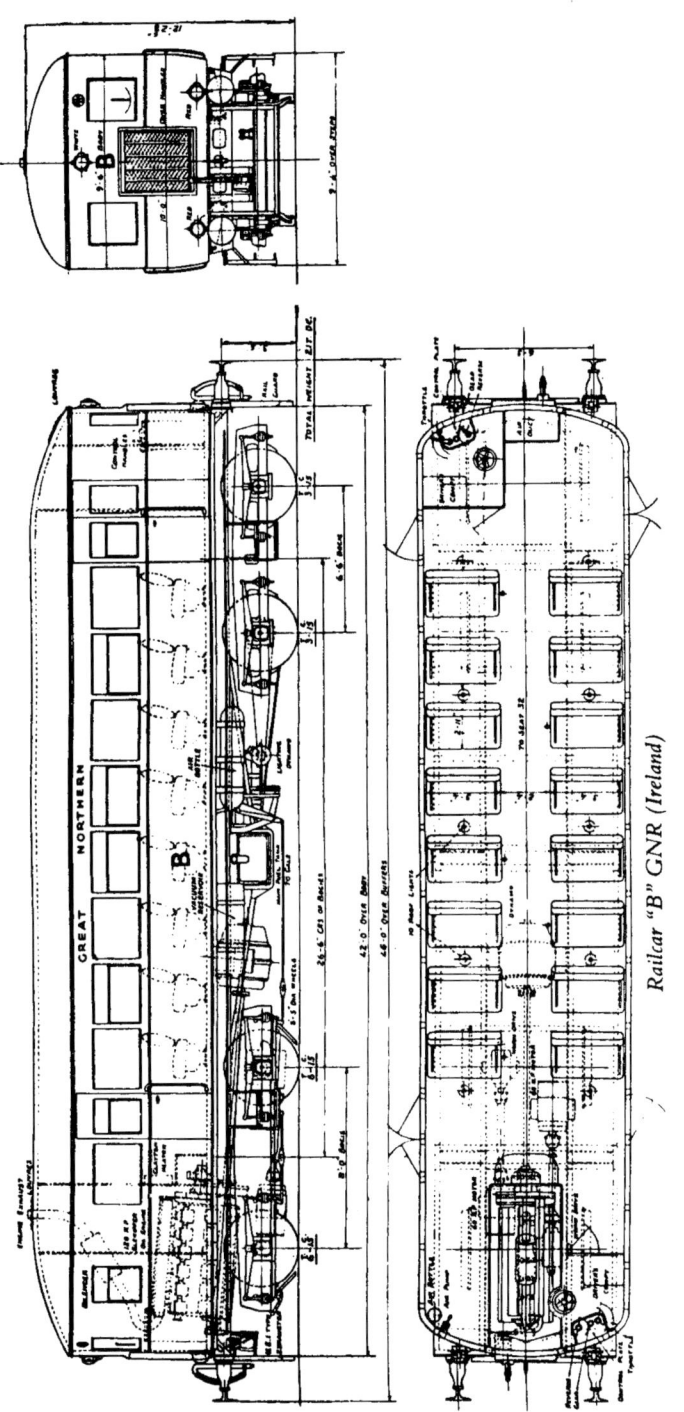

3 mm scale

Railcar "B" GNR (Ireland)

GNRI railcar 'B' as built with 2+2 seating. This was also the original seating arrangement of 'A'.

Railcar 'A' as UTA 101. For some years 'A' continued to wear the GNR livery of Oxford Blue and cream (as did most of the other GNR railcars). It was to be re-engined and repainted in 1962.

D Anderson

UTA railcar 101 at Porthall, Co Donegal, one of the stations on the GNR 'Derry Road' which was in the Republic of Ireland. The UTA used 101 on local services on the Derry Road, chiefly between Strabane and Derry, where it received the damage that was ultimately to lead to its withdrawal.

EM Patterson

for the Transport Museum but sustained serious damage to its bodywork in a shunting accident in October 1963, and was withdrawn in 1964 after a long and successful life for such an early vehicle. It was sold to the contractor lifting the Clonsilla Junction–Navan railway, and then later worked on the contractor's lifting train on the Derry Road (1966–67), after which it was stored at Portadown until 1970, when it was finally disposed of.

Railcar 'B' had a much shorter working life. Its experimental diesel-electric drive proved unreliable. The chief engineer, GT Glover, had seen an electric motor at an engineering show in England and had been very impressed, so 'B' had this fitted. However, it was underpowered for the work needed and it frequently overheated. The diesel generator was very heavy on the springs, and as time passed parts became difficult to get. The GNR preferred Gardner power units, and one of these was subsequently fitted in place of the

Gleniffer unit. Railcar 'B' was taken out of passenger service during the war, although in 1942 it was put to use on the Dublin–Belfast newspaper trains. In October 1946 the engine was removed and it became carriage No 500, where it was used on the Irish North West section until withdrawn in 1949. It lay out of use for some years before final scrapping.

The next railcar emerged in November 1934. 'C' was somewhat larger and had its 96-bhp Gardner engine mounted in a forward compartment (the GNR used Gardner engines in many of its road fleet). The passenger compartment was articulated using a bellows arrangement and a door. This was a similar arrangement to that being used on the County Donegal Railway, for whom the GNR had built No 12 earlier that year. Like the Donegal and Clogher Valley railcars, the four-wheel coupled power bogie was built by Walkers of Wigan. The wheel base was 7'3" and the top speed was 46 mph. The driver sat on the right of the engine and saw out of five curved windows.

Unlike the earlier cars, 'C' was single-ended. It had to be turned at each terminus although photographs show a curved rear end to the passenger compartment, perhaps evidence that there was some thought of making it double-ended.. The passenger compartment had 50 seats, 44 of these in bus-type seats arranged 2+2 and facing towards the front of the railcar (the driver's end); six seats were arranged as a horseshoe type seat at the rear. Doors were in the centre and at the passenger end, with steps to rail level. The windows had an unusual curved top frame which was also found on CDR No 14. The railcar was of lightweight bus-like construction. It was just over 48 feet long, but only 8'0" wide (compared to an average carriage width of 9'6") and weighed only 14 tons. This gave a bhp/ton ratio of 6.86/1.

A fuel consumption of 12 miles per gallon was achieved from this railcar, which was used on Bundoran–Enniskillen service. The main problem with it was that, having only one cab, it had to be turned at each end of the journey but this was less of a problem on a 43-mile cross-country run than on a short branch. Railcar 'C' went to CIÉ in 1958. It ran for a while in 1959 on a mail service between Dundalk and Cavan. After that, CIÉ could find little use for it and it

Railcar 'C' at Dundalk. This was the first GNR diesel railcar with an articulated layout. Unlike 'A' and 'B' it had a cab at only one end, but this was not considered to be a problem, operationally, as most termini had turntables anyway.

Duffner W84

Interior view of railcar 'C' at the time of its introduction to service in 1934.

Duffner W81

Right: *GNR railbus 'C' – now renumbered 'C1'. The driver looks back as he leaves it at Bundoran Junction in June 1950. The railcar has just worked the 6.15pm from Omagh. Possibly the fact that they required turning after each run meant that 'C1' and her near sisters 'C2' and 'C3', (unlike the earlier 'A' and later D-G) found little employment after the dissolution of the GNR.*

TJ Edgington 780

Opposite: *Railcar 'C2'+'C3'. With the arrival of these two railcars in 1935, very similar in design to 'C', the GNR had a two car diesel train with much increased capacity. However, the practice of hauling one unit "dead" was not a success and they spent most of their working lives separated. These GNR designs do not seem to have found much favour with their final owners, CIÉ or UTA. They were out of use for long periods and none survived to work into the 1960s.*

Duffner W85

was withdrawn in 1961.

The use of diesel railcar traction for little-used narrow gauge lines, or country branches, may have provided the impetus for initial development but it was inevitable that efforts would soon be made to try out the new system for suburban traffic. There would be all the usual advantages operationally and commercially. However, capacity would have to be greatly increased but how was this to be achieved? Could units run in multiple? On the NCC, special lightweight trailers were to be tried and we shall follow their progress later.

The GNR decided to adopt a different approach and built two more railcars of similar design to 'C'. These would run back-to-back, thus providing extra seating and obviating the need for turning or running round at termini – very desirable on an intensive suburban timetable. 'C2' and 'C3' emerged in June 1935 and were put to work as a two-coach train on the Dublin–Howth service with some runs to Balbriggan. They had the same major dimensions as 'C' (which became 'C1'), each weighing slightly more at 15 tons. The passenger ends were flat rather than curved to facilitate coupling up, though there was no corridor connection between the two units.

'C2' had a guard's compartment and seated 52 third class passengers (four seats were removed in 1940 to increase luggage space). C3 could seat 32 third with eight second class at the rear and six first class passengers in a small saloon in the centre – a total of 98 people in the set. Both cars were mechanically similar to 'C' but each had the slightly more powerful Gardner 6LW rated at 102 bhp, capable of 48 mph. As there was no method of controlling both engines from one end, only the power bogie of the leading unit was used, the other being left in neutral and pulled along.

The operation of 'C2' and 'C3' as a two-coach set was not considered a success for two main reasons. Firstly there was wear on the transmissions from being dragged regularly. Secondly, the power/weight ratio as a two-car set was unfavourable. The weight of 30 tons being powered by 102 bhp gave a ratio of only 3.4 bhp/ton which compared poorly with the earlier cars or even the NCC vehicles with a trailer. As a result, they were separated in 1937. They ran hence as two units, mainly on the Irish North Western section of GNR, frequently pulling small specially built 2.5-ton luggage wagons, similar to practice on the Sligo Leitrim Railway.

In 1958, after the breakup of the GNR, 'C2' went to CIÉ. It lay idle for many years before

Railcar 'C2' interior. *Duffner W80*

being finally scrapped. 'C3' went to the UTA and became their No 102. It was never repainted and lay derelict at Adelaide yard for two years before being finally scrapped at Queen's Quay in 1961.

While the GNR continued to build articulated railcars for the CDRJC, as noted earlier, engineers and traffic officials realised that this type had limited potential for development, so after the 'C' series they moved to a different configuration.

In May and June 1936 respectively the next two railcars, 'D' and 'E', emerged from the works. From the start they were planned as self-contained trains suitable for suburban use, with a driving cab at each end. These two railcars had a central engine compartment, with articulated passenger saloons on each side. A larger engine was required for this, and the GNR stuck with Gardner, this time the engine chosen being the 6L3 which developed 153 bhp at 1200 rpm. As stated earlier, the cooling radiators of both these cars and the following pair were roof mounted.

The transmission was via a fluid flywheel and Wilson four-speed epicyclic gearbox. This allowed for automatic gear changing, the first such application by the GNR. There was electro-pneumatic remote control for gearbox and the reverse box.

The engine section length was 16'5½" over body; it was mounted on a six-coupled chassis, with wheels 3'0" in diameter and a wheel base of 7'3"+ 7'3". The body was divided into two parts, one of which contained the engine, compressor and dynamo and the other the gearbox and reverse box. As in many later railcars, this was in effect a separate unit from the gearbox and, in the case of these GNR cars, had a three-position pin which could be locked in forward, neutral or reverse. The compartment was also intended to serve as guard's accommodation, and was connected by a corridor to the rest of the train (though access was for crew only). However, there is evidence that guards disliked this

Railcar 'D' May 1936. A major change in design – the three axle articulated power bogie (using outside coupling rods) moved to the centre of the unit, with passenger accommodation on either side. But despite its sleek look this design proved to be somewhat underpowered.   ***Duffner W82***

Both 'D' and its sister 'E' operated on Dublin suburban services for much of their lives; Here 'E' calls at Sutton, on the branch to Howth, north east of Dublin, in June 1948

JH Meredith

compartment and chose to travel elsewhere! (This is not a surprise – the noise of a 1930s diesel at full throttle was deafening in an enclosed space!)

The two passenger section coach bodies were 'very modern' with large windows and full width drivers' cabs. They were 124'5" in length over buffers, about the same length as two mainline carriages, but the weight for the whole unit was only 39½ tons empty, 50 tons loaded. The maximum speed was quoted at 42 mph in fourth gear, and the bhp/ton ratio was 3.9/1 when empty. Lower than standard carriages, they were nevertheless full width (9'6") and so seating could be in a 3+2 configuration. One coach had 82 third class seats, with the outer ones facing out and the inner facing centre. Doors were located at either end and in the centre.

The other coach section was a tricomposite: it had 19 third class passengers next to the engine,

1960 was not 'D's only excursion on to ex BCDR tracks. In 1944 the GNR traffic manager temporarily managed the County Down's operations and this railcar operated off peak services to Bangor and Holywood while the arrangement lasted. 'D' is seen here at Bangor on a snowy winter's day.

John Pollock collection

with doors at the engine end. Somewhat surprisingly, it was second class that had the view – though only 20 of the 30 seats faced forward; there were actually two bench seats against the window which faced inwards, like some buses of the period. This compartment had doors at the end. The first class had its own compartment in 2+2 configuration, with doors in the middle.

The capacity of 'D' and 'E' was 159 seats in total. They went into service on the suburban Dublin– Howth route, except rush-hour trains.

Up to 1956 they covered 555,000 and 628,000 miles respectively, about half the mileage that the later 'F' and 'G' managed. After 1938 they went north, one to the Newry–Warrenpoint branch and the other to the Belfast area. 'D' passed to the UTA who renumbered it 103. It worked at Newry until December 1962, then it broke a driving axle and was scrapped in September 1963. It was never repainted in green. 'E' went to CIÉ in 1958, but as the southern company already had large numbers of more modern AEC railcars, they sold it to the UTA for parts in 1961.

Judging by their long lives 'D' and 'E' were successful enough. However, with only one 153 bhp engine they were somewhat underpowered – and engine failure meant total failure of the train. To address these issues the Dundalk works team produced their final 'home-grown' development, railcars 'F' and 'G', which appeared in 1938.

These units looked very similar to the earlier two, but there were substantial differences 'under the skin'. The most significant of these was in the engine and transmission. Each of the new railcars had two engines, Gardner 6LWs (as in 'C1'– 'C3') which each provided 102 bhp at 1700 rpm. These engines sat at either end of a smaller 13'9½" central section, with two axles on a 12'0" wheelbase. Each engine drove one axle

'D' passed to the UTA when the GNR ceased to be in 1958. It was renumbered 103 and operated regularly on the Newry branch. In 1960 it received an overhaul at the Belfast Queen's Quay shops. In this photo it is stabled at the stations' 'Holywood bay'.

EM Patterson 84Q

'F' ex works in 1938. Although similar in overall looks and layout, this railcar and 'G' were longer and 50 bhp more powerful than 'D' and 'E'. Both had long and successful careers north and south of the border. 'F' was finally scrapped in the early 1970s.   *Duffner W120A*

via a Vulcan-Sinclair hydraulic coupling. The Wilson five-speed epicyclic gearbox had vacuum electric control. These changes meant that they had a total of 204 bhp for their overall (empty) weight of 41½ tons, giving a bhp/ton ratio of 4.9/1. Top speed was now 48mph and they had slightly better hill climbing ability.

'F' and 'G' were slightly longer overall (159'5") than 'D' and 'E'. The centre section was shorter but each passenger section was made a little longer, allowing a guard's compartment off the third class section. As a result, passengers found that there was slightly less knee room but no doubt the guards appreciated the more tolerable noise level!

There were minor changes in seating. At both ends there were two small transverse bench seats, each seating two. These faced the driver in the middle but gave a view out. Overall seating was for 164 people (51 second, 8 first and 24 third class at one end, and 81 third class at the other. Later, when second class was abolished, the second class section was re-designated first

class. Both of these railcars accumulated over a million miles in service and spent most of their life on the Howth branch.

One feature which could give rise to operational embarrassment was the fact that the direction of each engine/transmission unit had to be manually changed. With one engine running 'forward' and the other in 'reverse' anyway it was all too easy for an inexperienced or careless driver to set the railcar's two engines attempting to pull it apart or squash it together! In either case it went nowhere at all until the correct setting was restored.

In 1958 'F' went to the UTA and was renumbered 104. It operated on the Warrenpoint branch along with 103. This railcar was subsequently bought by the same contractor as 101 and was also finally scrapped in 1969 after being stored for two years at Portadown. 'G' had gone to CIÉ but, like their other pre-war railcars, the company had little use for it and it was sold to the UTA in September 1962. It was renumbered 105 and went to Warrenpoint in

'G' at Howth, on the suburban branch where the final design of pre war GNR railcars spent most of their lives until 1958. Although 'G' passed to CIÉ in 1958, CIÉ had little employment for non-standard railcars. It was sold to the UTA in 1962 and worked the Warrenpoint branch until its closure in 1965. It was destroyed by fire at Belfast's Grosvenor Road goods yard in 1968.

Real Photographs X 125

Ex GNR Railcar 'F', now UTA No 104, passes Newry South signal cabin on a working to Warrenpoint in July 1963. This railcar worked on the Newry branch until its closure.

DJA Young

1963 to replace 103. It did no work after 1965 and was destroyed by fire in 1968 while stored at Grosvenor Road goods yard, Belfast.

In their final form these articulated railcars were judged a success and if one compares them to their contemporaries they had greater seating capacity and must have been easier to work on.

One other significant pre war 'articulated' railcar was built, but not in Ireland. The LMS built a three-coach train in 1938 and it is described in the following chapter.

However, the GNR articulated-type unit did not provide a development platform for the future of railcars which was to belong, in one form or another, to the underfloor-engine unit. One problem was that through access for

passengers – and hence operational flexibility – was just not possible, and the limited power/weight ratio meant that making up longer or heavier trains was out of the question. Lightweight construction was necessary for the limited power available and this in turn meant a lower quality ride, especially at higher speeds – none of these articulated units could exceed a 50 mph maximum.

As a result, when in 1950 the GNR opted for more railcars, they turned to an underfloor design. It was to be the underfloor engine diesel passenger unit which was to conquer all but the main lines in Ireland and the UK, and for some 20 years to be the chief thrust of motive power development in Northern Ireland.

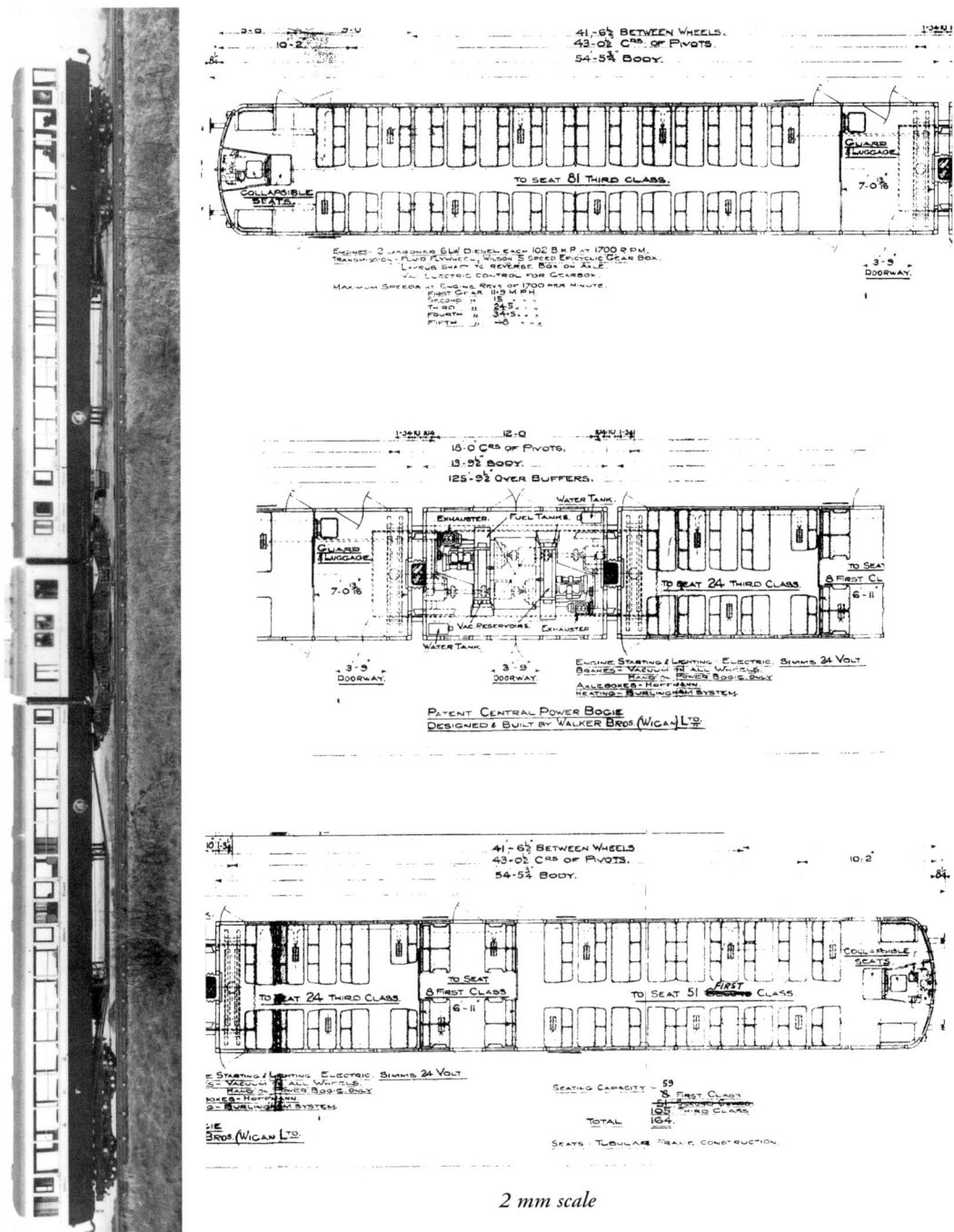

2 mm scale

GNR drawing of railcars F and G. Photo shows railcar F.
Real Photographs 88159

3 Railcars on the NCC (and in England) 1933-39

NCC No 1 at York Road in 1936. When introduced in January 1933, it was the first true underfloor twin engined railcar, albeit with petrol engines until 1947. No 1's transmission used a torque converter and it provided the traction prototype for much future development on the NCC, LMS, UTA and BR.

Real Photographs 6730

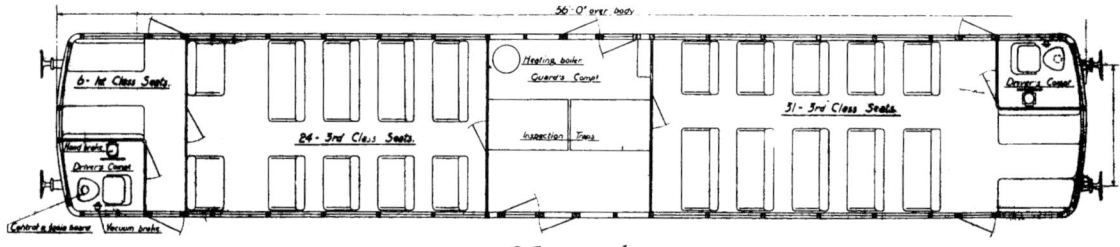

2.5 mm scale

Before we move to the post-war years it is necessary to look northwards from Dundalk and see what the GNR's northern neighbour, the LMS(NCC), was doing at its York Road works in Belfast.

In January 1933, the first NCC railcar emerged from the Committee's workshops at York Road. It seated first and third class, with driving cabs at each end and was turned out in the standard LMS coach livery of lined crimson.

NCC No 1 was the first in a line of 'railcars' (as they became known in Ireland) which, highly developed, have led to today's diesel railcars such as the Alstom 'Adelante', and the 'Virgin

No 1 in original livery at Carrickfergus with an old carriage attached. This allowed some extra first class seating, as the dedicated railcar trailers only provided for third class.

Real Photographs 88416

The makers nameplates on NCC railcar No1, showing the joint nature of the enterprise. Unusually, it was cast in aluminium. **Courtesy J Hunter**

Voyager'. Of course, these are capable of speed and comfort far superior to anything that might have been imagined in 1933.

No 1 was by no means the first or only railcar to run in the UK or Ireland, but its significance lies in its mechanical layout – it was the first generation of a line which has given us the sophisticated diesel trains mentioned above. The traction configuration used in No 1 – twin engines mounted underfloor, driving the axles of end mounted bogies – was to become the 'classic' layout for diesel multiple units worldwide, in particular the hundreds of diesel multiple unit trains of British Railways' huge 'Modernisation Plan' of the mid-1950s.

No 1's bodywork was built in a similar manner to traditional-steam hauled coaches. It had a 54'0" metal underframe and a wooden body with an overall length of 56 feet. The engines themselves were ten-litre petrol types, built by Leyland. They each developed 130 bhp at 2000 rpm. These were virtually identical to the engines which powered the single and double-deck buses for which Leyland were famous. In fact the project to build No 1 was a joint one between Leyland and the LMS(NCC) – the works plates had both names on them.

In the centre of the railcar was a guards and parcels compartment – the two engines were accessed by means of hatches here. They were vertically mounted and operated independently. Each had to be started separately and control was manual. Throttle, clutches and final drives were operated by a series of levers and bell cranks. Cooling was by means of radiators mounted centrally on the roof of the railcar. The use of roof mounted radiators was continued on the later NCC railcars, and on the GNR, which had used them on 'A' and 'B' and was to do so again on its articulated railcars 'D'–'G', though these of course had their engine(s) mounted in a central traction unit. However, the practice was not continued after World War Two, except on Sligo Leitrim railcar 'B'.

One of the benefits of the roof mounted radiator was the fact that airflow was assured, and it was easy to simply drain off water when the railcar was standing overnight in frosty conditions. The pipes could also be used to help heat the car.

The argument in favour of the later underfloor position was that it provided more protection against frost, although it was common for engines to be run up regularly if units were stabled outside in frosty conditions! Perhaps there was also a fear

No 1 in early UTA livery. In 1959 it was re-engined for the third time, with twin Leyland 0/600 diesel engines, possibly recovered from the MED re-engining programme. Note that the exhaust pipes now pass up the corners rather than the centre (see previous illustration).   **D Anderson**

of leaks into the passenger compartment from a roof mounted radiator system. The UTA MEDs originally had a header tank mounted above the doors and this was prone to either overflow or leak at times, with embarrassing results! Today, of course, with retention toilets and other waste storage requirements, tanks and air conditioning equipment mounted at roof level are once again common.

In No 1, power was transmitted to the wheels by means of a Lysholm-Smith torque converter. This use of torque converters was to be a feature of subsequent railcars from the York Road works. Its ability to transfer power smoothly more than compensated for the inevitable losses of power inherent in such devices. (See Appendix 1 for further information about the working of torque converters.) Top 'gear' was engaged from about 25 mph, at which point the engines were directly driving the axles. Petrol engines did of course have the ability to rev much higher than most contemporary diesels.

The two 130 bhp engines gave No 1 a very much higher power output than any contemporaries, and the unit weighed 32 tons. Its power/weight ratio of 8.1 bhp/ton gave No 1 a top speed of approximately 60 mph,

Ex NCC railcar No 1 approaching Whiteabbey on the 2.40 local from Ballymena, with a van in tow, on 14 September 1963.   **DJA Young**

considerably faster than any other railcar existing at the time.

The railcar was 56 feet in length, the bodywork carried on two coach-type bogies, similar to that on many LMS coaches of the day, resulting in good ride quality at higher speeds. To create a vacuum for the brakes, a motor-driven exhaust was used and vacuum was then maintained by an auxiliary exhaust, driven by the transmission. The same system was also used on railcars 2–4. Railcar 1 seated six first class and 55 third class passengers. In 1954 it was re-seated to give 72 third class seats.

Although the original thinking behind No 1 was that it would be used on lightly trafficked branch lines, its performance and worth led to it operating stopping services from Belfast York Road to Greenisland on the Larne line. Later it ventured as far as Ballymena on the main line and the Portrush branch.

In 1947, and then again in 1959, it was re–engined with diesel engines, latterly with similar engines to the MED railcars (Leyland 0600 125 bhp) and remained in service (eventually painted overall green with 'wasp' ends of yellow and black) until November 1965. During 1964 it was used to train drivers on the Lisburn–Antrim branch, at that time used only for occasional transfer trains (it had lost its passenger service in 1960). With the imminent use of the line for goods trains from Dublin to Londonderry, as a result of the closure of the GNR's 'Derry Road', there was a need for NCC section drivers to re-learn it.

No 1 was subsequently stored in the goods shed at Ballymena, still more or less operational. During its time there, a schoolboy friend of the author managed to start the engines in the shed. He quickly shut them down again for fear of discovery. No 1 has survived, though in decrepit state at time of writing. It is scheduled for ultimate preservation and has had some work done on it by the RPSI at Whitehead. Full restoration would involve new bus engines (the wheel turns full circle!) and also gearboxes from ex-BR DMUs. Of course Lysholm-Smith are long out of business and railway vehicle torque converters/transmission, as used on any modern vehicles, would be very difficult to fit, as well as expensive, for a vehicle never likely to see mainline use again. At time of writing it seems unlikely that No 1 will run again in the foreseeable future.

Nos 2–4 and the trailers

With the success of No 1, the team at York Road pressed on with development of the railcar concept, and shortly afterwards, in 1934, No 2 was rolled out. But not without a major problem.

Although petrol engines of the time had more power per litre than diesel, it was decided to go for the latter form of traction in future railcars. Despite its greater weight and vibration, the diesel engine is inherently capable of greater torque, especially at lower revolutions – this is to some extent offset by the fact that most diesel engines cannot rev as high as petrol engines – therefore they do need this 'pulling power' at lower revs. This 'pulling power' meant that hauling a lightly built passenger trailer might be possible, though up until now this had not been done. Although not really an issue at this time, the diesel engine was (and is) more economical on fuel, and also more reliable, largely due to the lack of high voltage electrics, needing no spark plugs. Diesels had already been used on the narrow gauge railcars and on GNR railcar 'A'.

But the downsides remained – and so the decision was made to make No 2 as light as possible. Traditional methods of construction were therefore abandoned and the quest to make the car as lightweight as possible began. They certainly succeeded – No 2's bodywork was significantly lighter than No 1's, by no less than six tons, despite the greater weight of its diesel engines and its greater length of 62 feet.

This was because of the use of aluminium extrusions and panels for the bodywork. However, when the time came to lift the new body onto the chassis, it buckled in the middle under its own weight! Extra stiffening had to be added, which added to the weight again. None of this improved the look of the bodywork, which was without doubt one of the ugliest to be produced, with slab sides and ends, made even more ungainly by the raised driver's cab sticking up from the flat roof. Even painted in Midland

No 2 in original condition at York Road after completion in 1934. It was the first NCC railcar to be fitted with diesel engines from the outset. The lightweight body proved to be too lightly built and bent when being lifted on to the bogies. The 'Turrets' must have been very cramped for drivers!

L&GRP 6731

crimson lake it hardly inspired, and when it later carried the UTA's unlined dark green, railcar 2 was an aesthetic disaster.

The same engine layout was adopted – two underfloor engines, but the engines in No 2 were diesels, once again made by Leyland. Each developed 125 bhp, and this set the norm for all future railcar development in Ireland and Britain. Petrol engines were not used in the future. The lighter body weight gave No 2 the best power/weight ratio of the NCC's four railcars. At 9.6 bhp/ton it was allowed to pull an extra two tons of a trailing load, compared with Nos 1 (when re-engined with diesels in 1949), 3 and 4.

All these railcars could pull some vans or wagons up to a certain permitted maximum weight, depending on the line they were operating over. Here the difference in pulling power of the diesel engine made itself felt. No 1, with her petrol engines, was only rated to pull 15 tons up the steep loop line at Bleach Green but No 2 was permitted 24 tons and Nos 3 and 4 could take 21 tons on this stretch of line. Other sections, such as the Larne line, where gradients were not so stiff, were allowed 18 tons, 28 tons and 25 tons respectively. However, no special 'luggage' trailers were built for these railcars as ordinary vacuum-braked vans could be handled, provided 'run round' facilities were available at termini.

Once again, on No 2 a torque converter was used. This time, however, developments in control systems allowed the use of hydraulically-operated throttles and an electro-vacuum system for operating the clutches and reverse mechanism. Such systems meant that increasing the power and weight of future vehicles would be possible. Multiple control would become a possibility (though not utilised at this stage). The mechanical system of No 1 would not have allowed such developments.

No 2 seated five first class and 75 third class passengers. The raised driver's cabs were designed to allow the use of low-roofed trailer cars to be pushed or pulled, or perhaps even both – one on each side. The idea was that the driver would be able to see ahead over the roof of the trailer, and for many years this practice was followed. The subsequent railcars, Nos 3 and 4, also had a similar set-up.

No 2 was the first of the NCC railcars to be withdrawn. Its very lightweight construction probably hastened its withdrawal from active service and in 1954 the engines and transmission were used to construct two tractor units for use in lifting closed lines. The body was stripped of anything useful and lay around York Road, being used for fire training purposes. It was still there in 1963 and could just be seen in the middle of a line of old cattle wagons. One observer remembers seeing it as late as 1966! Ironically it was to be destroyed by fire when a training exercise got out

No 2 at Portstewart after rebuilding by the NCC. It lost its turrets at this time. Due to its light weight it was the most powerful of the NCC designs.

Real Photographs X274

of hand.

At some point during its NCC career, No 2 lost its raised driver's cabs and its connecting end doors, which actually improved its appearance somewhat. Nevertheless, the basic mechanical design of No 2 was sound and was duplicated in the final two of the pre-war LMS(NCC) railcars, Nos 3 and 4, built in 1935 and 1938 respectively.

Nos 3 and 4 were virtually identical, the only noticeable difference being that No 3 (like No 2 in original form) had end doors, and so its headlight was mounted on the roof, just beside the driver's cab. No 4 dispensed with the end doors and had the headlights mounted below

window level. The only conceivable use for these doors would have been for ticket collectors – they would hardly have been considered safe for passenger use. By the look of the fitting it would have required a slim and very fit ticket collector to contemplate using it while on the move above walking pace.

The chief difference between these cars and No 2 was in looks. A new, more 'air smoothed' look replaced the angular lines of the earlier machine, although other details remained very much the same, including their length of 62 feet. Weight went up to 28 tons, so there were no problems with chassis buckling, and they seated

No 3 with an old coach acting as trailer, at Whitehead in NCC days. The final development of pre-war NCC railcar development, Nos 3 (1935) and 4 (1938) seated 12 first and 60 third class. They were much more successful than No 2, although the mechanical arrangements were the same. The 'Turret' driving cabs were still cramped but were retained to the end of their careers.

Real Photographs X 276

Railcar No 3 at York Road. The end door cannot have been much used in regular service. No 3's career ended when it was destroyed by fire at Whitehead in 1957.

Real Photographs
X 6536

No 4 and trailer at Bangor about 1953. With the exception of No 1, the ex NCC railcars all worked on the "County Down" for varying periods, and proved successful operating off peak services. However, their capacity was too limited for busy trains.

EM Patterson 225

12 first class and 60 third class passengers. Like No 2, they had the elevated driver position at either end, although the design had a more integrated look. Nos 3 and 4 retained this feature to the end.

In 1934 two railcar trailers had emerged from the works. These seated 100 people and were of especially lightweight construction, which gave them a weight of only 17 tons unladen – about half that of a normal steam-hauled coach. At first there was some thought that No 2 might push one and pull the other to make a three-coach train. However, despite their light weight, this arrangement limited performance to such an extent that it was rarely used in operation – one

trailer was the norm.

The idea that the driver, perched in his little cab, could see over the roof of the trailer when pushing, seemed to work, especially as the trailers themselves had a very low flat roof profile. It is possible that the idea was copied from some French railcars which used a similar layout.

However, an accident occurred after World War Two. Railcar 3 was pushing a trailer on the Portrush branch when the trailer hit a cow, one of a herd which had wandered on to the line. It was then decided that the angle of view from the cab left too big a blind spot for safety, just in front of the trailer. So the practice was discontinued. In

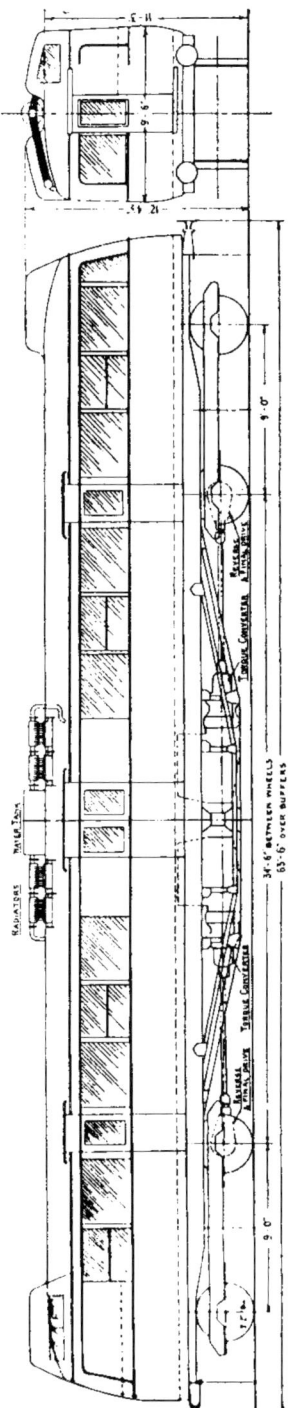

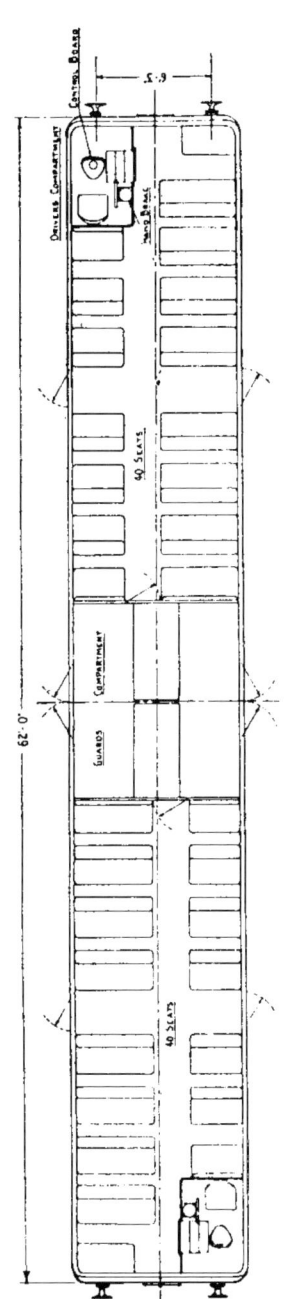

2.5 mm scale

LMS(NCC) railcar 3.

Railcar trailer No 1 as built; this and its sister, No 2, were built in 1934. Each seated 100 third class and weighed only 17 tons. The flat roof profile was to facilitate the driver's vision when it was being propelled.

L&GRP 6732

Railcar trailer No 1 in the second NCC livery in 1948. The trailers became Nos 544 and 545 in 1959. Both ceased to be used for passenger traffic with the withdrawal of railcars Nos 1 and 4 in the mid 1960s. No 544 was scrapped in 1968, but No 545 survived until 1978 as Signal Fitters van No 3109.

HC Casserley 51638, courtesy RM Casserley

Railcars 2 and 4 in 1950. No 4 is already in UTA livery. Railcar 2 was to have a short life under the UTA. It worked on the Bangor line for a while. After withdrawal from passenger service, it's mechanical parts only returned to the 'County Down' in 1954 to lift the remains of the BCDR main line to Comber.

Kelland collection, 24259

Railcar 4 at York Road in April 1964. It was the last NCC railcar to be built (1938) and differed from No 3 only in a repositioned headlight and the lack of an end door. No 4 survived in traffic until 1966, when it was stored in one of the carriage sidings at York Road. The end came in 1969 when it was set on fire by vandals.

Roger Holmes R0645

Railcar trailer No 2, by now numbered 545 and repainted in UTA livery, at Ballymena. It later became a signals department van, and survived until 1978.

CP Friel collection

future, railcars, if using a trailer, would have to run round. As time passed, and newer vehicles which could operate in multiple came into service, there was little need for the NCC railcars to be used on busier services and they increasingly worked on their own.

The original livery of NCC railcars 1 and 2, and the trailers, was standard LMS crimson lake. Later they were painted a lighter shade of red, with a cream band round the windows, and this livery was carried by Nos 3 and 4 from the start. With the UTA takeover in 1948, they were painted in a dark green livery with a pale green band at cantrail level, coming down the front in a curved pattern below the windows. From about 1955 on, the light green band and front was replaced by a cream panel at the end above waist

level. From 1961, a yellow and black 'wasp' panel was applied below waist level at the fronts and this was the final livery carried by No 1 and 4 and the trailers. None survived in service to get the post 1965 livery of deep red and oyster grey.

Railcar No 3 was taken out of service after a fire at Whitehead in July 1957. The railcar had worked an afternoon train from Belfast and was propelling a trailer into the excursion sidings (near where the RPSI now have their HQ) when it went on fire. Staff were able to detach the trailer, but No 3 was completely destroyed.

No 4 lasted the longest, coming out of service in February 1966 and the author remembers seeing her, in dilapidated but largely sound condition, in one of the carriage sidings in York Road two years later. There was even a plan to preserve her but this came to nothing and No 4 was scrapped after a fire in 1969. In the end, only No 1 survived.

The trailers both survived to be re-numbered in the 500 series, along with newer trailers. No 544 was withdrawn in 1968, but 545 survived, remarkably, as a signal fitter's van. Its last 'duty' came in 1977–8, when it was used as a mess room for contractors' workers engaged in building the new diesel running shed at York Road.

During this pre-World War Two period, English railways had been showing some interest in the diesel railcar idea, although only one, the GWR, embraced the idea with any degree of enthusiasm. The latter company eventually produced a substantial fleet of single-unit railcars (the 'flying bananas') with AEC engines and Self Changing Gears Co transmission and gearboxes. They were a successful design and were used for branch line and parcels traffic, some being constructed specifically as parcels vans and the last few being produced as two-car units. Surprisingly the GWR did not seem to make any further progress in railcar

GWR diesel railcar No 14, running in BR carmine and cream at Birmingham, Snow Hill in April 1958. No 14 was constructed at Southall and entered service in April 1936. It had a Gloucester Carriage and Wagon Co streamlined body and two 130 bhp AEC engines.

TJ Edgington,
Colour-Rail DE483

GWR AEC railcars 35-38 were designed as twin units with a cab at one end and a corridor connection at the other. They could also run with a non-powered intermediate as seen here. No 37 was destroyed by fire in 1947 and was replaced by No 33, seen here in 1955 on the rear of a set leaving Landor Street Junction (Birmingham) for Burton on Trent. No 38 is at the head of the train. Their evolutionary successors were the GNR AEC cars introduced in 1950 (see Ch 6).

C Banks collection,
Colour-Rail DE1565

The last Armstrong Whitworth railcar entered traffic in August 1934. This also had diesel electric drive, with a 95 bhp engine. Bodywork was by Park Royal - the rounded end windows are similar to some GNR railcars of that period. Seen here leaving Newcastle Central Station, it was withdrawn in 1939.

Armstrong Whitworth

development after the war, leaving this to the manufacturers, AEC, and the GNR in Ireland.

Not surprisingly the Southern Railway showed little interest in diesels – electrification of its densely populated system made much more sense. The LNER experimented with steam railcars and then seemed to lose interest, although four diesel electric machines, produced by Armstrong Whitworth between November 1931 and February 1932, were introduced on some LNER lines in the north-east of England. Although these were the first diesel electric railcars to be actually built in the British Isles, it seems that GNR railcar B did enter regular service before them.

The Armstrong Whitworth railcars were extensively trialled by the LNER and the first was not taken into stock until January 1933. The 250 bhp diesel engine fitted was a standard Armstrong-Saurer road vehicle design and the bodywork was by Cravens of Sheffield. Armstrong Whitworth developed their own electric drive for which they claimed low maintenance and great reliability.

One railcar, which incorporated a kitchen, operated a luxury 12 seat express service on the LMS for two weeks in 1933 between London and Castle Bromwich, near Birmingham, in connection with a British Industries Fair.

LMS four-wheel diesel railbus No 29951, possibly at Hamilton. This was one of a batch of three of these cars (22950–52) built in 1934. They had a 130 bhp six-cylinder Leyland engines, Lysholm-Smith hydro-mechanical transmission and weighed 10½ tons. After trials between Preston and Carlisle, they operated from Blackburn to Springvale and Clitheroe and subsequently at Hamilton in Scotland.

**N Stead,
Transport Treasury**

*The LMS three-car
articulated diesel train of
1938, seen leaving St
Pancras. Mechanically,
this train drew on the
technology of NCC diesel
railcars Nos 1–4. Each
car had two vertically
mounted 125 bhp
Leyland engines driving
the inner axles of each
bogie through a torque
converter. The
sophistication was in the
articulation and the
multiple unit wiring.*

Author's collection

However the diesel electric railcar was still somewhat ahead of its time.

The LMS, parent company of the Irish NCC, was, it seems, largely content to leave development of these new types of diesel vehicles to York Road, where the team was building up its knowledge of their construction and operation. However, three four-wheel railbuses powered by Leyland engines were introduced in 1934 and operated in the north of England, and there were some experimental cars which were tested from time to time, including a rather unusual vehicle produced by Michelin. But in 1937 the LMS did decide to produce a 'modern diesel train' for itself. This emerged from the Derby works in 1939, just six months before the start of World War Two.

It certainly looked the part. The three-coach train was a single articulated unit – the two outer coaches, each 64 feet long, rested on a 52-foot centre coach, and the cab end had five rounded windows. The engines were placed behind fairings and the whole train looked very streamlined. Thirty first class seats and 138 third class were provided, most of the latter being reversible. Luggage space and a toilet were also incorporated.

The articulation was an idea which Sir William Stanier had taken up for some of the LMS steam-hauled stock at the time, but mechanically this train was a development of NCC railcars 2–4.

Under each coach were two vertically mounted engines of 125 bhp each, driving the inner axles of each bogie through a torque converter, with a total bhp for the three-car set of 750. As the whole unit weighed 73 tons when new, this gave a power/weight ratio of 10bhp/ton, which provided mainline standards of performance. The train was tested at speeds of up to 70 mph, much faster than any GNR unit, though on a par with the speeds possible with the later NCC cars. However, this was a true mainline diesel train.

It was set to work on an Oxford–Cambridge service. A second unit was planned but never built and, with the advent of the war, it was stored and remained out of service until 1949. Unlike Ireland, where the diesel railcars played an important role in maintaining services during the war, the LMS clearly saw a new train of this type as a liability rather than an asset under wartime conditions.

The 1939 diesel train never re-entered passenger service. In 1949 it was converted to a two-car inspection unit for overhead electrical lines, the centre car being removed, and the driving cabs given flat ends. Two engines were left and all seats were removed, the roof being flattened. It was moved to a depot at Longsight in 1959 and came out of service soon afterwards, although it was still in existence in a derelict state as late as 1967.

4 Railbuses 1934-39

Before we go on to look at the development of diesel railcar units after the war, there was one other aspect of dieselisation which is worthy of some attention – the development of railbuses.

Essentially most use of diesel power for passenger traffic on railways, Irish and British, was by means of specially designed machines. In the beginning these did not, on the face of it, seem much different from the petrol railbuses of various sorts which had taken to the rails since the World War One era. But the railway companies, in particular the GNR, believed there was a need for vehicles which could run at even less cost than railcars, on lines which would otherwise have no passenger traffic at all and so the concept of the Railbus was born.

The narrow gauge County Donegal had some early units of this type, which proved to be successful, but quickly moved to specifically designed diesel units. On the broad gauge the railcars, such as 'A' on the GNR and '1' on the NCC were the first in the field – railbuses followed them.

In 1934 the Dundalk works of the GNR turned out their first true 'railbus' – by which I mean an actual road bus altered to run on railway tracks. The modifications concerned the tyres and entrances only – in virtually every other respect the unit was unaltered from the type of vehicle to be found on the roads.

The invention that made these vehicles a practical proposition was a special type of wheel. Two Dundalk engineers, Howden and Meredith, collaborated with the Dunlop tyre company to produce a wheel which would give the railbuses an acceptable ride on steel track without using a special railway chassis. Thus savings could be made in construction costs.

Essentially the Howden-Meredith wheel had a steel rim between the pneumatic tyre and the rail surface. The steel rim was profiled to normal railway outline on the outside but fitted snugly over the rubber tyre on the inside. it was made slightly smaller in diameter to ensure it stayed on when the tyre was inflated. This type of wheel was first tested on two permanent way vehicles and as a result the profile was slightly altered for passenger use. But punctures were practically eliminated and the safe axle load could be increased somewhat. An emergency brake system was fitted which ensured the wheel rim stayed vertical and cut the engine ignition circuits.

The first railbus came after railcar 'C' and was lettered 'D'. It entered service in September 1934 and was converted from a chassis of a 1929 bus numbered 5, the body coming from 186 – nothing was wasted by the frugal GNR! The engine, in common with the others, was the Gardner 4LW of 60 bhp, and originally the patent Howden-Meredith wheels were fitted to both axles. However, after some problems with the machines not operating track circuits, solid front wheels and axle were fitted. This can hardly have improved the ride of these machines, and still did not entirely cure the problem. Some had full-width front cabs and others half cabs, depending on the type of bus bodies they were converted from, but to simplify engine access they were converted to half cab. The livery carried by 'D' and the others built for the GNR was that carried by the railcars – Oxford blue lower panels and cream upper.

'D' differed from later models in having folding doors on each side, just behind the

The Howden Meredith wheel. This was an ingenious invention which allowed converted road buses to be used on rail without major re-engineering. It also allowed some extra degree of comfort compared with the standard railway rigid wheel arrangement! Of course, it was still possible for the tyre to be punctured.

Duffner R578B

driver's cab. The second railbus, 'E', had the same arrangement, but the later railbuses had the more common rear swing-doors and platforms.

'D' operated between Dundalk and Clones and was re-lettered 'D1' when railcar 'D' came into service in 1936. In 1939 it was sold to the SLNCR where it became that railway's 'A', replacing a previous railbus of that number on the SLNCR (the diesel engine from the original finding a new home in its successor). In 1950 it was sent to Dundalk for overhaul and the bodywork was scrapped and replaced with a second-hand body from another GNR road bus, with doors at the rear. By 1954 this railbus, and others on the SLNCR, were becoming increasingly difficult to operate due to lack of suitable spare parts. It ultimately shared the same fate as the other SLNCR railbuses, being sold for scrap after the line closed.

GNR railbus 'E' (later 'E2') followed in October 1934 and worked on the Scarva–Banbridge branch. It was similar to 'D' but had a reverse gearbox, so it could run in either direction – though this was not something often done, there being no cab at the rear end. In 1947

it became No 1 when numbers replaced letters on GNR railbuses. It passed to the civil engineer's department in 1956 as No 8178, and ultimately went to the UTA. It has survived to be restored in running order as No 1 (though it does not venture out on to the modern railway.) and can be seen in the UFTM, Cultra.

The third GNR railbus – 'F' – had a shorter

GNR railbus 2, previously 'F', presumably awaiting repair after an accident, judging by the rather odd angle of the cab. The flimsy nature of these machines would cause a modern safety expert heart failure. However they did usually operate at low speed on lightly used lines.

AM Wright

GNR railbus No 4 at Banbridge. The GNR Banbridge–Scarva branch line was a favourite haunt of these railbuses, until it closed in 1955. No 4 had been originally built by the GNR for the Dundalk Newry and Greenore Railway, which closed in 1951.

CP Friel collection

A rear view of No 4 showing the arrangement of the steps. These allowed the introduction of extra pickup and setdown stops, often at level crossings, to promote more traffic.

AM Wright, Author's collection

Dundalk Newry & Greenore Railbus No.1 in that company's livery, sometime during the 1930's before it returned to the GNR. Note the typically LNWR signal post in the background.

Lens of Sutton

career. It appeared in January 1935 but was totally destroyed in an accident at the Square Crossing at Dundalk on 26 April 1944. It had been relettered 'F3' in 1938 and its replacement, which entered service later that year, carried the same number/letter. It was renumbered 2 in 1947 and went to CIÉ in 1958 where it survived, mostly unused, until the early 1960s.

In 1935, the GNR also built two railbuses for the Dundalk, Newry and Greenore Railway. No 1 had front doors like 'A' and also had a 'route indicator' fitted above the cab, with a headlight on top. No 2 joined it in July 1935, both working on the DNGR section until after World War Two. Both railbuses were sold by the

DNGR in 1948 back to the GNR where they were given the numbers 3 and 4. No 3 was scrapped in 1955, while 4 became a permanent way vehicle numbered 8177, and went to CIÉ in 1958.

The other customer for railbuses built by the GNR was the Sligo, Leitrim and Northern Counties Railway. This railway ran from Enniskillen to Sligo across sparsely inhabited countryside straddling the border between Northern Ireland and Éire. The company had briefly trialled one of the GNR's early railcars in 1932 and decided to buy something even more cost effective. This vehicle was lettered 'A' but, unlike the GNR prototype, had rear entrance

The original Sligo Leitrim and Northern Counties railbus 'A' with its luggage trailer. This railbus was converted by the GNR and was originally petrol powered, changing to diesel in 1938. Only a year later it was destroyed in an accident. The Sligo Leitrim used small luggage trailers to increase capacity for parcels etc.

Real Photographs 88904

The second Sligo Leitrim railbus 'A' in 1950. Formerly GNR 'D', this railbus had been introduced in 1934, lettered in the railcar series – it had to became 'D1' when railcar 'D' was introduced. It had a 60 bhp Gardner engine, and entrance doors immediately behind the driver. Later railbuses were to opt for rear doors.

Kelland collection 24180

Sligo Leitrim railbus 2A at Manorhamilton. Like the others, this was built for them by the GNR. It was introduced in 1938, and had the usual Gardner diesel engine. 2A survived in service until the closure of the Sligo Leitrim line in 1957.
CP Friel collection

doors.It was originally fitted with a 40-bhp petrol engine, had a full-width front cab and seated 32 in total. In 1938 it received the benefits of diesel power and was re-engined with a Gardner 4LW. Fuel consumption was reported to have dropped from 9 mpg to 21 mpg. Unfortunately SLNCR 'A' was destroyed in an accident in March 1939.

By this time a second railbus had been placed in service. '2A' had arrived in 1938 and was powered from the start by a Gardner diesel engine, but had a half-cab body style. A replacement for the original 'A' was found, in the form of the prototype GNR railbus 'D' – which became the second 'A'. Its later career has already been recounted.

The LMS(NCC) had been an enthusiastic innovator of diesel traction, with its early railcars pointing forward to more sophisticated vehicles. However, they did experiment with two railbuses. In 1934 and 1936, two Leyland PLSC3 32-seat road buses were converted. They were similar in concept to the GNR ones, incorporating the Howden-Meredith wheel system and rear entrance doors, though these were part of the bodywork and there was no rear platform. As built in 1928–9, these buses would have had petrol engines and it is not known for certain if diesel engines were fitted when they became railbuses. They worked on the northern section of the NCC's system, between Coleraine and Londonderry and were painted LMS crimson below waist level and cream above – a livery also applied to the railcars. However, the

Sligo Leitrim Railbus 'A', seen here in 1955 after re-bodying in 1950. By this time it had not long to go in service. It was sold for scrap when the SLNCR closed in 1958.   ***EM Patterson 29B***

The NCC introduced two 32 seat railbuses in 1934 and 1936 which were used chiefly between Coleraine and Londonderry (and it seems, on the Dungiven branch also, judging from the destination blind shown in this undated photograph). They used their road fleet numbers but did not run after the war period.

Real Photographs X 272

NCC did no further development on the type and the ultimate fate of the railbuses is shrouded in mystery, although it seems they did not survive World War Two as there are no known (to the author) references to them after 1945.

Whatever the economics of running these small diesel railbuses, they could only maintain the railway's advantage while roads remained potholed and primitive, as the engine noise, vibration and (by railway standards) poor ride was not likely to win passengers who could find a more comfortable alternative. As roads were improved after the war and into the 1950s (except in the more remote areas) it is not surprising that the type was not perpetuated with any enthusiasm by railway companies after 1945.

Furthermore, they had limited capacity, which meant that on a branch such as that to Portrush, with seasonal fluctuations, a 'conventional' train was needed to take over. Running at 'high' (60 mph or more) speed was impossible, and these lightly built machines were liable to damage if accidentally shunted heavily – a more serious hit usually wrecked them.

Consequently, after the war the railbus concept lost favour in Ireland, although, in 1953 CIÉ placed a railbus in service which was to be the last of the type in Ireland for some years. Numbered 2508, it was a conversion of 1934 AEC Regal IV No A8 in the former DUTC road fleet. It ran in service on the Thurles to Clonmel section for two years, after which it was stored at Inchicore until withdrawal in 1961. Some four-wheel railbus-type vehicles were also produced in mainland Britain under the BR modernisation plan of the 1950s.

Much later, in 1982 NIR bought a railbus from BR. It was one of a series of experimental vehicles that ultimately led to the development of the four-wheel, two-unit diesel railcars known as 'Pacers' or Classes 141–3. The railbus bought by NIR was a single unit with cabs at each end, the bodywork based on the standard Leyland National bus design. There was a 200 bhp underfloor engine driving one axle of its four-wheel underframe. The unit was numbered RB3 on BR but carried no number on NIR. After many years out of service, it is once more in use on the preserved railway at Downpatrick.

A final reflection on the short-lived railbus phenomenon begs this question – If the traffic on a line is so light that a 30-seat vehicle is all that's needed, why keep a railway open at all? In the 1930s, freight on the railways was still relatively buoyant and lines could be kept open for this, with the passenger service a bonus, but in post-war Ireland freight decline was rapid and most such lines were quickly lifted.

5 Post-War experiments: SLNCR Railcar B and the UTA Ganz

The World War Two years were busy ones for the railways of the north of Ireland. Even those parts that ran through neutral Éire were affected by the 'Emergency', as it was known there. Fuel – both coal and oil – was in short supply and the economy of the railcars was much appreciated. However, there was no time available for experimentation, and the development of new types inevitably was delayed until the war was well over.

SLNCR Railcar B

The first post-war diesel railcar to appear on the tracks of the north of Ireland was on the Sligo, Leitrim and Northern Counties Railway, a rather ramshackle affair which ran between Sligo and Enniskillen. It had never had much money but, pre-war, had used two railbuses similar to those on the GNR, the latter once again providing a great deal of support through their works at Dundalk.

Neither is it fanciful to see the hand of the bigger company in the SLNCR's decision to order a new railcar from Walkers of Wigan. It was known simply as 'B' during its time on the Sligo Leitrim. It was delivered in 1947 and immediately gained the approval of the passengers who used it, accustomed as they were to either the very old steam-hauled carriages or the noisy railbuses. 'B' was in fact the first (and only) application of the basic 'County Donegal' design of railcar to the Irish standard gauge.

Like the last two Donegal machines, 'B' had a full-fronted cab power unit, the driver sitting on the right of the engine, which was a Gardner 6LW of 102 bhp @1700 rpm. The engine was mounted on a four-wheel bogie with coupled wheels, and the axleboxes were fitted with Timken roller bearings. Transmission was via a fluid flywheel and a Wilson epicyclic gearbox (the first of a new kind); gears were electro-pneumatically operated. Radiators were mounted on the roof in a box-like affair that was later removed.

This power unit was articulated by means of a corridor/bellows connection to the passenger section, at the other end of which was a further driving cab, this time a half-width one. This greatly increased the flexibility of 'B', though it did often pull a small trailer, which meant running round, but at least turning was not needed.

'B' was quite a lightweight, at 18 tons 12 cwt, and this gave it a reasonable power/weight ratio of 5.26 bhp/ton, and gearing sufficient for a maximum speed of 42 mph, though unofficially it could do a bit more! The relatively low top speed was hardly an issue on most of the SLNCR's line anyway because the timetable allowed two hours and five minutes for the 49 miles, although this did include a long and variable stop for customs at the two border stations. A contemporary account enthused:

> The vehicle is almost unique among railcars, in being almost entirely free from vibration, as well as being exceptionally free running, within the limits of its somewhat restricted compass of speed. The extractor operated throttle ensures a complete absence of jerk at starting.

The author travelled on this railcar in 1968,

SLNCR railcar 'B' at Enniskillen. This machine was the only Irish standard gauge derivative of the successful narrow gauge railcars built for the County Donegal. 'B' had a 102 bhp Gardner engine, and seated 59 people. The main difference from the narrow gauge machines (apart from the gauge!) was that it had a driving cab at either end – a great operational advantage.

Pearse McKeown

SLNCR 'B' went to CIÉ in 1958 after the Sligo Leitrim closed and was renumbered 2509. Unlike the inherited GNR railcars, it was used quite extensively as far afield as Limerick and Waterford. It was also used for enthusiast specials and driver training. It is seen here in 1969 at the then recently opened station at Kilbarrack, just south of Howth Junction.

CP Friel collection

while it was in CIÉ ownership, and can vouch for the accuracy of the statement about vibration. There can be no doubt that one of the advantages of the articulated system was isolating the passenger section from the engine.

Within its overall length of just under 55 feet, Railcar 'B' seated 59 people on bus-type turquoise leather seats in a 2+3 arrangement. There were also 15 straps for standing passengers, though it is hard to imagine it ever being that full! The floor was finished with blue linoleum. There was also a guard's compartment at the end nearest the engine, this being 8'6" long, with double sliding-doors. A further set of

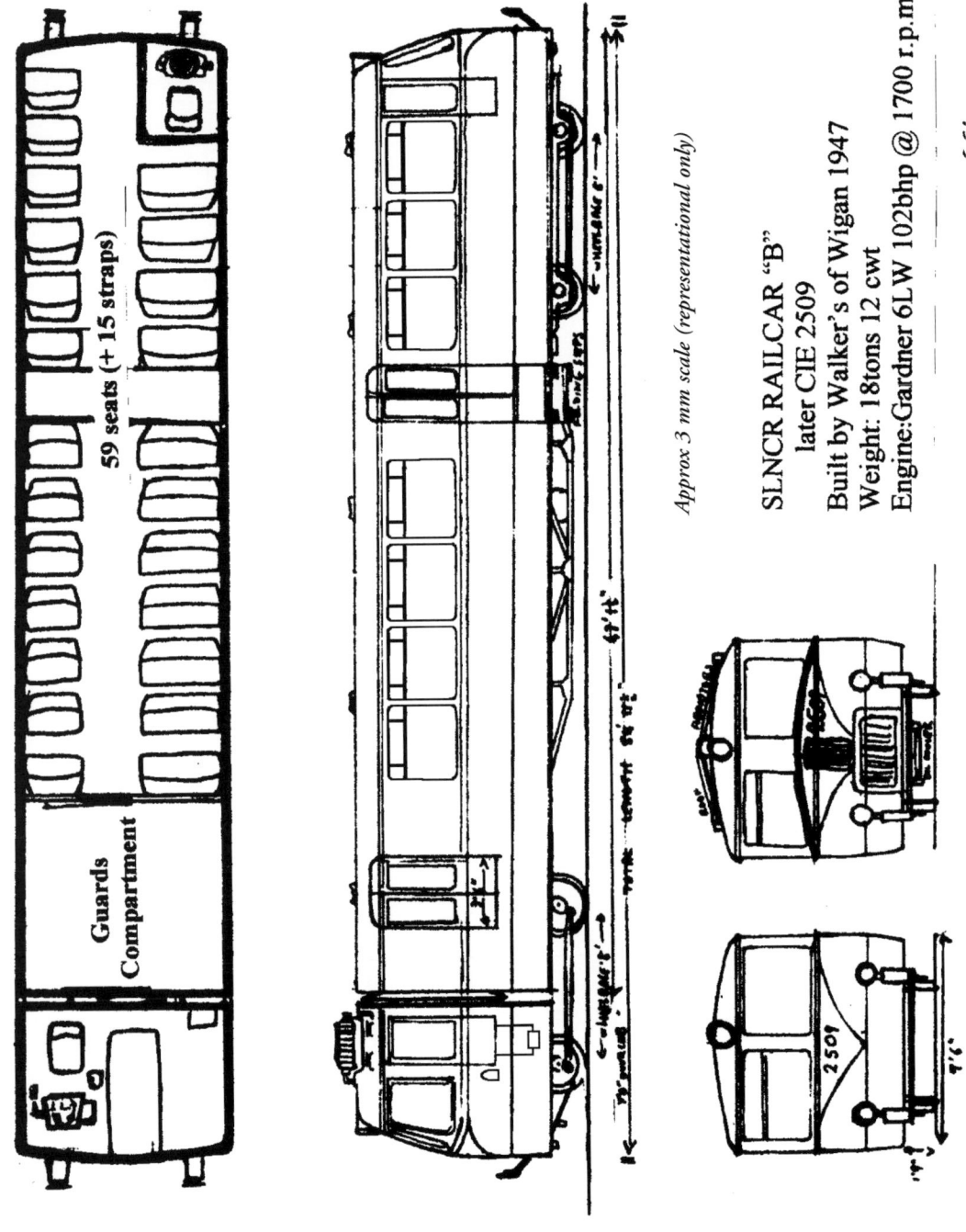

59 seats (+ 15 straps)

Guards Compartment

Approx 3 mm scale (representational only)

SLNCR RAILCAR "B"
later CIE 2509
Built by Walker's of Wigan 1947
Weight: 18tons 12 cwt
Engine: Gardner 6LW 102bhp @ 1700 r.p.m

such doors (manually operated) were situated halfway towards the other end of the passengers' compartment, these doors having folding steps for use at halts without platforms. The handrails of these entrances were picked out in a mid-blue shade. Railcar 'B' was mainly driven by one man, who looked after it with great care. It had a unique livery at first – the lower panels were a deep chrome green and the upper ones eau-de-nil, separated by a narrow black band; the roof was white. The letter 'B', picked out in gold, appeared at either end between the two cab windows.

The Sligo Leitrim closed finally on 30 September 1957 and the railcar lay at Enniskillen shed. CIÉ bought it in 1958, when it was towed to Inchicore, from whence it emerged in standard CIÉ green and bearing the new number 2509. It was then allocated to the Limerick–Nenagh local services, though also tested on the Loughrea branch. It received the new black and tan CIÉ livery in 1962. In late 1966 it went to Waterford but broke down after a few weeks, returning then to Dublin. It was used by various railway societies for rail tours from time to time, and for other sundry duties such as driver training, until 1971, when it was withdrawn. It lay out of use for years, and then was transferred to Mallow goods yard for possible preservation. Nothing was done to it, though, and it deteriorated over the years, until it was recently brought back to Inchicore and at time of writing is still stored there. It may find a home in a new Irish National Transport Museum. This railcar would certainly be a useful machine for any preserved Irish line.

This type of design was not repeated anywhere else in Ireland on the standard gauge. Although successful at the work for which it as built, its low speed and limited ability to haul other vehicles, or work in multiple, meant that the design wasn't capable of being developed for the main line or heavy suburban work that railcars would be handling in the not too distant future.

The 'Ganz'

A further single-unit railcar was purchased just after World War Two, and in some ways almost looked like a mainline version of railcar 'B', though its origins were very different.

This was the single-unit railcar built in 1937 by the Metropolitan Vickers Electrical Company and Metropolitan Cammell Carriage and Wagon Co. It was based on a design built by Ganz for use on the Hungarian State Railways between Budapest and Vienna.

The railcar was built in Birmingham and used on the LMS main line between Euston and Tring, where it achieved speeds of over 70 mph. However, the LMS showed even less interest in this type than they did in their own train. It was stored during the war and not resurrected afterwards.

Someone, somewhere in the recently formed UTA must have been aware of the existence of this machine, with its supposed good performance. Could it provide a platform for future railcar development? At this time the use of diesel traction for passenger services was very much on the agenda, and so in early 1951 the UTA purchased this railcar. It was provided with new 5'3" bogies and entered service on the ex-BCDR section in April 1951, with the running number '5', though usually referred to simply as 'The Ganz'.

The Ganz was powered by a single diesel engine developing 240 bhp at 1250 rpm, made under licence from the Ganz company. It weighed 38 tons and was 64 feet long. This gave it a power/weight ratio of 6.3 bhp/ton, which was not dissimilar to those of some of the GNR pre-war railcars but substantially less than the NCC cars. The engine and transmission was built onto the leading bogie, driving both axles. The engine itself (a pre-war design) took up considerable space behind the driver's cab where it was encased in a polished wood cover. It was articulated in the sense that the engine moved

Left: *In 1951 the UTA purchased a single pre-war railcar built in England to a design by Ganz of Hungary. It was simply known in Ireland as 'The Ganz'.*
It boasted a powerful 240 bhp engine, and could reach 70 mph under favourable circumstances, but lacked capacity. The design was not perpetuated by the UTA as it proved inferior to the underfloor twin engine design. The Ganz railcar, UTA No 5, is seen at Queen's Quay, Belfast, on its first day in service, 23 April 1951.
TJ Edgington

Right: *The Ganz at Queen's Quay. It was trialled against a NCC railcar and the pioneer Harland and Wolff diesel electric locomotive, No 202, in 1951. No records of the respective performances survive but the NCC railcar proved to be the best unit. The UTA had probably already made up their minds anyway, as Nos 6 & 7 were already being built during that year.*
Real Photographs X 9261

with the bogie inside the wooden case. This leading bogie was a long affair with a 13'0" wheelbase.

The Ganz had air brakes – the first vehicle to run on the UTA with these. There was a driving cab (like railcar 'B') at each end but no through connections. The Ganz seated 36 third class and 18 first class passengers and had a modern look, although it had a rather narrow body with straight sides.. Interior panelling was in polished plywood, with wooden flooring covered with cork-based carpet and rubber. In early service it had a two tone green livery similar to that adopted for Nos 6 and 7 and the first batch of Multi Engined Diesels (8–13).

The Ganz had a much more powerful engine than that of any of the twin-engined railcars and

it would be tempting to see it as a forerunner of the MPDs which were to follow much later. But its performance in Ireland does not seem to have been sparkling. Acceleration was less rapid than the ex-NCC cars with which it was compared but top speed was higher – up to 70 mph. True multiple-unit operation would have been awkward, with only a narrow access corridor past the engine – the Ganz was in any case double ended. However, a trailer was provided in 1954, numbered 215, which increased capacity. Of course this then meant running around at termini.

It turned out that there was little the UTA could learn from No 5, as in service the NCC railcars generally out performed it. The type did not lead to any further development.

The UTA designed trailer for the Ganz, No 515, at York Road in April 1964. This carriage (numbered 215 until 1959) was built in 1954 as part of the batch of trailers made for the MEDs. It outlasted the Ganz railcar by some years. Oddly enough its use with 6&7, which it matched quite well in looks, never seems to have been considered, probably because it was air-braked and conversion to vacuum was not worthwhile.

DJA Young

The Ganz at York Road in 1957. After some time on the BCDR, the Ganz made its way to the ex-NCC lines. While there, it worked the Portrush branch and occasionally ran to Ballymena before official withdrawal in 1965.

Colin Boocock

53

Many railcars and their trailers spent their final years in a kind of twilight – not in service but not officially withdrawn. It is obvious from this sad picture, taken inside the wagon shed at Adelaide in September 1964, that the Ganz is never going to run again.

DJA Young

No 5 was sent to the BCDR section and entered service on 23 April 1951. In 1952 it was used in comparative trials with ex-NCC railcar No 3 and the pioneer Harland and Wolff diesel electric locomotive No 202 (originally BCDR 'D1', then No 2).

However, by this time it would seem that a decision had been made to opt for a new type of railcar developed around a true multiple unit with underfloor engines. The test results did not lead to any startling change of mind. Later No 5 worked out of York Road for some time, on the Larne line. However, it was later transferred to the ex-NCC Portrush branch where it seems to have been well liked. One morning trip was made from Portrush to Ballymena, where it connected with another train for Belfast, and the driver spoke of it achieving 65 mph up Ballyboyland Bank, just south of Ballymoney. This was quite an achievement.

In the late 1950s it was given the then current railcar livery of dark green and off white cab and roof, modified around 1961 by the addition of 'wasp' end warning panels. After the takeover of the northern section of the GNR in 1958, the Ganz was transferred to Adelaide, but seems to have been little used. Being a one-off, parts were inevitably a problem throughout its life. Officially, it remained on the UTA's books until 1965, but really there was no long-term use for it by then, especially since the introduction of the three double-ended MPD railcars. It was quietly scrapped at Maysfield yard in 1965, having been stored out of service in the wagon shops at Adelaide for some years. The trailer coach survived until 1980, having been renumbered 515 in 1959. It was altered for use as an MED trailer in 1963.

At the time of the entry of the Ganz into service, a new fleet of underfloor engined diesel trains was entering service on the neighbouring GNR and these are the subject of the next chapter.

Simultaneously a similar train was being designed and built at the UTA's new workshops in Duncrue Street. This two-coach train was to be the prototype for the most numerous and advanced type to date on the railways of Northern Ireland and will be described in Chapter 7.

More than just an experiment: The GNRI and CIÉ AEC fleets

6

Its experience with the early railcars 'A' to 'G' had convinced the Great Northern Railway that diesel railcars made a great deal of sense for a company whose lines encompassed both intercity, suburban and rural lines. The high-capacity suburban railcars had performed well on the busy Dublin routes while the earlier units were found in border and branch line environments where their low running costs were much appreciated by management. The noise and vibration from the relatively unsophisticated engine installations and suspension must have been less attractive to passengers, though presumably no worse than that of contemporary buses – the main alternative in the days before universal car ownership.

In 1947 the GNR had embarked upon the marketing exercise which was to prove so successful – the 'Enterprise' trains from Belfast to Dublin. New steam locomotives capable of hauling this service had been ordered. But what of other mainline services? Could the diesel railcar provide the answer for the future here? The company approached the well-known manufacturer AEC who had had considerable experience of underfloor engine railcar traction on the GWR before World War Two. Just after the war AEC had produced for the same company a three-car unit – two power cars with an intermediate trailer. For some reason this was not developed by the GWR – nationalisation in Great Britain may have had something to do with this, because it was to be another five years before any serious new development was to take place on the UK mainland, and by then Ireland was already well on its way with dieselisation programmes.

However, this 1947 experimental train was to provide AEC with the means to develop the type, and the upshot of this was that in 1948 the GNR ordered a series of railcars from AEC to a design by Park Royal. These were to be used on longer distance services and had first and second class accommodation. They were constructed at Dundalk works.

The first of the new railcars, with power car 601 nearest the camera, poses for an official photograph in May 1950. The centre coach is a type K23 buffet car. Each power car had twin 125 bhp AEC engines and transmission was by a five speed pre-selector gearbox. These units were officially known as 'diesel trains' which reflected their much wider usage on the system.   *Duffner R629B*

Interior view of the first class section of an AEC car. These were very comfortable and some survived until the early 1970s in this form, although usually declassified.

Duffner R630B

Each GNR power car had two AEC A215 diesel engines developing 125 bhp at 1800 rpm, mounted vertically underfloor. These were 6-cylinder direct injection engines of 9.6 litres. Torque was rated at 430 lb/ft at 1000 rpm, falling to 380 at 1600 rpm. One was mounted vertically each side of the main frame. Each engine drove through a fluid coupling and a Self Changing Gears Ltd five-speed pre-selective gearbox, by means of an external coupling to a final drive on the outside of the inner axle. The pre-selection system (also used on the earlier GWR railcars) involved the use of a separate selector lever to 'pre-select' a gear, before the actual gear lever and clutch were operated. The power bogies had a 10'0" wheelbase with 3'2" wheels.

The GNR made trailers for these units, by converting existing mainline carriages, and they could run as three- or even four-car sets up to a maximum of 70 mph. However, each car was intended to work with a 'twin' facing the other way, which limited interchangeability, although later special jumper cables allowed this. Multiple unit working (ie with more than two power cars) was not possible.

Although brakes were vacuum type, there was a new form of 'quick release' brake. This was known as the Gresham and Craven system,

which proved very successful and was later adopted for virtually the all the DMUs built for BR later. The AEC trains used similar control systems to those of earlier vehicles. Each power car weighed 38¼ tons, those with boilers 1¼ tons more. There were two 50-gallon fuel tanks.

With an intermediate coach of approximately 30 tons weight, a three-car set had 500 bhp available for a 108-ton train, which gave a power/weight ratio of 4.6 bhp/ton. A two-car set could have 6.41. These figures did give rise to some discussion amongst engineers, and many felt that the power/weight ratio was too low – that higher power should be employed to avoid undue stress on engines and transmissions.

Of course, driven off the engine were various ancillary systems such as air compressors, electrical systems generator and the like, and these can drain as much as 10% of the engine's power. This meant that the bhp/ton ratio on AEC railcars could be as low as 3.5 bhp/ton and often less. As with the mechanical transmission, maximum efficiency was only achieved at full throttle settings.

Unfavourable comparisons were drawn between this and the high power/weight of the LMS three-car unit produced in 1938. It is significant that the UTA uprated the engines on

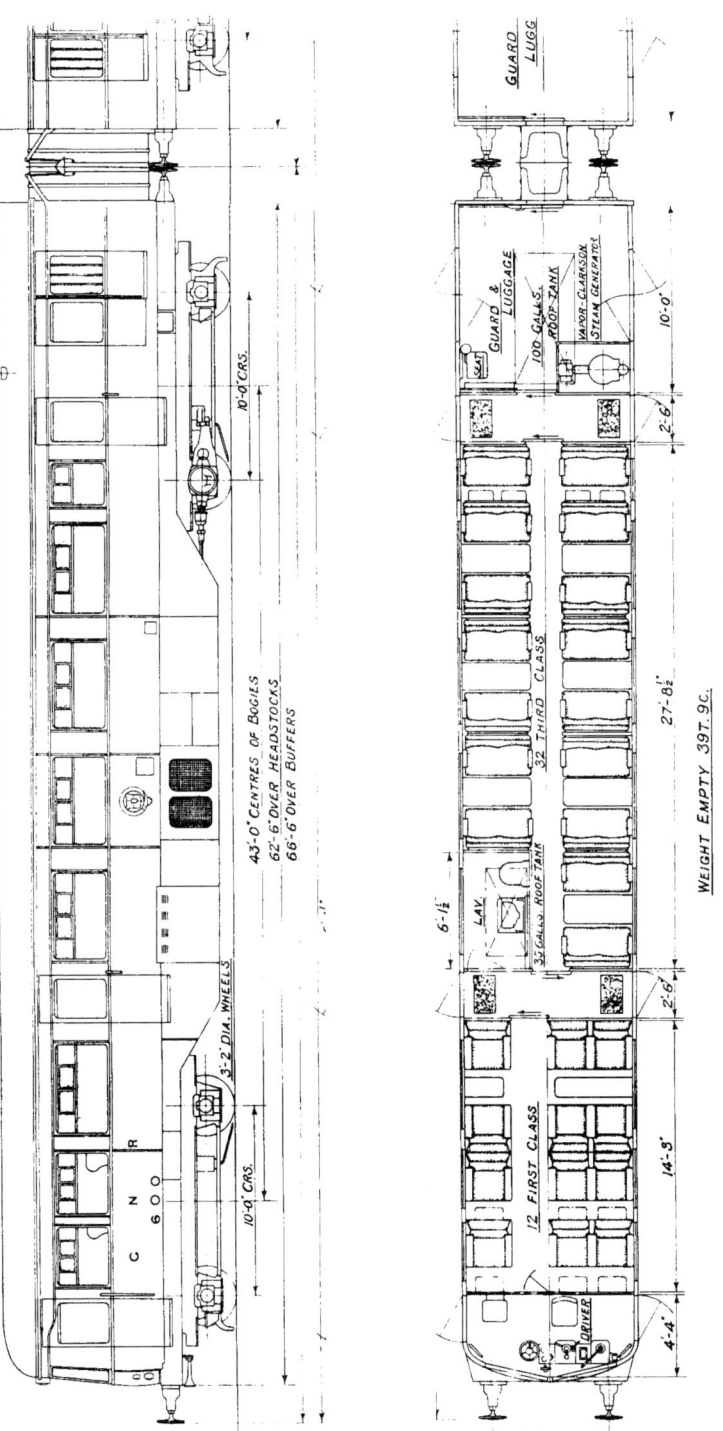

2.5 mm scale

GNR AEC railcar.

The final pair of AEC railcars, 619 nearest, stand outside the paint shop at Dundalk in 1951. With these cars the GNR took a great step forward into dieselisation. They were to prove a very successful design, if somewhat under-powered by later standards.

EM Patterson 15N

A three car AEC set at Clones. The AEC railcars travelled widely over the GNR system, and usually worked as three car sets with a trailer coach between two power cars.

CP Friel collection

its MED trains in 1956, whilst most BR railcars utilised 150 bhp engines, although the first batches stayed with the 125 bhp type.

Body length was 62'6", and width was 9'6". There were full-width cabs with two large front windows and a small centrally placed headlamp just below the cantrail. Behind the driver was the first class compartment with 12 deeply padded seats, two rows at the front facing forward, with tables in the seat backs, and the rear six arranged in a bay with a table between. Across a toilet-equipped vestibule, the third class section seated 32 in 2+2 seating with another vestibule leading to a luggage compartment/guard's van at the corridor end. The guard's compartment of even numbered cars was equipped with a Vapour

In March 1951 a three car AEC sets waits in the 'Howth' platform at Amiens Street station.

**Kelland collection
121**

Clarkson oil-fired boiler for steam heating. This system was rather expensive, and the boilers needed switching on some hours before the train went into passenger service, but it worked well. Later efforts at saving money on heating were to prove less successful, as the UTA was to discover.

The 20 cars were numbered 600–619 in the coaching series. They were delivered between June 1950 and April 1951 and were finished in a livery of Oxford blue and cream, similar to that of the earlier railcars. They originally had deep skirts, which covered much of the mechanicals, to give them a very modern streamlined look. In common with many other such attempts to streamline the look of the underfloor area, these were considered a nuisance by maintenance staff and were later often left off! But, being the first of their type, a number of modifications needed to be incorporated.

Firstly, the engines had no ability to free wheel – drive was engaged at all times and this had potential problems for overspeeding engines on down gradients. A significant incident highlighted the problem. One railcar set hit some tools which had been left on the line and these damaged one engine. As there was no way this engine could be disengaged while the set was travelling, it began to overheat as the axle forced

it to keep turning and it ultimately caught fire. So a free wheel was added to the drive train of the GNR cars and also to the majority of the CIÉ vehicles, which by then were being built to the same design.

However, this then led to a further problem. The batteries were charged from the drive train so that if this was idling there was no charge, resulting in problems with starting and so on. This problem was never entirely solved on the GNR AEC railcars, but was overcome in their BUT successors by having a separate external drive working off the axle for the generator. Railcar development could be, and often was, an expensive, time consuming and frustrating business.

The basic design was undoubtedly sound (whether underpowered or not). Many AECs ran up large mileages before withdrawal and they were never re-engined – it seems the larger-capacity engine was less stressed than some of the later versions. Nevertheless, in these as in all other railcars, regular engine overhaul was necessary at about 50–60,000-mile intervals. At the time, this was considered a very satisfactory performance, given their usage.

Some of the faults which did occur, mainly with transmission, were due to drivers not understanding the different techniques in

Interior view of the driving cab. Driver comfort was not a high priority, though the view ahead was much better than any steam engine!

Duffner 630D

1 Deadman's handle. 2 Engine revolution. 3 Reverser–forward neutral reverse. 4 Gear selector lever – 5 speed.
5 Clutch. 6 Vacuum and air pressure gauges. 7 Hand brake. 8 Train brake. 9 Throttle (foot operated). 10 Horn.
11 Oil pressure, lights for engine.

'driving diesel'.

In this regard, one aspect of the development of diesel power for rail use, was the widespread change needed in driving techniques. For most of my generation, brought up with the ambition to drive a motor car from the age of 17, the use of gearbox/clutch and accelerator is something which comes almost second nature – and of course diesel and petrol transmissions are basically the same.

However in the 1930s, and even in the 1950s, railway engine drivers accustomed to working steam locomotives were faced with an entirely new type of traction. Not many drivers could afford cars in those days so the engine/transmission of a diesel train came as something

revolutionary. The practice in the railways which operated railcars before World War Two had largely been to allocate the diesels to a smallish group of drivers, or even an individual, as was the case on the SLNCR with Railcar B. But with more widespread introduction of diesels this was no longer feasible and in due course all drivers were expected to learn the ways of the new traction. Some never took to it at all, while others were less than enthusiastic – despite the better working conditions.

A common problem was overheating due to the units being kept in too high a gear when travelling uphill, the engines consequently labouring and placing great strain on the gearbox, etc. Drivers used to steam were inclined to be reluctant to change gear downwards, as they believed that it was easier to allow speed to drop, and therefore (as they thought) make less demand on the engines.

Occasionally a failure of the control system could lead to one engine running in reverse – with disastrous results! With so many interlinked systems, both mechanical and electrical, a diesel railcar train was a very much more complex item than a steam train. It was inevitable that there would be many down sides to their development, but the advantages outweighed them in the eyes of operating departments and of course the accountants of the companies who saw the difference in their fuel and manning bills! And so, it is undeniable that these railcars were a substantial step forward and that they were viewed with interest by other companies, in particular the UTA in the north (of which more later) and CIÉ.

The GNR made very wide use of its ten new diesel trains, concentrating them on services where passenger traffic was under threat from competitors. They took over most services on the Banbridge–Newcastle line and were commonly used on outer suburban workings from Dublin.

However, the GNR cleverly used them to develop new traffic. The Dublin-based Enterprise express went over to diesel operation – the first intercity diesel express in the British Isles. A new direct Enniskillen–Belfast service was inaugurated, removing the need to change trains at Clones, and diesels were also made available for excursion work, complete with buffet car refreshments. Well aware of the dated appearance of many of its steam trains, the GNR spread the 'diesel experience' far and wide, so that diesel traction was available on some services on virtually every route

The GNR made full use of its railcars for excursions. Here a three-car set, including buffet car, arrives at Bangor on such a trip, date unknown.   *Bryan Marshall*

Developments on CIÉ

In 1950 the Republic of Ireland's state transport company had a far from modern motive power stud and, once again, management there thought railcars might provide at least part of the answer. AEC were quick off the mark. Between 1952 and 1954 they supplied CIÉ with 60 railcars that were virtually identical to the GNR ones, although they did incorporate many minor detail improvements

which the company had made, as a result of operational experience with the earlier cars.

These units were numbered 2600–2659 and each had first and second class accommodation and a guard's compartment – even-numbered units had a Spanner Swirlyflow boiler fitted. These AECs could be run in multiple and the free wheel facility was included from the start. It has been

CIÉ used their AEC railcars as four-car units, with two unpowered trailers. Here such a formation, using two standard CIÉ carriages as trailers, is working a Tralee–Dublin express in 1960. Working this way meant a lower acceleration rate, and on steeply graded lines performance suffered accordingly. As time passed the number of trailers used dropped to one, and in their closing days on main line services, such as the Rosslare line, the AECs often worked as 'power twin' sets.

EM Patterson 80G

Driving trailers allowed the AEC cars to run as two-car sets, although this was not a common occurrence. However, one such is seen at Ballinderry Co Antrim on a stopping train to Lisburn in early UTA days, unusually in plain Brunswick green, before the application of yellow 'wasp' ends to these railcars from 1960.

EM Patterson 83G

reckoned that AEC made little if any profit on the 20 GNR cars, thanks to after-delivery alterations. They did better on the 60 CIÉ ones, we may be certain.

Six more (2660–65) of the same basic mechanical design were subsequently built at Inchicore works in 1956 with a body shell designed by O V Bulleid. In 1961 these were rebuilt as non-driving vehicles (the only Irish railcars to be true 'powered intermediates') and three of the earlier cars which had been damaged in accidents were similarly rebuilt in the same year to become 2666–68.

One area where CIÉ differed from the GNR was in its practice of train makeup. Whereas the GNR operated the AEC cars as two- or three-car sets (a practice followed largely by the UTA), the southern company ran them as four-car or even eight-car trains with an equal number of trailers and power cars, hence the low power-weight ratio referred to above and the stresses it must bring. It is the author's opinion that this is what led to the

earlier wearing out of the CIÉ cars – there is a limit to how often something can be overhauled or rebuilt!

Most of the CIÉ railcars were used for longer-distance services and came in three different batches. The first, from 2600 to 2647, were for mainline services and had a similar layout to the GNR cars. The next nine (2648–2656) had four extra seats in place of the toilet and were mainly for Dublin and Cobh suburban services. The last three cars, Nos 2657–9, went to the Waterford and Tramore section and worked there until its closure in 1960. They had high density bus-type seating and were third class only.

All the CIÉ railcars were initially painted in dark green, but later received a lighter shade than hitherto which looked very smart. In common with other stock, all the railcars were repainted after 1961 in the then new livery of orange and black, with a white stripe just under the cantrail.

Many of these CIÉ AEC railcars had long lives, though not in their original format. Some were

A UTA three car set leaves Lisburn on a local train to Portadown in the mid 1960s. Today the 'third line', constructed in the 1970s, which curves away at Knockmore Junction to Antrim would be on the left of the picture.

CP Friel collection

given new suburban-type seats, starting in the late 1950s, and increasing numbers were turned out in this style as traffic increased throughout the 1960s and their mainline duties passed to GM locomotives. Most were worn out by the early 1970s (the ex-GNR ones on NIR struggled on for a little longer).

The author can remember travelling on AEC railcars on the Dublin suburban services in 1969 and 1970 (some still with their original first class seating – much appreciated because first class tickets weren't issued!) and by then they were becoming rather asthmatic – performance was far from brisk. The intermediates in each four-car set were standard CIÉ coaches, either Park Royal wide bodied types or wooden bodied 1950s coaches made redundant from mainline work. The power/weight ratio of these sets was therefore quite low, but this was not a problem on the relatively flat sections around Dublin. However, units employed on longer-distance services such as Dublin–Rosslare ran as two-car sets.

On the break up of the GNR Board in 1958, ten AEC railcars went to CIÉ and ten to the UTA. The CIÉ cars were given a suffix 'N' but otherwise retained their GNR numbering (600–619) while the UTA cars were re-numbered in the series 111–120. The UTA railcars remained on their parent GNR section, even working to Dublin occasionally if needed. A brief excursion by a set of AEC railcars on to the NCC section in early 1969 proved unsuccessful. They seemed underpowered and crude to men used to the newer, more sophisticated MED units, and the steeper gradients of parts of the NCC lines were a challenge. They were soon returned to the GNR Belfast–Portadown section.

The UTA's AEC railcars were all finally disposed of with the coming of the second batch of diesel electric railcars in the mid-1970s. Exact data is hard to come by but most seem to have been withdrawn progressively in 1973–74 and were cut up in 1975. The ones that went to CIÉ were sent to Mullingar scrap yard about the same time – unlike their slightly newer CIÉ brothers, they were not converted into push-pull units. The reason for this would appear to be that they were not fitted for 'multiple' running, as were the CIÉ cars. No 601N was noted down as due to be converted but never actually appeared.

Railcars without engines

As they finally expired, the CIÉ AEC railcars were taken to Inchicore and became part of an ingenious low-cost exercise to provide basic transport for commuters. By the early 1970s Dublin was already beginning to have traffic problems and people were rediscovering the railway. With increased services the elderly railcars were still needed in some form.

CIÉ had 34 largely redundant locomotives – the unsuccessful C class, which had Crossley 550 bhp engines. CIÉ got agreement from General Motors in America to supply them with new 1100 bhp GM engines, as fitted to the very successful locomotives they had been building for CIÉ since 1961. The traction equipment was basically sound and so the new 201 class came into being.

To operate with these, the AEC railcars were converted into cut price push-pull trains. They were not very attractive and were not very comfortable – with so much less weight the ride was very bouncy. But they were cheap and could be quickly produced.

These units survived, deeply unloved by those travelling, until the coming of the DART electric trains in 1984.

So ended the career of what was numerically the largest railcar type in Ireland – 86 power cars (if one includes the Bulleid variations) and many more trailer carriages. Most of their passengers in their final days would have been surprised to learn that the tatty, spartan, plastic-seated old carriage they were travelling in had, in the mid-1950s, been the acme of modern comfortable rail travel!

7 The UTA investigates further: AEC cars 6 and 7

On taking over the railways wholly within Northern Ireland in 1948–49, the Ulster Transport Authority found itself with a network which covered most areas of the north-east but which had been badly run down during the war years. (The GNR, being a cross-border railway, was not included in the UTA. However, it was purchased by the Northern Ireland and Republic of Ireland governments in 1953 and administered until 1958 by a board, with representatives from the UTA and CIÉ.)

The NCC had some modern equipment ordered just after World War Two, such as the excellent 'Jeeps', 2-6-4 tank engines designed by Ivatt but based on an original Fowler design, and some modern carriages. However, the Belfast and County Down Railway, never a byword for innovation or investment, was in a badly run down state. Only one new locomotive had been ordered since the end of the war and this was a repeat order of a type acquired in 1924. Two new coaches were built in 1938, but that was all – much of the BCDR's rolling stock dated from before World War One! Yet its Bangor line was one of the busiest suburban railways in the whole island.

As a stopgap measure, now that the two operations were combined, some more modern NCC locomotives and rolling stock were drafted to the busy Bangor line. It quickly became clear that large chunks of the rail network would be shut down. The first to go was the BCDR system, which closed except for the Bangor line in 1950. Large sections of the NCC's more rural lines followed a few months later. The UTA was charged with making railways pay, but this was in fact an impossibility given their infrastructure. So closures were inevitable.

The remaining bit of the County Down – the Bangor line (technically a 'branch' – the main line was the now closed one to Newcastle) – carried a great deal of commuter traffic. Despite the run down nature of the system, trains often comprised up to 12 six-wheelers, well filled, and timings over the steeply graded line were smart. Would diesel railcars 'do the job' there? Nothing suitable existed 'off the shelf'.

The UTA carried out some trials on the Bangor line using railcars 3 and 5, and the ex-Belfast and County Down diesel locomotive 202. The latter had only 250 bhp anyway and had been built back in 1932, so it clearly was unlikely to shine. Ex-NCC railcar No 3 could cope reasonably well with the level runs to the town of Holywood, a distance of about four miles, but lacked capacity – something which was even truer of the 'Ganz'. Nevertheless, the Ex-NCC railcar was the winner, confirming for the UTA engineers that this basic design was the one to go for.

However, single-unit railcars, with or without trailers, or even three-car units, wouldn't be enough. The unpowered trailers helped them carry more people but eroded performance, especially on the steep grade out of Holywood, with stops along it. As so many Bangor-line trains needed more seating, any attempt to pull more trailers up these steep grades and sharp curves beyond Holywood was going to be out of the question, unless a more powerful vehicle could be acquired. Diesel locomotives might solve the problem, but would need to have about 1200 bhp to handle trains of the size needed, with a suitable fast start-stop performance, and in the early 1950s most such locomotives were themselves experimental. They were also expensive, hard on track, and operationally not much better than steam, with a need to run round at termini as before. CIÉ were to discover a few years later for themselves just how poor a choice a British-built early 1950s design might be.

However, just about this time the GNR was ordering its ten new diesel trains from AEC/Park Royal. These looked promising, though they were seated for mainline running. Deciding that they might be worth evaluating and developing, the UTA purchased sufficient components to make a pair, similar to those on the GNR, but with some significant differences.

The new Chief Engineer of the UTA was a man named James Courtney. He had previously worked in the Northern Ireland Road Transport Board, which managed bus services in Northern Ireland, and he believed that the application of road bus technology to railways would provide the answer to these problems. Articulation and bogie mounted over floor engines were out – both reduced flexibility in operation. Underfloor

engines were in. Both Leyland and AEC were introducing new types for the bus market in the UK. Could these engines, with NCC or GNR-style transmission, provide the motive power? The advantages would be obvious – having a 'standard' engine type would lead to economies of scale and maintenance at the newly built integrated workshop facility at Duncrue Street, Belfast, where bus and rail vehicles were built and serviced side by side.

In the first of a long series of such conversions, two ex-NCC third class coaches of modern design, built just before World War Two, were selected as guinea pigs. The original underframes, bogies, body and even some windows were re-used, with the addition of cabs and a guard's compartment. The two new railcars were given the numbers 6 and 7 and were identical twins designed to run back to back. An intermediate compartment coach, No 279, seating 120 was converted to run with them. It

UTA railcars 6 and 7, with trailer 279 (later 528) at Queen's Quay Station Belfast in August 1951, shortly after entering service. These railcars, each powered by two horizontally mounted AEC 125 bhp underfloor engines, were to prove a very successful design. In the early 1950s great efforts were made to produce a 'streamlined' look with mechanical parts hidden behind fairings. The realities of maintenance soon led to their partial or complete removal!
D Coakham

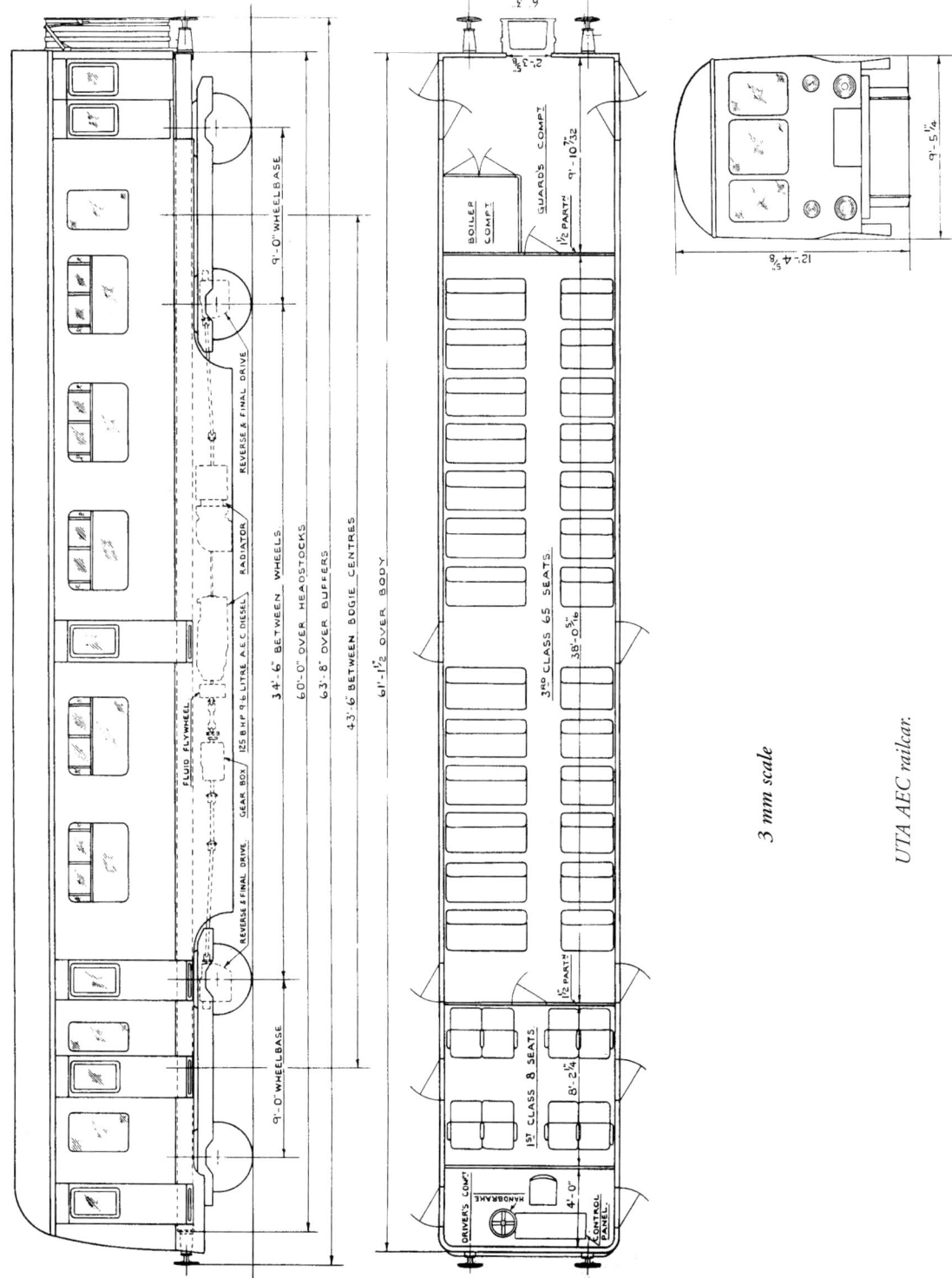

3 mm scale

UTA AEC railcar.

had no corridor connections and a different profile, which rather spoilt the appearance of the three-car set. However, each power car had seating for eight first class passengers in a saloon (accessed by its own doors) just behind the driver's cab, and 65 second class (old third) seats in 3+2 layout. With its trailer, this gave the set 16 first and 250 second class seats, a substantially greater capacity than anything hitherto.

As mentioned earlier the mechanical components were AEC but, unlike the GNR cars, these first UTA designed railcars had their 9.6-litre AEC 125-bhp engines mounted horizontally instead of vertically. This was a major development which needs some explanation.

The reason for choosing a horizontal engine in a rail vehicle is not so apparent as on a road one, where the floor height needs to be kept as low as possible to ease entry and exit to street level. The pre-war NCC railcars, as well as the LMS articulated unit, had vertically mounted engines, and the GNR retained them to the end. But the UTA (and later BR) opted for the horizontally mounted engine.

There were a number of arguments in favour (or otherwise) for each way of mounting. In favour of the vertically mounted engine was that anything mounted at the outside of it could be readily accessed by removal of any side valances. In later years these were usually left off anyway by busy fitters! On the pre-war NCC railcars, access to the top of the engine (cylinder heads etc) was by means of hatches in the passenger compartments, while the engines on the later GNR units could be slid out to allow work to be carried out on them.

However, one downside of vertically mounted engines was that the underside of the engine could be rather close to the rail head, and if track was uneven, or the suspension bounced excessively, there was the possibility of damage from flying objects kicked up from the track or ballast. If the engine could be mounted higher up, this would prevent such problems.

A horizontally mounted engine meant that despite being mounted higher up under the frames, the valuable passenger-carrying space above was

The cab interior of UTA railcar 6. This appears to have been similar to those of the GNR AEC cars. However the driver sat centrally.

EM Patterson 23A

UTA railcars 6 and 7, running with intermediate coach 528, leave Bangor station. From an aesthetic point of view, 528 ruined the modern 'look' of these advanced diesel railcars. However it increased seating capacity by 120, giving a total of 16 first and 250 second class seats in a three-car set!

Bryan Marshall

preserved – the floor did not need to be raised. Also in its favour was that cylinder heads were more easily accessible. On some later UTA railcars the engine mounting was organised so that the engine could be removed on a cradle for any work needed (however, a pit was still needed for bigger jobs). A year or two later, British Railways opted for the horizontal engine for its first generation of DMUs.

Once again fluid couplings were used on 6 and 7 but with a four-speed drive to the inside axles of each outer bogie. Instead of five-speed gearboxes, the UTA units had a four-speed, and its operation was somewhat different. Only the

Evening sunlight catches the UTA pioneer railcar set at Adelaide, working the 5.55 pm from Lisburn. The enthusiast on the left was photographing the railcar – not all that common a sight in the early 1960s, when most railway photographers were concentrating on the passing of steam!

DJA Young

In June 1964, Nos 6 and 7 are still working with trailer 528 as they pass Adelaide, working the 2.40 pm Belfast-Lisburn. No 7 is leading the set..
RF Whitford

With car No 7 nearest the camera, and running as a pair, the UTA's prototype railcars are seen here in the mid 1960s on an Up train near Adelaide on the ex GNR line to Great Victoria Street.

RHG Simpson,

first gear of the four needed 'clutching' as in the GNR's AEC cars – the other gears were simply selected without any need for this. The drive was taken to the centre of the axles, not the outside – which was to become the norm for future UTA railcars. Their braking system was the same as the GNR units – the quick release Gresham and Craven-type vacuum brake that had proved very satisfactory.

Each unit weighed 35 tons – their power weight ratio of 7.14 bhp/ton (when running as a two-car unit) was therefore somewhat higher than that of the Great Northern's AECs. This made 6 and 7 more suitable for the Bangor line for which they were mainly designed. Heating was by a boiler in the guard's compartment of No 6.

The trailer was a 1933-built non-corridor ten compartment third, seating 120, with the usual quarter lights and slam doors. Retaining its original number 279 at first, it became 528 in 1959. It was scrapped in 1971. It always looked somewhat odd sandwiched between the two modern-looking power cars.

As built, the AEC units could not run in multiple – ie no more than two power cars could be operated together. Although in fact 6 and 7 did not run with any other railcars in multiple,

their control systems were experimented with to develop the system which came to fruition with the later UTA railcars.

Nos 6 and 7 entered service in August 1951 on the Bangor line and were an immediate success. Later they were transferred to the NCC section and ended their days on suburban duties on the GNR section, mostly on stopping trains to Lisburn. By this time the trailer had been dispensed with and they ran as a two-car set. The Operating Department also apparently liked these cars and so they set a precedent. Their longevity and the ruggedness of their mechanical systems is shown by the fact that even in the mid-1960s one of the fastest recorded times (28 minutes) on the boat train from Larne Harbour to York Road was recorded on these units!

They were withdrawn from service in July 1966 and stored at York Road, where they were destroyed by a fire in December 1969, at the same time as NCC railcar No 4. Nos 6 and 7 provided much useful operating data and, along with the earlier NCC railcars, meant that the UTA had experience that was to stand it in good stead when the issue of large-scale dieselisation was raised.

8 The UTA MED (multi-engined diesel) railcar fleet

The first six car train as originally built in April 1952. Nos 8–13 were converted from the same type of coach as were 6 and 7. In 1953 the second and fifth coaches, 12 and 13, were given cabs and converted into driving cars.

Official UTA photo, courtesy Stan Myers

The poor state of Northern Ireland's railways after World War Two has already been referred to, and the UTA was tasked with the job of seeing what could be done. In particular, what about those 12-coach commuter trains on the BCDR? A line as busy as that could hardly be shut down. (Though there was a proposal to do just that at one stage. It was estimated that 20 double-decker buses would be needed to replace the trains! Fortunately for all commuters using the already crowded Belfast–Bangor road today, this proposal did not go forward.) No, diesel railcars it would have to be, but trains of six (or even more) coaches would be desirable – and not just a few sets but a complete fleet, running a much more intensive timetable than anyone had

yet considered.

The experimental AEC train of Nos 6 and 7 has already been discussed. Now the lessons learnt from its operation would be put into large-scale practice, with some alterations made. The new units became known as Multi-Engined Diesel trains (MEDs). The first four trains of three coaches each (two power cars and a trailer) entered service just a year later, in 1952.

At this point it is worth noting that the term DMU (Diesel Multiple Unit) as used in the UK mainland was not generally used in Ireland – the Great Northern referred to their AEC units as 'diesel trains', although the term 'railcar' was much more widely used in Ireland throughout the period described (and indeed even today). In

Top right: The engine
and transmission system set
up to show the relationship
of the main units; each car
had two sets.

CP Friel collection

Lower right: Railcar
underframe showing the
layout of engines and
transmissions etc.

*Official UTA photo,
courtesy Stan Myers*

fact, strictly speaking the term DMU would
probably have been more technically correct,
especially for the later machines. These MED
railcars would revolutionise thinking as regards
the capability of diesel railcars and therefore
their design is worth a closer look, serving also
to explain some of their features.

The MEDs would follow a similar pattern in
terms of drive train to the earlier NCC railcars
1–4, the layout being engine/clutch/torque
converter/with direct drive followed by final
drive on the inside axle of each bogie. However,
the power plants used, unlike the prototype cars
6 and 7, would be essentially bus engines. This
was undoubtedly due to two main reasons. The
NCC workshops and engineering team (which
the UTA had of course absorbed) had had a
relationship with Leyland going back to the
1930s and the earliest NCC railcars, while the
UTA itself was building a major new
engineering and production plant at Duncrue
Street, connected by rail to the NCC line outside
York Road. There were benefits to be had from
integrating road and rail workshops, and
therefore why not use the same basic power
plants for road and rail also?

The two Leyland 0600 engines, each of 9.8

The left hand side of the Leyland O/600 engine. The sump was specially shaped to allow space (!) for a fitter to stand between the two engines and work on the fuel pump, oil filter or starter motor. Presumably the man had to be slim! Each MED car had two of these engines.

Official UTA photo, courtesy Stan Myers

litres, used direct injection of fuel; ie the diesel was injected into the main cylinders and there compressed, leading to ignition. This is the original and more widely used from of diesel fuel injection. Its advantage is economy; its disadvantages being noise and vibration. Later, as diesel motor cars became more popular, it was supplanted by the indirect injection form where a small amount of fuel was pre-ignited in a smaller chamber first – this gave a 'softer' ignition sequence and less noise, at the expense of fuel economy. In 1952 though, diesel engines were used only in buses and lorries, neither of which were expected to be particularly quiet – the same applied to trains! (The direct injection diesel is potentially capable of much lower exhaust emissions also, although again in 1952 no one was overly concerned about this!)

Each engine provided 125 bhp at 1800 rpm, with a maximum torque of 410lb/ft at 900 rpm. In terms of diesel technology, they were considered a definite advance on the earlier and physically bigger AEC engines, and developed 12.75 bhp/litre. (It is interesting to compare these figures with a typical modern diesel injection car engine, which can develop in excess of 45 bhp/litre!). They sat horizontally almost side by side in the centre of the car. The engines, clutch and torque converter were mounted to the frame, as a unit, on flexible link-type couplings. The engines were of course water-cooled, with double banked radiators mounted forward of each engine, air being drawn in by fans driven from it. The torque converter fluid, which also required cooling, had its own radiators in tandem with the engine cooling ones. A third radiator segment cooled the engine oil.

These engines, though modern, were typical of the time, in terms of power output, but the arrangements for transmission were sophisticated. A clutch was provided on the engine and this transmitted power to the torque converter and then to an auxiliary gearbox, before entering the final double reduction final drive. The clutch was double acting – this allowed it to engage the converter, or direct drive, at the appropriate train speed.

In the MED railcars there was also an auxiliary gearbox fitted after the torque converter. This had two ratios which allowed for maximum speeds of 55 mph or 73 mph. The

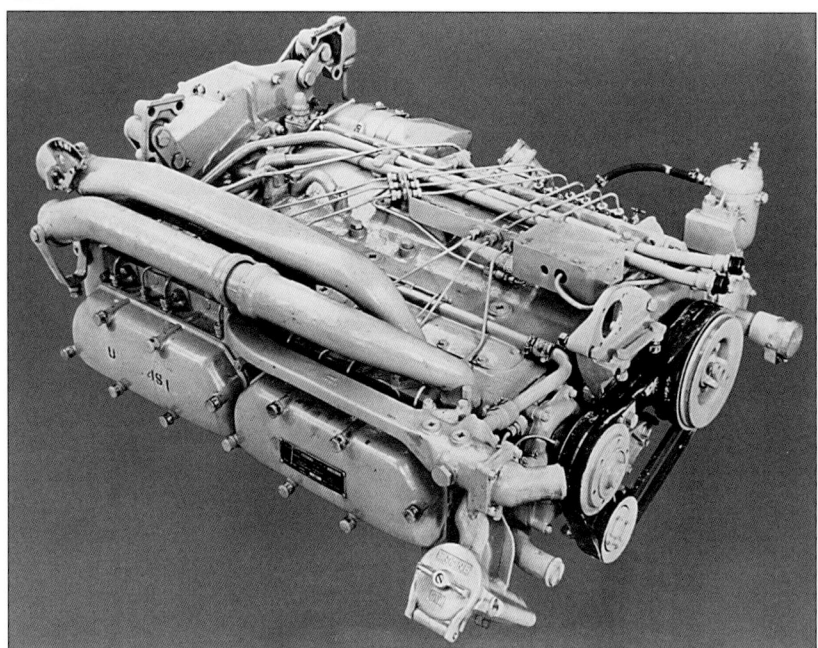

Top: *The right hand side of the Leyland 0/600 engine. One of the advantages of the horizontal engine was ease of access to cylinder heads. The oil filter was moved to the far (left) side in this application.*

Below: *An MED radiator, front showing the fan mounting and the top engine/oil cooling elements, with torque converter fluid elements at the bottom.*

Both official UTA photos, courtesy Stan Myers

lower maximum was expected to be more useful and the gearboxes were usually left permanently locked to that. The lower top speed was sufficient for work on the Bangor (and later Larne) lines, where acceleration from the numerous stops was more important than a high top speed. This gear was not accessible to the driver from the cab. From the gearbox the drive passed to a double reduction final drive via a sliding gear system, which allowed forward or reverse motion to be selected.

It was important to provide safety devices to prevent damage to engines and transmission, and so each engine had a low oil pressure and high water temperature switch and also a low cooling water switch, all associated with the appropriate warning lights. The operation of any of these switches stopped the selected engine and returned its clutch to neutral. If faults occurred while the train was running, then the stopped engine could only be re-started once the trip switch was re-set and if the problem had been rectified.

In the final drive reversing mechanism a switch informed the driver via a light whether the final drives had engaged in the required direction. Each engine drove the inner axle of its bogie, as on Nos 6 and 7, which meant that the two powered axles had half the weight of the vehicle (about 18 tons) available for adhesion. All of this equipment fitted into the underframes of ex-NCC coaches and determined the length of the new railcars – 60 feet over headstocks.

The controls in the MEDs were very simple: a throttle to control engine speed; a clutch controller to select neutral, converters, or direct drive; and a direction controller to select forward or reverse direction. There were of course various other controls such as the deadman's handle, brake controls etc, and separate engine stop and start buttons, warning lights and so on. A windscreen wiper, electrically operated, also featured on the centre window of the cab. (The driver was centrally seated.) This was described as a 'dual horizontal squeegee' type, which traversed the screen horizontally rather than being on a pivot. The type was widely used in the 1950s (the GNR and CIÉ AEC railcars had them too) but seems to have fallen out of favour by the early 1960s. Many MEDs had more conventional wiper blades fitted later, although the UTA fitted its MPD types with the earlier wipers to begin with. Ultimately all railcars were fitted with the more common (to us) pivoted types.

The cab layout of these new trains took a major step forward in what today is known as 'ergonomics'. In the GNR railcars the controls

The electrical connecting sockets on MED No 10. These sockets enabled multiple working to take place, which introduced a flexibility not seen before. The driver holding up the flaps is Paddy Megaw, who in steam days was the regular driver of 4-4-2T No 17 on the Donaghadee line. Note the three pipe air brake system.

EM Patterson 230

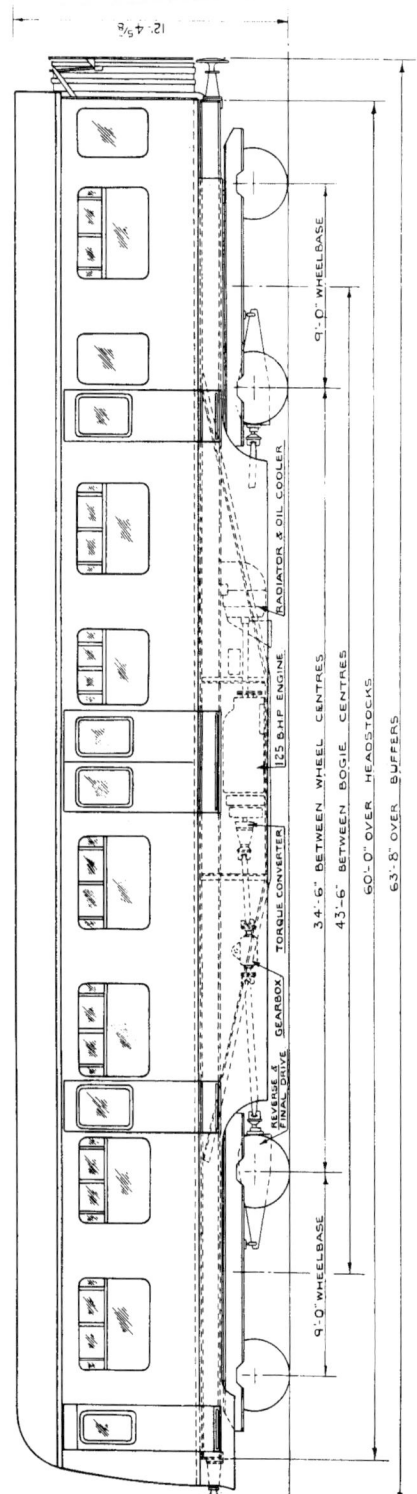

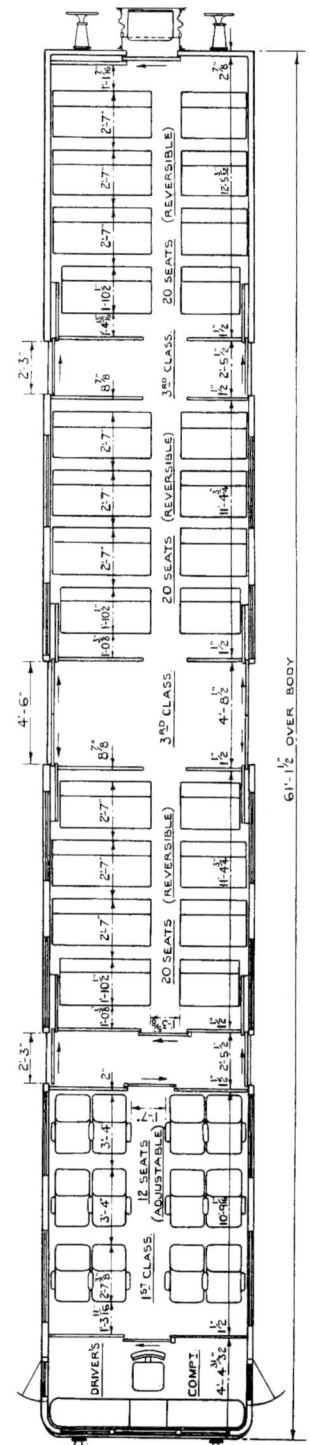

3 mm scale

MED railcars 9/11/13.

Below: The cab layout of a UTA MED. Compare with the photos of 6 and 7 and the GNR AEC cars! The location is a siding on the so-called 'back line', the former NCC main line between Greenisland and Monkstown.

Official UTA photo, courtesy Stan Myers

1 Interlocking master switch. 2 Deadman's handle/throttle (push down). 3 Main air reservoir. 4 Speedometer. 5 Engine start [top row (eight)]; Engine stop [bottom row (eight)]. 6 Rev counter. 7 Train pipe air and brake pressure. 8 Horn. 9 Forward or reverse. 10 Direct drive, torque converter drive, neutral, off. 11 Train brake. 12 Lighting switches.

were scattered about and the cab environment looks (to us today) decidedly 'old fashioned' – the foot throttle, for example, was particularly inconveniently placed and the large pedestals, upon which sat selector levers, look almost like steam controls.

In the MED cab, the driver sat centrally, with engine controls laid out in a style which again was to be largely followed in many later BR DMUs. Even shunting movements were considered and an auxiliary panel was placed on the left (looking from behind the driver), which allowed the driver to look back out of his window while operating a shunting throttle and brake – a special override was provided for the deadman's handle which would otherwise have prevented such movements. On the left was the deadman's handle and throttle, combined in a single control, and large instruments showing engine revolutions and speed. On the right, a similar handle served as a gear selector between neutral, forward and reverse, and torque or direct drive. There was also a telephone to the guard's compartment. The uses to which the telephone was put included, according to one young passenger, enabling the driver to alert the guard about children travelling 'first' who shouldn't have been!

However the simplicity of the driving controls belied the fact that control circuits and wiring were very complex. Before the advent of the MEDs, all multiple unit trains (which practically speaking means the previous generation of Irish railcars from AEC) had been wired on the north/south principle. That is to say, a car built to face Dublin must always do so, and a car facing Belfast, if being repaired, couldn't be replaced by a Dublin-facing one turned around on a turntable. Only another Belfast-facing car would do. Furthermore, these earlier cars used steam-heating which meant that you had to have at least one power car with a boiler; otherwise there was no heat.

Obviously this had detrimental effects on availability – if two Dublin-facing units go down then two sets are idle, even though there are two perfectly satisfactory 'other end' cars which could provide a set. The GNR operating authorities got round this difficulty by using special jumper cables to ensure that the correct connections were made.

The UTA engineers wanted to eliminate this problem so that any MED power car or railcar could be turned around and marshalled in any position in a train. Obviously each end would need a driving car with a cab, as there were at first no double-ended cars. They also wanted to have up to eight power cars operated by a single driver, without needing engines to be left in 'neutral', thus not adding to the power available. All cars, including trailer cars, would need sockets at each end. In an effort to persuade the UTA to purchase their products, the AEC company had arranged a trial in Dublin with two sets of the GNR-type cars to show that they could be run in multiple. Cables were apparently run through open windows in the drivers' cabs to connect two sets together for a demonstration to the chief UTA engineers. It did work, but they decided to build to their own design rather than buy from AEC.

So a method of 'spiral' wiring was adopted which enabled the circuits to be picked up in whatever order cars were coupled up. For example, No 2 start button would always start the engine in No 2 position, and No 7 stop would always stop the engine in No 7 position. This system allowed complete flexibility and was subsequently patented by the UTA. All the control circuits took current from the battery in the car operated by the driver, but the starting current for each car's engine came from its own.

The UTA engineers decided to fit the new railcars with air brakes, and the Westinghouse Co developed a straight air brake, with electro-pneumatic operation and an emergency valve. A requirement of the system was precise control, and simultaneous operation throughout the train. Emergency brake operation could be via the deadman's handle, the engine speed controller and the passengers' emergency valve, accessed in the passenger compartments by means of a release cable or in the event of a breakaway. A linked governor circuit would automatically cut the electrical current to the engine speed controller, bring the engines to idle speed and the clutch to neutral. In this case, once the brake had been applied the driver could not start the train again until the emergency air pipes were fully charged again.

The railcars incorporated air compressors, belt driven from the front of each engine. Each was electrically connected to the others so that they charged or unloaded at the same time. Air from the main reservoirs operated the throttle motors and cylinders, which operated the clutch and reverse mechanisms. Air at a lower pressure also operated the sliding doors.

Passengers in the new railcars were to be quite pleasantly surprised – especially those who had been used to former days on the Belfast and County Down with its antiquated and bad riding six-wheel stock. Even getting in was a novel experience. These new trains had power doors! Inside they were trimmed in bright colours and had an open aspect. Seats were at least as comfortable as in the old BCDR second class, even though they were similar to those fitted on

Left: *The telephone has now been mounted in the cab. The driver could use this to communicate with the guard's section of the railcar. In this photo the driver is Walter Geary.*

EM Patterson 23H

Below: *Interior view of an MED second class passenger saloon. Despite the plaudits at the time, these were very much short haul type seats.*

Official UTA photo, courtesy Stan Myers

Interior view of an MED first class passenger saloon. Some MEDs lost their first class compartments in 1956, when they were re-seated with standard second class 3+2 seating. **Official UTA photo, courtesy Stan Myers**

the UTA's buses. On one side of the centre aisle were two seats and on the other side, three. MED second class seating was green and fawn coloured moquette, while the floor was covered with brown linoleum. One power car had 40 reversible second class seats and a guard's compartment. The 'other end' car had 60 seats and the trailer seated 78 second class in three saloons. A six-coach train had 404 seats in total which compared reasonably with the capacity of most steam trains on the line. However, the superior performance of the new trains gave hope that a more intensive service could be offered.

The first class compartments, situated at the end of the composite cars, had an excellent view ahead (unless the driver pulled the blinds down, as some did – presumably disliking the feeling of

eyes boring into the back of their heads!). Seating here was 2+2 and each of the 12 seats was individually adjustable. The seats were originally trimmed in blue moquette, the backs in beige Vynide leather cloth. Linoleum was again used for floor covering here, this time in a blue shade although between the seats, carpet of the same colour was fitted. In the first class section, hardwood mouldings were used to give a touch of extra luxury. Plastic finishes were used extensively throughout the vehicles. Lighting came from four circular fittings in first class, with the other saloons being lit by bulbs recessed into the ceiling, with open reflectors. Lights could even be dimmed by the guard.

Train heating was not by boiler, as hitherto. The UTA engineers decided that there was heat

Close up of the centre section of an MED car showing the power operated central doors, with 'No Entry' and 'entrance only' signs. This arrangement was largely ignored – people came and went by whatever door was nearest. In any case, when the doors were open the instructions were invisible!   ***CP Friel collection***

The coke fuelled heating stove in an MED train, "neatly housed in an asbestos lined cupboard"! It was part of the guard's duties to check this stove at layovers. Many units later received alternative and additional heating.

Official UTA photo, courtesy Stan Myers

going to waste from the engines, so why not use this hot water? So engine heating water was pumped around the power car through pipes, which allowed heat to escape as required. In the trailers there were stoves to provide heating. These burned coke or anthracite and were of a novel design, with the combustion chamber below floor level, completely surrounded by fireproof material. The flue ran up through the passenger compartment, and heating was by a series of pipes throughout the vehicle.

In an article featured in one technical publication at the time, it was stated that "the problem of diesel train heating has been successfully overcome". These were brave words, because the problem of heating was to haunt the designers and engineers of diesel railcar trains in Ireland until it was finally laid to rest with the introduction of electric heating on the 1966 diesel-electric railcars. As the MEDs grew older, so the problems of using engine water to heat passenger saloons became more of an issue. The coke stoves gave way to paraffin 'smith's' heaters in the trailer cars, and proposals were made in the early 1960s to fit the MEDs with heat exchanger devices (which will feature later) to boost heating.

Part of the problem was the power doors.

These were operated by air from a compressor driven from a pulley off the radiator drive shaft. Above each door was an air cylinder, and valves controlling their operation were situated in the guard's compartment, one for each side of the train. These controlled all the doors on one side except for the guard's own door. A light in the guard's compartment indicated whether doors were open or closed and there was an electrical interlocking system to prevent the signal bell to the driver being sounded before they were closed. Emergency release valves were situated in the vestibules at each door.

From a passenger and operator's point of view this was one of the novel features of the railcars. Such doors and their modern successors are now standard on suburban and intercity coaches but in 1952, when the first MED appeared, they were very definitely 'modernist'. Indeed they were far ahead of the BR Modernisation plan DMUs which began to appear soon afterwards. None of these had power doors and it was the 1980s before such features appeared in British Railways DMUs. Even then, they were the rather flimsy bus-type affairs fitted to the Class 141 and 142 Pacer units, reliable enough but frequently draughty.

The MEDs had single doors at approximately one-third and two-thirds the way down the vehicle, with double doors in the centre. The idea was that entry would be by means of the single doors and exit by the double. In fact this did not work out in practice – the Northern Ireland travelling public went in and out as it pleased.

However, the power doors had one unexpected problem – heat, or rather lack of it. Unlike modern doors, which are opened on demand by boarding passengers, these doors had to be opened by the guard – all or nothing. So they were usually left open at termini, which in the frequently cold and wet conditions Northern Ireland experiences gave rise to considerable discomfort. Ultimately bulkheads with internal doors were fitted in an effort to overcome this problem and some seating capacity was lost as a result.

A great deal of attention was paid to the introduction of these advanced diesel trains at the time and Leyland and the other manufacturers involved hoped that bulk export orders for the type would follow. This doesn't seem to have happened, although most European countries over the following years developed diesel railcars which owed much to the basic design.

MED No 9 heads a six coach train at Bangor West in 1952. These cars were converted from the last six NCC J¹⁰ type open thirds of 1936–39. Two others had become Nos 6 and 7 and a ninth had been lost to enemy action in 1941. The centre trailers shown here were later converted to driving power cars.

EM Patterson 271

Development and construction of the MED railcars

It has been remarked that the UTA seemed incapable of building two railcars alike in all details. The GNR and CIÉ had purchased their railcars 'off the shelf' virtually – hence they were of one of two types, at first, anyway and that was that.

Although all the UTA MEDs shared the same sophisticated mechanical arrangements and could of course operate with each other, their actual bodywork and seating arrangements, etc, were very varied. The reason is, I think, not hard to find. They were essentially a DIY job from the start, made in what I might call the great Irish railways 'self-help' tradition.

Put simply, there was no government money worth the mention coming to the UTA in Northern Ireland. Unlike the government in the mainland UK and the BR Modernisation Plan of a few years later, the government in Northern Ireland had a very consistent policy for many years – little money for public transport and in particular no money for trains. The UTA was charged with 'making the railways pay'. Railways impoverished by five years of war, followed by five years of austerity and closures, had no hope of generating the large amounts needed for capital investment in new trains. (This didn't stop them hoping, as chapter 10 will show!) So the UTA rail engineers had to improvise. They went back to the first NCC railcar for inspiration – take a steam coach underframe, sling engines, etc, underneath, build a 'new' body and, hey presto, you have a

Conversion work on J10 class coach No 203 or 204 at Duncrue Street works in early 1952. These were to become railcars 13 and 12 respectively. However initially they were not given cabs and ran with their new numbers as non-powered intermediates until early 1953, when the new J18 trailers, 201–14, began to emerge.

CP Friel collection

MED No 8 at Bangor in October 1952. This three coach set is in original condition with the narrow waist band. A new livery variation was introduced with Nos 14–35 which had a broad band at waist level and different front end treatment.

Kelland collection 24085

modern looking state-of-the-art diesel railcar.

The new trains did look the part. They were fitted were deep valances over the front buffer beams and also over the engines, giving them a modern streamlined look. However, maintenance staff didn't seem to have liked the valances so much, and they disappeared progressively over the years! The same thing happened with the AECs on the Great Northern and CIÉ as well. One thing they all shared was the fitting of bus-type seats. Some of the second class seats in many of the power cars were reversible, so that passengers who wished could see ahead, but not necessarily the same number in each vehicle.

As you might expect from the description 'bus-type', the seats themselves were less than luxurious, with three on one side of the aisle and two on the other. The backs were low and the padding fairly meagre. The seats themselves were all finished in UTA-style green fabric and did not compare favourably with those fitted to the GNR and CIÉ railcars, though it has to be remembered that the UTA cars were designed for a trip which was less than half an hour end to end, whereas those on the other companies undertook much longer journeys.

Of course, the bus seats also allowed greater seating capacity in an era when standing was definitely not the thing – except on the London Underground. This is in contrast to today when,

for example, the latest version of the DART electric suburban trains are coming out with fewer, rather than more, seats. In fact the number of seats in the MEDs was reduced in 1962 when the bulkhead doors were fitted to reduce draughts.

There were first class sections of eight or 12 seats at the front of some of the cars, which gave a good view ahead. (This layout was to become standard for most early railcars.) First class was in 2+2 configuration and, again, was somewhat less luxurious than those fitted to contemporary GNR and CIÉ cars, although they were commented upon favourably by the railway press at the time. First class was removed from half of the power cars in the late 1950s, the remainder of the Bangor line MEDs losing theirs in 1964 and those on the NCC lines following suit when NIR abolished first class on all routes except the Dublin line.

Sixteen of the power cars were converted from existing ex-NCC coaches, though given the drastic changes made, the underframes of some must have been about all that was actually used! The first six, Nos 8–13, had smooth sides, and were conversions from the pre-war NCC J10 open thirds. There were originally nine of these modern vehicles (202-09). No 209 had been lost to enemy action in 1941 and Nos 205 and 208 had become AEC cars 6 and 7. The remaining six became Nos 8–13. They retained most of the original bodies, including the ventilated windows, but were reskinned, as the original coaches, though modern in layout, had full panelling. The even-numbered cars had a guard's compartment.

The first two three-car trains used Nos 12 and 13 as the centre cars. One of these is shown under conversion on page 82. It is unclear from the photographic evidence whether they were fitted with engines from the start and were therefore effectively 'powered intermediates' or the engines were added in 1954 when they received cabs.

Although numerically the next group, the other conversions, Nos 14–23, were not built until after Nos 24-35. These were converted from much older ex-NCC coaches than the first six – J4 and J5 centre corridor thirds of 1925–30 vintage! The conversion was much more drastic and probably only the frames and the wooden body ribs were reused, which would account for the higher roof profile on these cars, compared to Nos 24–35. Externally they were to the same body style, with metal body panels and a very modern ribbed appearance.

An anomaly has come to light during the research for this book in terms of establishing the length of these coaches. There is no doubt that the UTA planned the whole class to be 60 feet long, and the new vehicles (to be described later) and the original six cars were all of this length. However, the J4 and J5 class coaches which provided underframes for the second series of conversions were 57 feet long. Yet UTA drawings made in 1954 show their length as 60 feet. Seating capacity was the same, so did these cars have slightly closer seat spacing and 3 feet less length than the others in the class? Or were the underframes lengthened during conversion – a process which no one now remembers? Proof cannot be found either way – it now rests in a flooded quarry near Crumlin – and some aspects of UTA drawings suggest a lack of attention to detail, another example being one of a 2-6-4 tank which shows an incorrect shape of the tank sides.

It is the author's opinion that the coach underframes were probably lengthened. The mechanical layout of the underfloor drive shafts, etc, was planned for a 60'0" coach with a longer distance between the bogies and would presumably have needed modification for a 57'0" frame, as there was little enough room under there for the engines, gearboxes, compressors, fuel tanks, radiators etc.

The remainder of the power cars (24–35) had bodies similar in appearance to the later conversions but were built new with lightweight metal bodies. However, they had a lower roof line.

Nos 24–31 were built on LMS-designed 60 foot underframes which the UTA had already acquired in 1950 from Wolverton (formerly the LMS carriage works which had produced most of the NCC's carriages).

The final four power cars (32–35) looked the same but this masked one significant difference –

MED No 17 at Queen's Quay in April 1955. This illustrates the new livery introduced for Nos 24-35 and trailers 201–14. It has been slightly altered from the original on the leading car, with the white roof confined to the dome.

Kelland collection
24081

Left: A worm's eye view of the underside of an MED car – not much space under here!

Official UTA photo, courtesy Stan Myers

Below: A brand new three car set with Nos 29 and 28 at Bangor on 1 January 1953. This is the earliest known photograph showing the striking livery used for Nos 24–35 (and later Nos 14–23). Note that initially the whole roof was pale green. The front number has not yet been applied and, on No 29 at least, the UTA roundel was set one panel higher than on most cars. This roundel was mounted on a separate metal disc (see page 103 upper).

EM Patterson 22T

power cars weighed 36 tons.

A further difference in Nos 24–35 was that their windows could only open to allow ventilation – but not sufficiently to allow passengers to put their heads out of window!

One interesting point has been made regarding the number of cars built at this time. Given that they would be formed into three-coach sets, this would give much more capacity than the Bangor line alone needed. (Indeed, later on, 12 cars were to be permanently transferred away.) It has been suggested that the railway engineers had hopes that the line to Comber, closed in May 1950 but not lifted until 1953,

rather than having conventional carriage frames, they were built from new with integrated body and chassis from Metal Sections Ltd. This made their weight even less – 34 tons as opposed to the 36 of the earlier units. Incidentally, it seems that the 'lightweight' bodies weren't all that much lighter than the conventional ones – most MED

Continued on Page 89

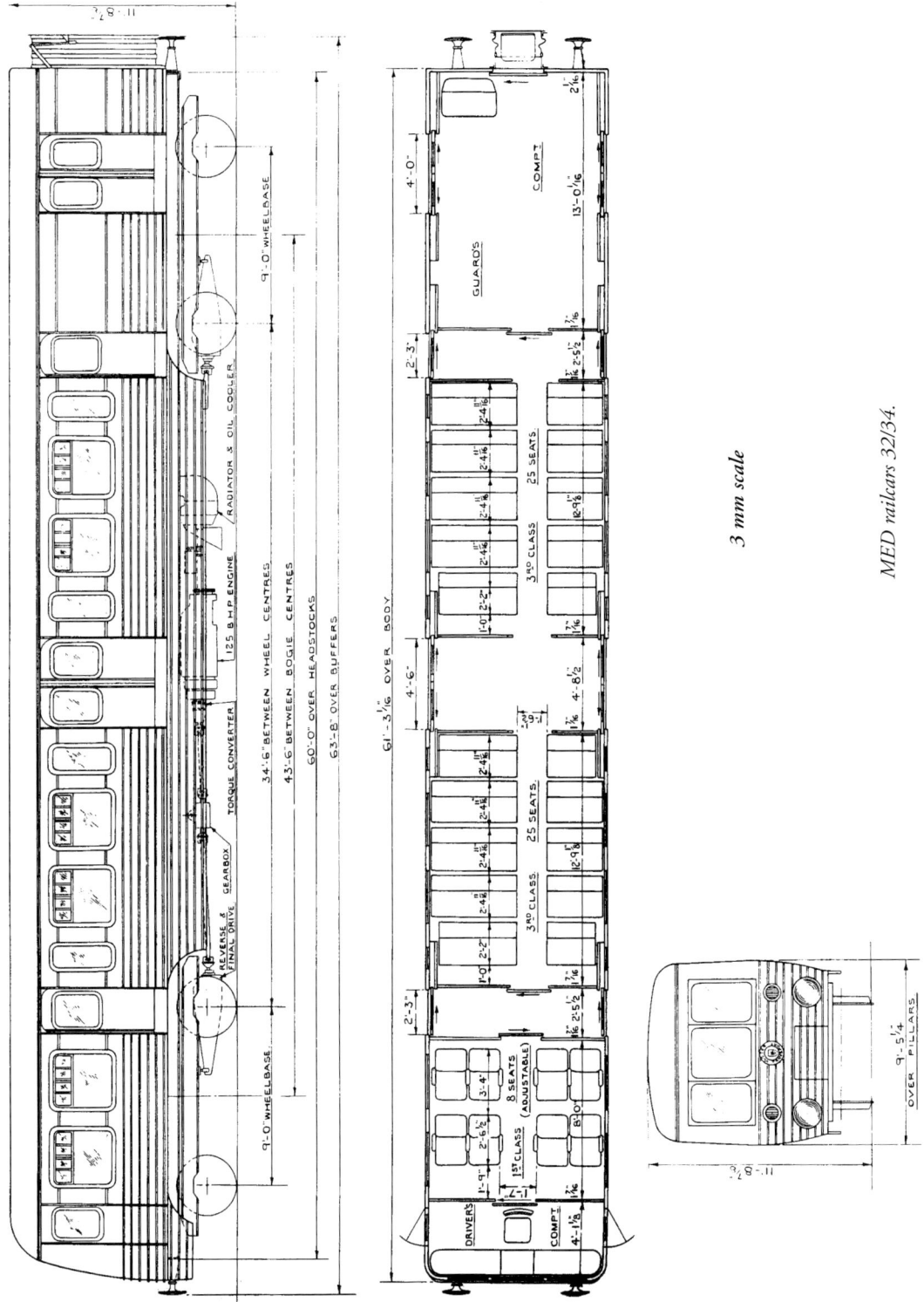

3 mm scale

MED railcars 32/34.

87

'Lightweight' body, with the low roof profile, under construction at Duncrue Street. Nos 24–35, and trailers 201–14, were built totally new with steel body frames, whilst Nos 14–23 used the underframes and wooden body ribs from J4/J5 centre corridor thirds dating from 1925–30, clad in steel panelling.

CP Friel collection

MED trailer No 506 (originally 206) just out of shops after an overhaul at Duncrue Street works in April 1964. The footsteps under the doors are picked out in silver paint. The inset lights can be clearly seen. This useful safety feature was not repeated on the later MPD and DE railcars and is still relatively uncommon today.

DJA Young

would be reprieved, and some of the new units used to provide services on this once busy stretch of the old BCDR system. But it was not to be.

Each 'set' was to be formed of two power cars and a trailer and the main batch of trailers were built in the same way as the final four power cars, with an integral design of chassis and underframe. Fourteen trailers (numbered originally 201–214)

were delivered between August 1952 and April 1954, as the power cars emerged. Each seated 91 people in a 60 foot vehicle and weighed 26 tons. They had an identical body style to that of power cars 24–35 and were renumbered in 1959 as 501–514. The Ganz trailer, No 215, had a similar body style but had nine fewer seats and a brake compartment. It became an MED trailer in 1963.

With the completion of the building programme in April 1954, the UTA arranged this publicity photograph. Under overcast skies, seven six-car trains were assembled at Queen's Quay Station, all those visible in the same livery with the pale green 'loop' round the front UTA symbol. In this striking finish the horizontal ribs were picked out in the lighter shade (except for the area within the loop). By then the pale green roof had given way to grey, except for a stripe just above the cantrail. No 29, with its higher UTA symbol, is on the right. The earlier smooth sided units in the original livery were placed inside the station out of view.

DJA Young collection

In-service modifications

Four years after the arrival of the first units, a programme of re-engining began in 1956. The original engines were of 125 bhp which was pretty well the norm at the time. But new Leyland engines, of an improved design known as the 0/680 type, gave another 40 bhp and it was decided to make use of these to allow the running of four car trains. The new engines gave much greater torque (475 lb/ft at 1150 rpm

compared with 410 at 900). Surprisingly BUT/Leyland information of the time gives its power rating at 150 bhp and as such it appeared in many BR railcars. Where the UTA got the extra 15 bhp is not clear, but by the mid-1960s the figure of 150 bhp was also being quoted for the MED trains – statistics can be misleading!! The greater power now meant that that four-car sets were possible. As a result, extra trailers were needed, but these were very basic conversions from older ex-NCC hauled stock.

These carriages were 57 feet long and, with two exceptions, were of the ex-LMS J11 non-corridor type, with higher pitched roofs. Apart from cabling, no alteration was made, the cars even retaining their original numbers until 1959. The ten compartment coaches were of varying age too. Four (later 517–19 and 525) were fully panelled coaches from the 1920s. The others were steel panelled, though two (later 520/21) were in the earlier LMS 'Period 2' style. In fact these coaches actually held more travellers than their newer counterparts – 108 seats. The rather sleek look of the original power cars, with their smooth front ends and skirts, was certainly not helped by the addition of older compartment coaches in the middle of a rake, with their higher roofs and different panelling.

The two exceptions – Nos 255 and 261 (later 526/27) – were J5 centre corridor stock from 1929–30, seating 80 and having two lavatories each. These were in fact the same type as had been rebuilt into power cars 14–23. MEDs were always seen as suburban units and toilets were fitted to only one other trailer, 523, which had them after rebuilding in 1969. All of these carriages were fitted with Westinghouse air brakes. With 12 four- and two three-car sets now available, some were now transferred to the NCC section.

In fact, running four-coach trains does not seem to have been a very long-lived feature – the steep banks and curves of the ex-BCDR line provided a stiff test to any railcar and although the new sets had a similar power/weight ratio as the older three-car ones, there was no more weight available for adhesion. By the mid-1960s three-car sets became the norm again, which probably reflects the ageing process for engines and transmissions.

However, it was not in the nature of things that the homogeneous class of 14 MED trailers built new would remain unmodified. Between December 1957 and April 1958, 204–209 (as they were then) were fitted with drivers' cabs at the expense of four seats to allow short formations of one driving car and one trailer to operate off-peak services. These cars were reclassified J19.

In December 1961, the driving equipment was removed from Nos 505–07 (as they had become in 1959) and placed at the No 2 end of power cars 24, 26 and 28, thus allowing them to operate as single units. In 1963–65 the cabs were removed as well. Controls remained in Nos 504, 508 and 509. The number of seats also fluctuated as the original boilers were removed in 1960–61 and replaced by Smith's heaters as mentioned earlier. This restored two seats as the original boilers in the trailers had taken up space equivalent to two seats.

In 1962, Nos 526 and 527, along with 518, had the unusual distinction of being fitted with through vacuum pipes so that they could work with MPDs as well as MEDs (see page 139).

MED No 19 leading a six car train at Tillysburn in July 1964 – with a four car set strengthened by a trailer and power car at the front. The train includes two of the non-corridor J11 trailers converted in 1956. These did nothing for the aesthetic appearance of the set!

EM Patterson 1060

An MED set, led by an unidentified driving trailer, approaching Helen's Bay. It was found that there was not really much benefit in using these. The controls were removed from three of them in 1961 and fitted in power cars but Nos 504, 508 and 509 retained their driving cabs until withdrawal.

EM Patterson 95R

A rare view of an MED operating as a single unit. No 28 is seen operating a Sunday service at Helen's Bay in January 1967. Despite appearances, this is a down working using the up line to pass the permanent way train visible in the distance.

RF Whitford

MEDs were rarely used on what would be considered high-speed longer-distance services – the lack of toilets on most of the cars and bus-type seating would have made that a dubious pleasure. Nonetheless they were capable of good performance, especially when the sets were reduced to three again with the heavier engines. Ride could be 'lively' at higher speeds – certainly the author would rate the MPDs better in this respect. Maximum speed on the Bangor line was 60 mph and the governed speed of 55 was adequate for this.

At one point, one of the sets that worked on the NCC was used for an experiment. The gearbox was locked in the higher setting (73 mph top speed) and a three-car set was taken to Londonderry. The purpose of this was presumably to evaluate the type for use on the NCC main line to enable passenger services to be dieselised. Quite clearly the internal setup would not be satisfactory but, if the mechanicals worked, then maybe they would have been developed. However, it seems that the trial was not deemed a success, with overheating of the torque converters generated by the higher sustained speeds and stiffer gradients encountered. A different type of unit would be needed and its story is told in Chapter 12.

The other major development in service was that, between 1966 and 1969, the original hydraulic transmission (using Leyland/Lysholm Smith torque converters) was replaced by mechanical gearboxes manufactured by Self Changing Gears Ltd which incorporated Wilson four-speed epicyclic gears. The torque converters had proved to have a limited lifespan by railway standards – this may have been partially due to the increased power they had to absorb since the re-engining in 1956. Spare parts were also becoming difficult to obtain.

Rather than fit new Schneider torque converters similar to those on the MPDs, it was decided to fit gearboxes, similar to those fitted to the majority of British Railways DMUs. These would be easy to obtain and spares would not be a problem. Gearboxes would do fine for the MEDs as there was never any question of them being used for freight haulage, unlike their younger sisters the MPDs. It was also clear that mainline services would be handled by the new diesel electric railcars which began to arrive in 1966. After this there were no major mechanical modifications carried out on any of the MED class.

In 1969 the introduction of conductor guards meant that non-corridor carriages were no longer suitable in traffic. Two of the non-corridor trailers, 519 and 523, had their bodywork rebuilt with centre corridors, and 523 had toilets added.

Livery

As described earlier, the MEDs, when first introduced, appeared in two liveries, both 'Deep Brunswick' green. Nos 8–13 had a narrow body stripe below and a broader one above the windows, similar to Nos 6 and 7. The colour of the stripe was not cream as is often supposed but a very light green, in fact the same colour as used on the roofs of UTA buses. The cab area was picked out in the same colour.

The 'ribbed' cars, Nos 14–35 and trailers 201–14, had a quite striking livery, with a wide body stripe below the windows which turned down at the front of the cab to form a loop around the UTA 'Red Hand' symbol, placed centrally on the front. The ribs were picked out in pale green, except within the loop. The roof received the light green too but this quickly weathered and was soon replaced by grey apart from a stripe just above cantrail level. Even this disappeared from around 1955 (see photo page 85).

On repainting, the elaborate livery was replaced by plain Brunswick green, apart from a light green cab front above the window level. Only No 14 received the 'Catherwood blue' livery which was applied to some of the MPDs in 1959–60. In the case of No 14 the upper body was white (page 103).

From late 1960, yellow and black warning panels were added to the front of all driving cabs on railcars. Around the same time, the cabs, on repainting, ceased to be picked out in light green.

In 1965 UTA railcars began to appear in three striking new liveries. The UTA was experimenting with different liveries for the various lines. The NCC section railcars came out in a deep red and oyster grey livery, those on the GNR in blue and cream. The MEDs on the Belfast and County Down received a livery of olive green and cream which looked quite well, although it bore no resemblance to any livery actually carried by the BCDR, whose locos had been a dark green and whose coaches had been maroon. This livery was not carried by any other stock.

The regional variations were short-lived and by 1967, the NCC section livery became standard for all NIR diesel trains. No MEDs were repainted into the post-1970 livery of dark blue and maroon, although the trailers which survived to be made into parcels vans, working on the Larne line, were painted unlined maroon in their last years.

From the mid-1950s, the MED livery was gradually simplified. The body stripes disappeared , though the cab areas retained the pale green rectangle (see colour section). From late 1960 the livery was as seen here – plain Brunswick green, relieved only by the yellow and black visibility panel. MED 32 leads a six coach train through the disused halt at Tillysburn, just outside Holywood, in July 1964.

EM Patterson 106P

The last years

In June 1969, following the introduction of conductor guards by NIR, the remaining non-corridor trailers were stored and subsequently broken up in the early 1970s.

Having been originally specifically designed for the BCDR line to Bangor, the MEDs were the only form of motive power to be found on the Bangor line between the closing of the link line through Maysfield in 1965 and the opening of the new Central Station in 1976. Generally 14 units were to be found here with the other 12 used chiefly on the NCC line to Larne, where the MEDs worked a number of services. They were also to be found on stopping services to Ballymena, though rarely north of there.

The GNR section was largely worked by AEC and BUT railcars until these began to be withdrawn shortly before the MEDs themselves and they were rarely seen on that section either, though occasionally units would be transferred to deputise if there was a crisis of availability, something which did become much more common as the older ex-GNR railcars wore out From 1976 they became much more common on the GNR section.

One trailer (506) was withdrawn after a bomb explosion in October 1973, as was power car 12. Four (508, 511–13) were converted to luggage vans around 1975. Windows were removed and new larger (manual) sliding doors fitted. They had a capacity of 7 tons and became Nos 631–634. They joined two similar vans (621 and 622) converted from old AEC railcars, as well as some ex-LMS design vans dating from 1936. Surprisingly enough, the ex-Ganz trailer (515) was also converted, in 1973, retaining its original number. All finally disappeared in the early 1980s, being scrapped along with MPD railcars withdrawn at that time.

As the MEDs were being withdrawn a major problem presented itself. They, like many other vehicles of the 1950s, contained blue asbestos. No one had thought anything of this at the time – blue asbestos was commonly used for insulation in those days – but in the late 1970s new legislation introduced strict regulations for the disposal of any vehicle with this material. Of course, many vehicles had already gone for scrap

MED 10 (probably with MED 21) on the Larne line near Whitehead, in July 1977. By this time most MEDs operated as 'power twins'.   *JM Allen*

Some MED units survived to carry a short lived NIR 'Citytrack' branding. One such was MED 33, seen here near Hilden on the ex GNR line to Portadown, in 1977. The re-opening of the Belfast central line meant that they were to be seen on the ex GNR main line from time to time.   *JM Allen*

A number of MED trailers were converted into luggage vans by NIR. No 511, seen here at Antrim in 1980 as luggage van 634, was converted in 1975.   *JM Allen*

or disposal at Magheramorne near Larne, but for those left, a number of alternatives had to be investigated.

Unfortunately there was no specialist contractor in Northern Ireland who could dispose of this material safety. Consequently many out-of-service MEDs lay for some considerable time while plans were made for their safe disposal.

Burning under controlled conditions was possible but the nearest place for this was in Newmarket, England. In any case, the cost of transporting the large number of redundant vehicles – MED, MPD, and the body shells of Class 70 diesel electrics power cars and trailers – would have been very high. Another possible option was dumping at sea off the Copeland Islands – an idea that was rejected as such dumping was now contrary to international conventions. The possibility of setting up a plant to strip the asbestos was considered, but again ruled out on grounds of cost.

So, dumping somewhere in Northern Ireland it would have to be. Two possible dumping grounds were considered where it was felt the environment would not suffer. Interestingly, one of these was a long-disused railway tunnel on the old Markethill to Goraghwood line (closed in 1955) – the Lissummon Tunnel – which was still in a satisfactory condition. The idea would be to re-instate a section of the line and deliver the vehicles to the site using this temporary line. On completion, the tunnel mouths would be sealed. However, a former quarry at Crosshill, County Antrim, near Crumlin, was found to be ideal for the burial of the contaminated vehicles. It was only a short distance from the railway, and vehicles travelled to a specially constructed siding where the bodies were cut off the underframes. They were finally taken by road a short distance and tipped into the flooded quarry – filled with water to depths of up to 80 feet.

One small group of MEDs almost made it into preservation. Power cars Nos 10, 19 and 21 (which did not contain the blue asbestos of some of their later cousins) were transferred to the Railway Preservation Society of Ireland. It was planned to refurbish them using parts from BR. Sadly, however, this scheme did not proceed and the bodies were used at storage huts at the former Nutts Corner Airport until September 1980. They were then cut up – a dismal ending for the last of a significant class which pioneered wide-scale dieselisation in the British Isles.

Next stop, Crosshill Quarry. MEDs 24 and 30, and numerous BUTs, await their final disposal at Antrim in April 1980.　　　　　　　　　　　　　　　　　　　　　*JM Allen*

Ex GNR 204 bhp railcar 'G' running over the Gormanstown viaduct on a Dublin-Drogheda train in late spring 1959. Built in 1938, railcar G passed to CIÉ in 1958 but was never re-painted by them. It was sold to the UTA in 1962, becoming No 105, and finished its working life on the Warrenpoint branch in 1965.

Colour-Rail

Ex NCC railcar No 1 at Templepatrick on a local working from Ballymena. It was permitted to haul up to 21 tons trailing weight on the line between Belfast and Antrim (as were Nos 3 and 4). By the time this photograph was taken, in 1965, No 1 was nearing the end of her active career with the UTA, being withdrawn officially later that year.

DJA Young

Ex NCC railcar No 4 at York Road No 2 platform in April 1964. Judging by the mop and bucket on the platform, someone has been cleaning the windows while the railcar waited for its next turn of duty; something never seen on today's railway.

RH Whitford

Railcars 6 and 7 in original condition, arriving at Belfast (Queen's Quay) in June 1953. This experimental three-car unit was powered by AEC engines similar to those of the GNR 600 class, but had a new control system and transmission. Their success led to the widespread introduction of diesel railcars on Northern Ireland's railway system. The units are in their original livery – used also on MED cars 8–13.

JM Jarvis, Colour-Rail

Railcars 6 and 7, pass Magheramorne signal box with an afternoon boat train from Larne Harbour near the end of their active career in July 1966. Although the oldest of the UTA designed railcars, they were still capable of a good turn of speed. They were never re-engined, nor was the transmission system changed during their service life of nearly twenty years! The siding in the foreground was being laid for the now famous spoil contract. **DJA Young**

Ex GNR AEC unit No 112 leaves Finaghy station in May 1959. Although it carries its new number, it has not been repainted, with only the UTA 'Red Hand' symbol on the front to denote its new owners. The area around the three car unit has completely changed today, and semaphore signals and wooden halt shelter have also long gone. No 112 was withdrawn in 1970. **JG Dewing, Colour-Rail IR 492**

Ex GNR AEC unit No 113 heads an excursion train away from Bangor station in May 1962. The UTA converted all its ex GNR AECs to allow multiple unit working. This seven coach train includes four power cars and three trailers. 113 has been repainted in the final UTA green livery with 'wasp' panel and green upper front panels.

RH Whitford

At Derriaghy halt on the Belfast-Lisburn section, AEC car 115 brings up the rear of a Belfast bound train in July 1969. It is wearing the 'suburban' version of the 1965 'regional' livery,, with a narrow white band at window levels. The 'regional' liveries were a welcome change from the previous UTA green but were to be eventually swept away with the introduction of the NIR livery of deep red and oyster grey.

Colour-Rail

CIÉ adopted a green livery for its AEC diesel railcars, although it was a brighter shade than that of the UTA. Here 2607 is leading a four-car set comprised of two power cars and two trailer coaches (the usual formation south of the border) into Killiney station south of Dublin. This area has been called 'Ireland's Bay of Naples' and it looks delightful on a sunny June day in 1959. **JG Dewing, Colour-Rail IR 336**

CIÉ initially used its 60 AEC railcars on main line services and in June 1963 No 2627, in the tan and gold livery, passes Limerick Junction on a Cork–Dublin train. The two green vehicles are of particular interest. They were built using AEC parts under the direction of O V Bulleid. Although originally fitted with driving cabs, by 1963 they were being used as powered intermediates, as in this eight coach train. **JD Fitzgerald**

UTA Multi Engined Diesel railcar No 28 at Belfast's Queen's Quay station in May 1957. In 1953 the Bangor line became the first suburban line in the British Isles to see total dieselisation of its services. There were many variations over the years in the UTA green livery. This was the late 1950s version. Nos 24–35 had Metal Sections Ltd bodies. No 28 was introduced to traffic in December 1952 and was withdrawn in 1978.   **Colour-Rail IR 183**

Six MED trailers (504-509) had driving cabs fitted in 1957-8. The introduction of these allowed two-car sets to operate. Here an unidentified one heads a four-car train towards Bangor near Helen's Bay on Easter Monday April 1962. In general, the ratio of two power cars to one trailer was more satisfactory on the steeply graded line beyond Holywood.   **RH Whitford**

So far as is known, No 14 was the only MED car to receive this short lived variation in livery, with a much paler shade of green, similar to the 'Catherwood Blue' or 'eau de nil' applied to the UTA's bus fleet in 1959-60. Some MPDs received it as an all over colour (page 173).– the MED version had a white upper band from below window level to cantrail, which improved it somewhat. Note the metal disc which previously carried the UTA roundel.

Colour-Rail

In 1965 the UTA experimented with different liveries for the three 'regions', each having two variations. The 'Down Region' got an attractive olive green and cream scheme. At first this had a narrow cream band to denote 'suburban' and this is shown applied to units 26 and 27, and one trailer car, at Helen's bay in May 1966, passing 34 (still in the older UTA colours) on a works train.

RH Whitford

During 1966 the distinction between 'suburban' and 'mainline' was abandoned and one MED set got the broader cream band as seen on 16, 17 and trailer 509 at Queen's Quay in February 1967. This paint was of very high quality and lasted much better than the dark green. However it was soon to be superseded by the deep red and oyster grey of Northern Ireland Railways.   ***RH Whitford***

When the UTA introduced 'regional' liveries in 1965, they chose deep red and oyster grey for the ex-NCC section. Very few vehicles were ever painted in the 'suburban' variation of this. One example was MED trailer No 518, seen here at York Road in February 1967, sporting the narrow grey band. No 518 was a conversion from an LMS coach transferred to Northern Ireland to replace coaches destroyed in the Blitz.   ***RH Whitford***

9 The British Railways connection

Ireland's railways have not always been recognised for their contribution to the pre-eminence of the British railway industry. It is certainly true that in many cases they followed rather than set trends from 'across the water'. There was a certain amount of 'people export' in steam days – the names of Ivatt and Maunsell, for example, come to mind. These were among other men whose careers began on an Irish railway – in the case of the first, the GNR(I), and the latter, the GSR – though in neither case were their Irish efforts particularly distinguished.

Perhaps the most interesting example of someone who made the journey in the opposite direction was OV Bulleid who came to Ireland in 1951 from British Railways as CIÉ's chief engineer. His innovative mind led to the procurement of CIÉ coaches, wider than anything else anywhere, and to experiments with turf-burning locomotives.

However, unlike the situation regarding conventional steam traction, it is interesting to note how for a period dating from the early 1930s to the late 1950s Ireland led the way in diesel traction, especially railcars. In one sense, the reason isn't hard to discover. Ireland had (and has) a much smaller population than mainland Britain. Most of her railways were under earlier pressure from road omnibus and freight services. It is therefore not surprising that they should have embraced the concept of the 'bus on wheels' in an effort to stay in touch with the passenger market. It was also realised quite early on that the self-powered diesel train could be much more than just a branch line affair. Only on the GWR in England was there any comparable interest, and the GNR's AEC cars of 1950 could well be seen as a synthesis of their own pre-war development and that of the GWR in developing a three-car set which was capable of mainline operation.

It is also worth remembering that the NCC's railcars, in particular, were capable of running at mainline speeds of 60 mph and over. Some of those involved in the development of these railcars have argued that the parent LMS was happy to allow the small team in Belfast to work on development and collect data on the technical aspects of running diesel units before the LMS itself got involved (as it did, just prior to World War Two).

It was to be the period just after World War Two, as recounted in chapters 6–8, which really got things moving, with units on the GNR taking over mainline services with high-speed timings and the UTA's fleet of MEDs in 1952-53 taking over the complete operation of what, for years, was the busiest suburban line in the island of Ireland.

British Railways had undoubtedly been watching these experiments with much interest, and Irish railwaymen from this era remember regular visits and interchanges of information both on technical and operational matters. Therefore it was not surprising that, when they did finally decide to introduce railcars on a wide scale, the British Railways team, headed by RA Riddles, should produce initial designs which, in the author's opinion, had UTA/GNR written all over them. A further connection was that the Leyland and AEC companies were also heavily involved in the development of these BR units.

The first British Railways' DMUs were known as the 'Derby Lightweights' and ultimately numbered 219 vehicles. The first eight cars entered service in the West Riding in June 1954,

The pioneer two-car 'Derby Lightweight' set on test at Melbourne on 1 April 1954. The first eight 'Derby Lightweight' sets had 125bhp Leyland engines and were strongly influenced by the MED design. They used the same engine and transmission system (Lysholm-Smith torque converter) as the MEDs, but after the first eight sets the simpler mechanical gearbox was adopted.

J Robertson, The Transport Treasury

fitted with Leyland 125-bhp horizontally mounted engines driving the inner axles of the bogie. This was precisely the layout adopted by the UTA for its MED fleet of two years before.

The similarities continued in the transmission system – once again Lysholm Smith (Leyland) Torque converters were employed, with a double-acting clutch which allowed the engine to be connected to the true converter drive or direct to the output shaft. Freewheels were incorporated once again to prevent engines being overrun. Leyland Motors and Walkers of Wigan jointly developed the final drive systems, as well as the controls, which provided for four engine speeds as well as idle, exactly as on the controls system of the MEDs.

Maximum speed was set at 62 mph, somewhat slower than the higher top speeds specified for the MEDs, although higher than those units

lower-gear top speed of 55 mph, a change which reflected the different use for these railcars. They were intended for cross-country lines rather than intensive suburban or mainline use. The remainder of the Derby Lightweight cars used gearboxes and 150 bhp engines, and this became more or less the standard for later units as the diesel train became more widely used across the UK.

The control system patented by the UTA for operating up to eight engines was also used in many BR railcars, though of course as time passed, such systems were further developed. Many later BR railcars could not work with other than their own classes and sub-classes, though as they were spread widely over the British Railways extensive network this was not seen as a problem.

Later batches of these BR railcars had BUT

A two car set of Cravens Class 105/106 railcars, headed by M51751 at Skipton about 1960. This type was introduced in 1956 and most had two 150bhp BUT or Leyland engines, similar to those later used in the GNR BUT cars, with which their front end treatment had parallels. A hundred of this type were given single 8-cyl 238 bhp Rolls Royce engines with torque converters.
The Transport Treasury

engines of 150 bhp similar to those of the units which the GNR was ordering about the same time (see Chapter 11), but in the British Railways' units these were horizontally mounted. They were connected to a four-speed gearbox provided by Self Changing Gears who also supplied the GNR BUT drive trains and later supplied automatic gearboxes for the UTA's new Multi Purpose Diesel railcars.

The only significant area where British Railways chose not to follow the UTA lead was in doors, BR staying with the traditional slam door rather than opting for the sophisticated air door system used by the UTA. In this they may have been wise – later railcars in Northern Ireland also found this innovation one step too far and it was not until the 1980s that power doors were seen again on Irish railcars!

For some reason the Irish input to the British Railways DMU programme does not seem to have been much recognised, even though it predated and was developed throughout the Modernisation Plan itself. There are occasional references in some publications to design 'from other countries' being studied before the first units were produced, but who else was working closely with Leyland and Walkers in the early 1950s? Certainly the occasional railcar unit was produced for overseas, but where were there significant numbers of diesel railcars operating

on lines essentially similar in most respects to British Railways, and less than 12 hours away by overnight ferry? The answer to all these questions is Northern Ireland, of course.

Almost as if to rub salt in the wound of 'non recognition', a publicity brochure *Railcar Progress Around the British Isles*, produced by the Self Changing Gears Co Ltd in 1957, has fascinating 'gaps' despite its purporting to be 'impartial'! In a section on Ireland (north and south), reference is made to the Donegal railcars, the GNR and CIÉ machines, and an account of the latest GNR BUT railcars, then just being delivered.

But what of the advanced diesel trains described in the last two chapters? Well, they are mentioned as follows, "These trains operate services between Belfast and Bangor . . . the general layout of these railcars is similar to that used by British Railways when they produced their first diesel cars in 1954". The Derby Lightweights entered service in June 1954 and were all withdrawn by 1969, although a few survived in departmental use. The first UTA MED entered service in May 1952 and the complete fleet of 28 power cars was in service by the end of 1953. They lasted until the mid-1970s. So who copied who? I think the answer is fairly obvious.

Later, as development continued, there was

One of the 'Derby Heavyweights', or Class 114 units, introduced in 1956. These had 6cyl 230bhp Leyland engines of the type later used in turbo-charged form in the UTA MPD cars. Front end treatment reflected the 1952 MED design. Here E50006 leads the 14.58 ex-New Holland Pier at Town Station on 5 May 1981.

RH Whitford

more in the way of cross-channel two-way traffic – the UTA MPD railcars of 1957 onwards originally used a similar Leyland engine to those of a two-car BR DMU, produced under the Modernisation Plan in 1956–57.

Unit No 50049 (of what would become known as Class 114 under the TOPS classification) was fitted with two 230-bhp Leyland engines as the original engines of the class proved to be underpowered for their weight. It was also fitted with a new SCG four-speed automatic gearbox (though not the torque converter). The first railcar of this type (known as 'Derby Heavyweights') – Unit 50000 – had been built with two of the experimental Rolls Royce 8-cylinder 238-bhp engines with a torque converter, a high-power railcar indeed. Once again, however, this design was not perpetuated and 50000 was withdrawn early due to its non-standard nature. It is not known whether 50049 retained its automatic gearbox or for how long.

In the 1960s the UTA's MED trains would receive Self Changing Gears (SCG) Wilson four-speed gearboxes which were in all respects the same as those fitted to many BR DMUs. There was even a proposal, which was not taken entirely seriously by management at the time, to re-gauge the Bangor line and run it using second-hand BR DMUs! By this time BR had a surplus of the type, due to the closure of so many

of the lines for which they were designed.

Today it is realised that innovation is both expensive and risky, something which the engineers of the 1950s were to learn the hard way. In the case of the UTA, they did not have the luxury of 'scrap and start again' which the larger British Railways did – the number of units involved just wasn't big enough. So designs which BR would undoubtedly have withdrawn (as they did many of the Rolls Royce-engined railcars) were perforce kept in service in Northern Ireland long after they would otherwise have been. This situation led to general dissatisfaction from engineers, operators and public alike. It was particularly the case with the Multi Purpose Railcars to be described in Chapter 12.

And yet a quick look at the specification of the Class 150 and Class151 'Sprinters' which BR and Metro Cammell respectively developed in the mid 1980's, is fascinating when compared to the ground breaking MPD design of 1957, over 25 years earlier.

1957	UTA MPD	Leyland (later RR) 275 bhp
1984	BR 150 001	Cummins 285 bhp
	BR 150 002	Rolls Royce (Perkins) 285 bhp
1985	BR 151 001/2	Cummins 285 bhp

An MPD Mk 2? The natural development of the UTA MPD type railcars of 1957–62 were the 'Sprinters' introduced by the old BR in 1984, which had a very similar engine and transmission layout (see Ch 12). On 15 August 1988, set 150 126 pauses at Harlech on an afternoon train from Aberystwyth to Pwllheli.

WN Johnston

(Ultimately the Cummins engine became standard for all, including later class 155/6 'Supersprinters'). The 1957 Leyland was way ahead of its time in terms of output per litre.

The transmissions on each type were as follows:

1957 UTA MPD – Hydraulic/mechanical - Torque converter and automatic four speed gearbox.

1984 BR 150.001 – Hydraulic/mechanical: Voith transmission – torque converter with three speed 'gearbox' (actually all contained as a single unit, Type T211)

1984 BR 150.002 – Mechanical SCG gearbox – not a success, unlike the earlier BR 'first generation' units.

1985 BR 151.001/2 – Hydraulic/mechanical : Torque converter and three speed 'Hot shift' gearbox – this gearbox was also troublesome and finally the Voith system was adopted for all later designs and production runs of Class 150. The 151 sets remain in existence but out of use at Crewe.

So the changes were rung with various alternatives but essentially there is some truth in the comment referred to later in Chapter 12 that the 'Sprinter' type is essentially an 'MPD Mk2'. However, I have to admit that in this case there is no evidence that UTA development of the type many years earlier played any part in the development of the universal 'Sprinter' family of DMUs which still operate so many suburban and secondary services in the UK mainland.

10 Diesel locomotives of the UTA and GNRI

Although the main theme of this book is the Irish contribution to the development of the diesel railcar, the story of GNR and NCC/UTA dieselisation would be incomplete without reference to the small collection of unique diesel locomotives operated alongside the railcars. Unfortunately there is no space in the present volume to tell the story of the much larger fleet of CIÉ diesel locomotives introduced from as early as 1947. Their story deserves a book in its own right.

From the foregoing chapters you might be forgiven for assuming that there was no interest in diesel locomotives, as opposed to railcars, in either the GNR or UTA. But this was not so. Recent research has turned up documents which suggest that the victory of the diesel railcar for mainline passenger haulage was by no means as foregone a conclusion in 1952–53 as it seems with hindsight.

The use of diesel power for haulage of both passenger and freight had started more or less simultaneously with the early efforts to produce passenger-only vehicles, and units such as the Clogher Valley rail lorry, which used an identical power bogie to that of the company's railcar, provided what might be termed the first 'diesel traction unit.'

Then there was the *Phoenix*. The Atkinson Walker steam tram locomotive, bought in 1927 by the Clogher Valley Railway and found to be a waste of time, was sold to the County Donegal Railway in 1932. Here it underwent a metamorphosis so complete that it was given the name *Phoenix*. What eventually emerged from the works at Stranorlar was a small 74 bhp diesel-powered tractor unit (or locomotive). This was numbered 11 in the railcar series and spent much of its long life shunting at Strabane with occasional trips to Letterkenny and Stranorlar. It

Phoenix *shunting at Stranorlar in August 1950. It was converted from a Clogher Valley Railway steam engine and powered by a 74 bhp Gardner diesel engine.* Phoenix *can be seen at the Ulster Folk and Transport Museum at Cultra, near Belfast.*

GW Sharpe

Harland and Wolff's pioneering diesel electric locomotive D1 (later 2) at Ballynahinch station. Its massive marine style diesel engine produced 270 bhp. Twenty five years later this level of power was being produced by an engine mounted under the floor of a carriage.

Real Photographs X716

was withdrawn when the system closed in 1959 and can still be seen in the Ulster Folk and Transport Museum.

On the broad gauge, the UTA inherited a few diesel electric and diesel hydraulic locomotives from the County Down and the NCC. The oldest of these locomotives dated from 1933. No 'D1' (renumbered '2' in 1937) on the BCDR was a diesel electric 1-Bo locomotive built by Harland and Wolff. It had an 8-cylinder two-stroke engine delivering 270 bhp at 850 rpm and weighed 33 tons.

On D1's inaugural run in June 1933 there were great hopes for it, as it had attained a speed of 60 mph pulling two coaches on the way to Newcastle. Grandiose statements about the future, envisaging a fleet of such locomotives, were made on that occasion, proving that the substance of 'hype' (although the modern term was unknown) was with us many years ago!

However, reality in due course set in and D1 did not live up to the great expectations expressed at that inaugural dinner in the Slieve Donard hotel. The locomotive spent its life on the BCDR's Ballynahinch branch, pulling a couple of six-wheel coaches at modest speed, with occasional visits to Belfast for servicing. After virtually the entire BCDR was closed in

1950, No 2 (officially renumbered 202, though it never actually carried the number) ran a shuttle service for some months on the Newcastle–Castlewellan section, which remained open. In May 1950 it took part in the trials previously mentioned (Chapter 5), but it did not work for the UTA again.

In 1951 it was returned to Harland and Wolff and became their works shunter, with the centre wheels removed to negotiate the very tight radius curves in the shipyard. The locomotive carried its County Down green livery to the end, apart from the H&W logo on the tank sides, and was cut up sometime around 1969, when road vehicles replaced the rail system within the shipyard.

A more modern machine, also from Harland and Wolff, was numbered D2 and appeared on the BCDR in 1937. This was the only pre-war diesel locomotive which was more than a shunter. D2 (soon to be renumbered 28) was a double bogie 1A–A1 with a nominal 500 bhp from its Burmeister and Wain type engine, and an official top speed of 55 mph. There is some evidence that it was originally planned as a Bo-Bo with four traction motors but in the event only two were ever fitted. The County Down used it principally on the Ardglass branch.

Harland and Wolff 500 bhp diesel electric locomotive No 28, newly in service on the BCDR in June 1937. No 28 turned out to have a very long career, although it is reputed to have been troublesome in service with the BCDR.

HC Casserley 14226, courtesy RM Casserley

Harland and Wolff's No 28 in UTA days, arriving at York Road on a train from the Larne Line, probably about 1951. The three bogie coaches make up the maximum load for this locomotive. Though the photo is undated it is assumed it was a summer train – No 28 had no heating apparatus. The NCC had built a special 20 ton heating van to run with it, but it isn't on this train.

Lens of Sutton,

In December 1944, No 28 was returned to Harland and Wolff (the BCDR had never actually bought it) and then in 1945 it passed to the NCC. It worked there for some years and was well thought of. It was here that the 60 mph speed was recorded – it certainly would not have run at that speed on its original County Down branch line! As No 28 had no train-heating equipment, a 20-ton heating van was built to run with it, though this meant that its maximum load was a rather puny 80 tons. The locomotive worked on the NCC section of the UTA until

1952 when it seems to have been returned once again to Harland and Wolff – the engine was apparently 'hired' under a long-term arrangement. Then in 1957 the GNR hired it for shunting work around Great Victoria Street and the Grosvenor Road goods depot. An older steam locomotive with the number 28 had just been withdrawn, so no number change was needed.

When the GNR was divided in October 1958, the UTA took over the hire arrangement on No 28 and subsequently bought the veteran machine

In NIR days, No 28 shunts carriages for a Belfast-Dublin train at great Victoria Street. It was finally scrapped in 1973, still carrying the number 28, which it had held under five companies!

Martin Baumann collection

in 1962 for £2,800. It survived through UTA ownership to pass to NIR in 1967 and lasted until 1973 when, sadly, this pioneer diesel electric locomotive was cut up. It might be noted that No 28 worked under no fewer than five companies, yet never had a number change.

On the BCDR, No 28 was originally turned out in the BCDR lined-green livery but, after it ceased to work there, was painted in a black unlined livery which lasted throughout its remaining long life, although the sides of its cab

were at different times adorned with the letters/crests of its subsequent owners, ending with NIR.

The NCC had three other diesel locomotives, all 'shadowy shunters' as I would dub them, since they spent much of their lives in the works, out of use at the ends of sidings, and certainly largely out of sight of enthusiast cameras. They were also all products of Harland and Wolff, although one had the remarkable distinction of being a 4'8½" gauge locomotive re-gauged to 5'3".

LMS(NCC) No 22, a Harland and Wolff built 0-6-0 shunter, at York Road in September 1946. It was originally built for the LMS in 1934, and had a 150 bhp engine. Operated at Chester and Heysham, it returned from the LMS in January 1945 and was hired to the NCC a year later. By this time the engine had been changed and now provided a more useful 225 bhp.

AW Craughton,

This engine had been built in 1933 for the LMS at a time when shipyards across the UK were looking for other products to offset the loss of shipbuilding work during the depression years. It was a 27-ton diesel hydraulic shunter with a 0-6-0 coupled wheel arrangement and was powered by a H&W-built Burmeister and Wain engine of 150 bhp. Transmission was via a fluid coupling and a two-speed gearbox. The leading axle was driven via a cardan shaft and a worm gear. It was given the number 7057 and worked for the LMS in England for 11 years before returning to Harlands in 1944. Possibly its low power output and the fact that spares would be more easily obtainable from its home works were factors in this move. In 1944 Harlands re-engined it with a new 225-bhp engine, re-gauged it, and it went to work on the NCC as their No 22. In this latter form its top speed was given as 10 mph in high gear and 5 mph in low. It was scrapped in December 1965.

The second of the 'shadowy shunters' was a more powerful machine. In 1936 the NCC took delivery of No 17. This was another diesel hydraulic machine but with 330 bhp available. It weighed 49 tons and had a starting tractive effort of 24,000 lbs – substantially more than the 15,000 lbs of No 22. It too had an 0-6-0 wheel arrangement, although drive in this case was from a jackshaft mounted forward of the leading coupled wheels. As delivered, it had the name *Harlandic* on a plate just under its front

No 22 shunts at Belfast in April 1948. It was a 'pure' shunter, with a top speed of only 10 mph. No 22 was scrapped in 1965.

HC Casserley 51811, courtesy RM Casserley

On the same day, No 17 shunts at the docks in Belfast. The jackshaft drive can be clearly seen. This was a more powerful diesel hydraulic machine of 330 bhp.

HC Casserley 51804, courtesy RM Casserley

In May 1950 No 17 has been freshly painted in UTA livery, and displays it's Harlandic 'brand name' on the bonnet front. No 17 was to pass into NIR ownership in 1967, though as far as is known it never ran after March 1966. It was scrapped in 1970.

Kelland collection 24253

headlight and it was designated 'Class X'. No 17 passed into NIR ownership in 1967 but saw little or no work before its final scrapping around 1970.

The third shunter which ran under the UTA management had the smaller 225 bhp engine – indeed it seems to have used the same powerplant (B&W 6-cylinder two-stroke) with which No 22 was later fitted. However, this machine had originally been built by Harland and Wolff in 1937 as a works shunter and, due to the sharp curves into some of the shops at Queen's island, the unit was an 0-4-0 with four-speed mechanical transmission. It weighed 28 tons and had a top speed of 20 mph.

In 1945 this machine ran on the NCC for a while and was temporarily numbered 20 there. It returned to H&W in 1946 when No 22 arrived. Then in 1951 it was sold (or exchanged) to the UTA in place of 202 (D1) and renumbered 16, taking the number of a small 0-4-0ST which was retired at the time, and retained that number until final scrapping in 1967.

None of these units (with the exception of D2/28) could be seen as being prototypes for mainline development and indeed they weren't. But they provided useful operating experience and their potential was not forgotten.

The smallest of the Harland and Wolff shunters, 0-4-0 No 16, is seen here in typically grimy condition. It was powered by the same type of engine as No 22, generating 225 bhp at 850 rpm. However, it was geared higher, with a maximum speed of 20 mph.

CP Friel collection

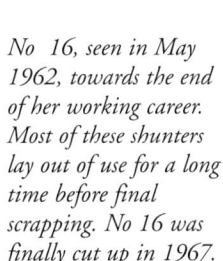

No 16, seen in May 1962, towards the end of her working career. Most of these shunters lay out of use for a long time before final scrapping. No 16 was finally cut up in 1967.

J Oatway 19/3

The UTA/GNR full dieselisation proposals of 1953

In 1951 the Great Northern Railway of Ireland was the largest independent railway company in Ireland. It operated services on an extensive network both north and south of the border. This meant that it could not be absorbed into the UTA or CIÉ, the southern nationalised company.

In 1952 the company got into serious financial trouble and a Board was set up, with both UTA and CIÉ representation. Known as the GNR Board, this arrangement lasted until 1958.

Working in collaboration with the UTA engineers, a study was carried out on behalf of both the UTA and the GNR Board with a view to discovering how best to dieselise both networks. The report presented to the UTA Board in 1953 made some startling reading. Although the new UTA railcars were now entering service and proving successful, they were not considered to be the answer for mainline operations or rural lines. Neither was it proposed to go for large-scale acquisitions of railcars from AEC, who had supplied the GNR with 20 in 1950–51. Mainline services, and freight, it was concluded, would need locomotives.

The study group, known as the Diesel Traction Committee, was given a brief to report upon:

> The number of diesel traction units (whether locomotives or railcars) – specifying types required to operate UTA and GNR lines; sources of supply, prices, delivery dates etc. Proposals for maintenance and repairs were to be considered, and some calculation was to be made of estimated economies in permanent way maintenance and renewals.

> Finally, how long was all this to take, realistically?

The underlying assumption was that all services would be operated by diesel. It must be remembered that the rapid and disastrous loss of freight by railways had not yet happened and that cattle traffic was still a major feature of Irish railway operations, particularly on the GNR sections. Therefore diesel locomotives were very much 'in the frame' and a number of manufacturers were approached to see what might be available.

The requirement was for four types of motive power – two of locomotives and two of railcars, which were under consideration for some mainline and branch services. The first type of locomotive, for mainline and freight services, would have been medium powered (800–1000 bhp), capable of hauling 600-ton freight trains at 30–35 mph, and express passenger trains of six coaches (approx 180 tons) at 70–75mph. They should be capable of double heading, and a weight limit of approximately 58 tons was decided upon, due to track limitations on many parts of the network of both systems.

It was felt that 40 such locomotives would be needed for the GNR sections and 16 for the UTA. No such locomotives were then in service in Ireland – or anywhere in the UK for that matter – except for a few British prototypes and CIÉ Nos 1100 and 1101.

The second type would be light locomotives for shunting and trip work at 30–35mph were required. In all, 24 of these would be needed.

Mainline railcars capable of operating up to eight coaches (four power and four trailer) were also to be acquired and railcars for branch line services were contemplated too. If possible, they should be able to work with each other and with the mainline cars. The pre-war and newer AEC railcars of the GNR and NCC were still operating. The new MED diesel railcars would also naturally remain in service.

Firms in the USA, Europe and Britain were all approached for the mainline locomotives and a total of 19 proposals were received. In the end, four types were shortlisted – one was diesel mechanical, two had hydraulic transmission, and one was diesel electric. It is interesting to note that most diesel electrics (the type which was ultimately to triumph just about everywhere) were rejected either on grounds of cost or weight – the 58-ton limit proving unattainable for most designs of this type in 1953. Indeed, the weight

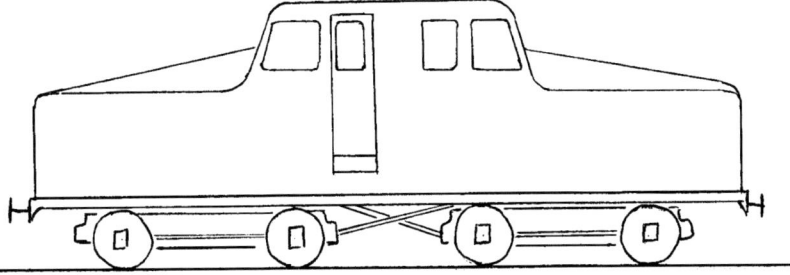

British United Traction Ltd proposed mixed traffic diesel locomotive for the Ulster Transport Authority.

Type:	Diesel mechanical	Max speed:	75 mph (high), 35 mph (low)
Engines:	4 x 200 bhp @ 1800 rpm	Weight:	40 tons
	AEC or Leyland	Max. axle load:	10 tons
Transmission:	4 fluid flywheels & 4 Wilson	Length:	34'0"
	epicyclic gearboxes with auxiliary	Price:	Two prototypes £30,000 each, then
	& transfer gearboxes; all axles driven.		£25,000 excluding heat; freight extra.

problem was one that had a great deal to do with the short-lived success of diesel hydraulics on the ex-GWR lines in Britain.

The first type of mainline locomotive considered was from BUT (British United Traction). This company's rail division had been formed in 1953, being an amalgamation of the engine makers AEC and Leyland, who had of course provided railcars and engines to both the GNR and UTA. Their locomotive proposal showed its railcar heritage very clearly. They proposed a centre-cab diesel mechanical double-bogie locomotive with four 200-bhp engines, two under each 'bonnet'. The locomotive weight was only 40 tons (a very low weight!), while the engines – turbo-charged developments of the existing 125-bhp engines – would develop 200bhp at 1800 rpm, driving through gearboxes. These locomotives would have been cheaper than any of the other types shortlisted, at an average cost of less than £30,000 each. The company also promised very quick delivery – just over a year from first order.

However, this design was considered to be very much experimental, though one advantage of it would be that if one engine failed the loco would not be a total casualty. However, it required the uprating of existing engines from 125 to 200 bhp, a tall order, and there were

concerns about braking capabilities on freight because of the low weight. Given the later unsuccessful uprating of the Multi Purpose Diesel engines, it seems unlikely to the author that these machines would have been particularly reliable in service. Even if they could have kept running when one engine failed, their performance would have suffered and, as was later found, one failure would lead quickly to stress on the other engines, with consequent serious problems. The low weight would also have had repercussions on adhesion as well as brake power.

The North British Company took a different route and put forward plans for a diesel hydraulic double-bogie locomotive, with a Paxman 16-cylinder supercharged engine developing 833 bhp at 1250 rpm. Transmission would be by Voith North – through three torque converters, low, intermediate and high speed direct drive to the final axle. An outline drawing shows that the single cab of this locomotive was situated towards one end, rather like some shunters. Starting tractive effort of this design was quoted at 29,000 lbs and the price was approximately £50,000. This design was the most expensive of the types shortlisted.

From Germany came a design by Henschel and Sohn Ltd. This was considered very promising

North British Locomotive Co Ltd proposed mixed traffic diesel locomotive for the Ulster Transport Authority.

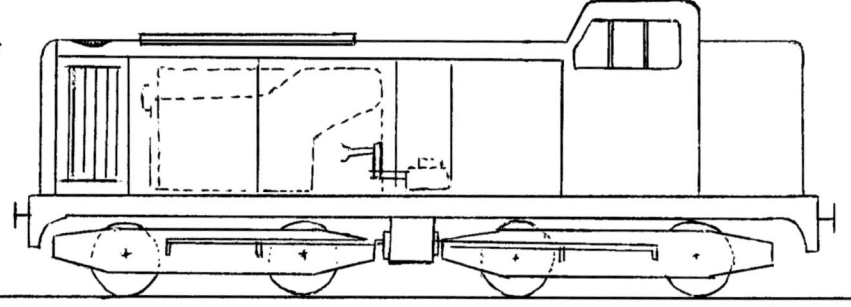

Type:	*Diesel hydraulic*	*Wheel arrangement:*	*Bo-Bo*
Engine:	*Paxman 16RPHXL 4 stroke supercharged 833bhp @ 1250rpm*	*Weight:*	*56 tons*
		Length:	*34'6"*
Transmission:	*Voith North British L36R - 3 torque converters*	*Axle load:*	*14 tons*
		Price:	*£49,750 incl Vapor Clarkson boiler.*

and looked similar to the North British offering. It would be a diesel hydraulic double-bogie locomotive with a 6-cylinder MWH engine developing 860 bhp at 750 rpm. It would have had Voith Turbo transmission and a two-speed gearbox for freight or passenger work. The Committee noted that the engine was widely used in Europe and had scope for uprating, but the transmission was new to Britain. Starting tractive effort in low gear was to be 37,000 lbs and in high was 23,000 lbs. The price was competitive at just under £40,000. However, it was felt that the heating cost (which was quoted

as £5,000) was much too high. It would be better to buy the locos without heating and fit this locally later on! Once again, delivery was quoted at just over a year from order for the first one, and subsequently four to five per month. However, there were questions about possible problems with import restrictions and spare parts.

The only diesel electric design to meet the criteria (almost) came from Metropolitan Vickers Electric Co Ltd. They proposed a twin-cab diesel electric Bo-Bo locomotive with a Paxman 16-cylinder supercharged engine developing 833 bhp at 1250 rpm – the same engine as North

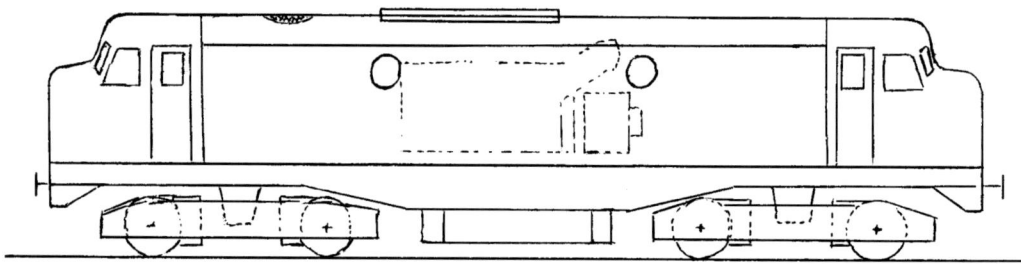

Metropolitan Vickers Electrical Co Ltd proposed mixed traffic diesel locomotive for the Ulster Transport Authority.

Type:	*Diesel electric*	*Weight:*	*60 tons*
Engine:	*Paxman 16RPHXK 4 stroke supercharged 833bhp @ 1250rpm*	*Length:*	*45'0"*
		Axle load:	*15 tons*
Transmission:	*Four force ventilated traction motors*	*Price:*	*£44,625 excluding heating (£1050 extra)*
Wheel arrangement:	*Bo-Bo*		

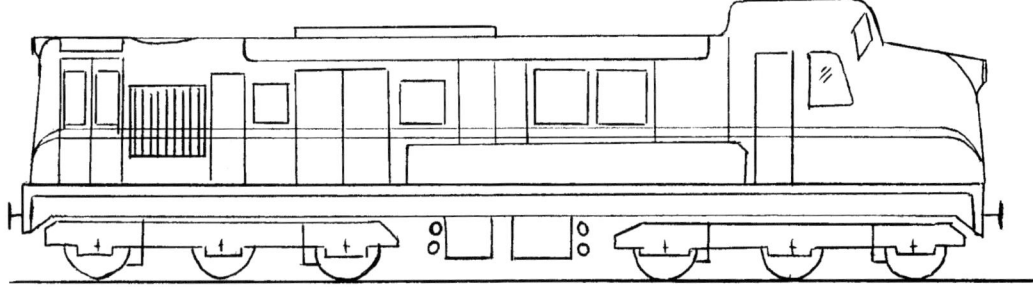

English Electric Co Ltd proposed mixed traffic diesel locomotive for the Ulster Transport Authority.

Type:	*Diesel electric*	*Weight:*	*84 tons*
Engine:	*EE 8SRKT supercharged*	*Length:*	*47 feet*
	1000 bhp @ 850rpm	*Axle load*	*14 tons*
Transmission:	*4 force ventilated traction motors*	*Price:*	*£51,850 excluding heating;*
Wheel arrangement	*AIA-AIA*		*freight extra*

British proposed. As an option, they also offered the same loco with a Crossley EST Vee 12 two-stroke. Starting tractive effort for this design would be 35,000 lbs.

The great advantage of the diesel electric system was (and is) that engine output and speed remain steady, and of course no gear changing would be needed. The weight of this locomotive would have been 60 tons. This was slightly in excess of the limit stated and the locomotive was longer than could be accommodated in the Dundalk works of the GNR. It was also the second most expensive, at a cost of £46,000 including heating, with a longer delivery time than the others – 21 months for the first, then two per month for four months and finally three per month until completion of the order.

The other 'proposals' came from many different British companies such as Brush Bagnall Traction, Metro Cammell and English Electric. The latter's offering showed some interesting characteristics. An outline drawing (above) shows what appears to be a single-ended locomotive with one cab looking over a high bonnet with a headlamp, very much like the prototype 'Deltic' engine. But a closer look at the other end reveals a small cab which is inset into the end of the engine bonnet. Presumably this was intended for shunting use or where turntable

facilities were not available. The company had built some locomotives for overseas with this configuration.

Also included were General Motors of America, and German manufacturers such as MAK and Krupp. Harland and Wolff, the Belfast shipbuilders, put forward two designs using two engines in each loco with a centre cab (some of their locomotives were already in service on railways in Northern Ireland as described earlier). However, all of these designs were either too heavy, too expensive, or both.

Of the four shortlisted engines, which would have been the successful type if the UTA had gone to tender and how would they have performed? Sadly, we shall never know. With hindsight, the experiences of other railways with British-designed diesels at this time did not prove encouraging. Yet the CIÉ experience, with re-engining the Metro-Vicks in the late 1960s, showed what could be achieved to turn a poor locomotive into a good one.

Shunting engines were also considered. The specification for these called for engines of 300–350 bhp, and 24 would be needed. Estimates from the firm of Drewry suggested a cost of around £15,000 each.

Finally, as part of plans for the overall dieselisation of the network, it was proposed that a number of steam engines might be converted to diesel. Though no details of this somewhat unusual proposal have come to light, the idea of a mixed traffic diesel with six-foot driving wheels from rebuilt 'Jeeps' would certainly have been a remarkable – if not bizarre – sight! The author's assumption is that these were shunting types – using an 0-6-0 wheel arrangement and mechanical transmission, similar to that pioneered by English Electric and subsequently used by BR in large numbers as Class 08. The steam locomotive frames and wheels would probably have been the only parts used, though given the work involved, it would hardly have seemed a great saving over buying new.

The report was received but never acted upon – the money was not available and the government preferred to spend what resources it had on other things. It would be much cheaper to let rail freight die off (and be transferred, they hoped, to the UTA's lorries) and then let railcars run the passenger rail services throughout. Had this committee made a final recommendation and a locomotive fleet been purchased, the results could have proved invaluable. The Republic of Ireland was shortly to embark upon its own disastrous designs from Metro-Vick. Yet the Crossley engine, which caused so much grief south of the border, was not even among those proposed by anyone at this time. Perhaps the more popular Paxman engines might have fared better – although subsequent experience with some early BR diesels would suggest that it had its problems too.

Perhaps the BR Modernisation Plan might have benefited from the UTA experience in locomotives, though the 750 bhp specified would not have sufficed for mainline work in Great Britain.

The MAK diesel

In the event, the GNR Board ordered some more railcars of the BUT type (see Chapter 11), and a solitary locomotive from MAK in Germany, though not one of the designs offered in 1953! This final diesel locomotive to run during the period covered by the present work was the result of a tendering process into which the GNR Board had entered. High capital costs meant that there was no possibility of any major order being forthcoming.

However, it led to a tempting offer from a German firm, Maschinebau AG of Kiel, who were willing to construct, and ship at their own expense, an 800 bhp diesel hydraulic locomotive for trial on the GNR. This offer was accepted and the locomotive arrived at the North Wall, Dublin, on 14 December 1954. It was painted in a blue livery, relieved by a horizontal white band just below bonnet level.

By any standards the 'MAK', as it was soon dubbed, was an unusual 'animal'. Germany was the biggest user of Voith hydraulic transmissions and the engine certainly looked German. It weighed 57½ tons and was unique for a diesel engine in these islands in having eight coupled wheels instead of bogies. In essence it was really a very powerful shunter rather than a serious mainline locomotive. Lacking bogies it would not have been capable of maintaining stability at high speed – its maximum rated speed was 50 mph.

For most of 1955 it ran trials, mainly on freight workings on the main line and Portadown–Londonderry, though it was also tried on outer suburban passenger services out of Dublin. The Germans sent over two engineers and, such was the skill needed to drive it, only a small number of men got the experience. The MAK also did some trials on the UTA's lines before the GNR Board decided to purchase it for £29,500, but no more were built, although the Board pushed for a follow-up order. However, by this time the

The MAK diesel shortly after delivery. Small headlights were fitted to the top of the engine bonnets soon after it's arrival in Ireland. It had a power output of 800 bhp and a top speed of 50 mph. No others were ordered.

Kelland collection 113

governments were wary of more expenditure on the loss-making GNR and it was hard enough persuading them to finance the proposed BUT railcar fleet let alone freight locomotives.

The MAK entered GNR stock as No 800 reflecting the locomotive's horsepower and distancing it from the steam loco fleet. It was something of a white elephant and passed to CIÉ in 1958. With the exception of the crane tank, it was the only item of GNR stock to be actually renumbered by CIÉ, becoming K801 in 1959. Its career with CIÉ took it to Cork where for some

After the break up of the GNR the MAK went to CIÉ, where it worked at Cork for some years. It is seen here in April 1960. The design proved satisfactory enough in service but the limited top speed prevented it from being a true mixed traffic type.

Kelland collection 114

End of the line for this unusual locomotive. MAK K801, by now painted in the later CIÉ black livery, has lost its coupling rods (at least) as it awaits disposal.

CP Friel 7718C

time it operated on the city's suburban lines, but eventually the fact that it was a 'one off' worked against it and it was withdrawn in 1967. It lay out of use for a number of years until being briefly reinstated for a month or so in late 1974, when it operated briefly as station pilot at Drogheda. Final withdrawal took place in 1976, after which it was sold to a Galway scrap dealer for use as a stationary generator.

In the event, the GNR was to order more railcars, developments of their AEC type, instead of locomotives, while the UTA devoted its energies to a new railcar design, and in 1957 embarked on its most technically ambitious design yet. It is to this 'third generation' of diesel railcars that we will now turn.

11 The GNRI develops: The BUT fleet

The final development of diesel railcars on the Great Northern Railway of Ireland came with the 24 units put into service towards the end of the GNR Board's existence, between 1957 and 1958.

The Board had been pleased with the performance of the AEC railcars, but higher performance would be useful. As well as more power, the ability to work in multiple, with up to four power cars in a train, was considered by operating departments to be a necessary development.

The ambitious scheme to dieselise the entire UTA/GNR network for passenger and freight with locomotives, referred to in the previous chapter, was clearly never going to happen. There was no doubting the usefulness of the existing railcars, but could the type be further developed? If it could, this would allow dieselisation of most if not all the mainline passenger operations.

So, in 1954 the GNR engineers began to plan for a third generation of diesel train – but it would be evolutionary, not revolutionary. The design work continued over a long period because there was no certainty that the funding would be available even for this.

By the time orders could be placed, AEC had become part of the company known as British United Traction, and the new company was having considerable success in producing railcars for the British Railways Modernisation Plan, in which the by now well-established layout of two engines underfloor driving four-speed gearboxes was common. So it was this format that was to be used for the second batch of railcars, the most significant difference from most BR designs being that the GNR retained vertically mounted engines with outside drive shafts. Once again Park Royal developed the design and they were built at Dundalk works.

GNR BUT railcar No 701. The first batch to emerge were the double ended second class type. They were longer and more powerful than the AEC cars which preceded them, with 300 bhp available. Gearboxes were four speed. Note that for this official photograph the wire valances over the engines have been removed to show the layout.

Duffner L1177A

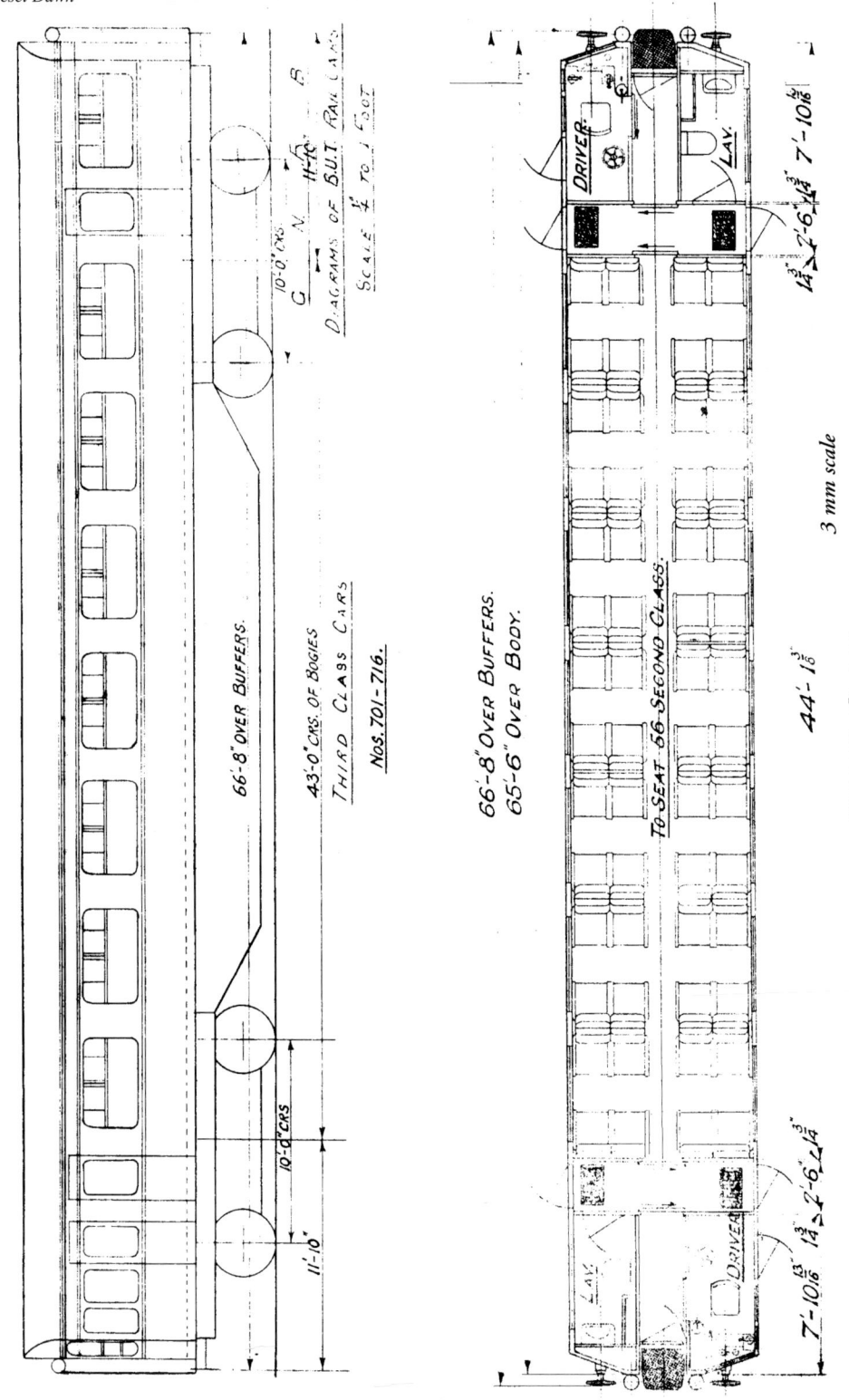

G.N. H.C. B

DIAGRAMS OF B.U.T. RAIL CARS

Scale ¼ to 1 foot

66'-8" OVER BUFFERS.

43'-0" CRS. OF BOGIES

THIRD CLASS CARS

Nos. 701-716.

10'-0" CRS

11'-10"

DRIVER

LAV.

66'-8" OVER BUFFERS.
65'-6" OVER BODY.

TO SEAT 66 SECOND CLASS.

44'-1⅜"

SECOND CLASS

3 mm scale

LAV.

DRIVER

GNRI BUT '700' series railcar. Interestingly, the elevation diagram describes the car as 'Third Class'. The GNR had gone over to two classes in 1951! Modellers should note that the BUT windows are much squarer than shown here. This seems to be a concept drawing dating from 1956.

An official photograph of a six coach train for 'Enterprise' services in 1957. From the start it was intended to use these railcars on the prestige workings of the GNR. Until the arrival of the single cab variety, first class and guards accommodation had to be provided in side corridor trailer coaches (third and fifth here). The fourth vehicle in the formation is the dining car.   ***Duffner R500H***

The new railcars were longer than their predecessors – 65 feet – and had two BUT A230 engines of 150 bhp each, still developed at 1800 rpm. Transmission was similar to the AEC cars but with a four-speed gearbox produced by Self Changing Gears Ltd.

The 16 'standard class' railcars (701–16) were built first. If the mechanical specification looked similar to the AECs, the bodywork did not – the new cars were quite different. The underframes and other mechanical parts were delivered to Dundalk in the summer of 1956 but it was to be April 1957 before the first completed railcar appeared, one subsequently appearing approximately every three weeks.

The most obvious difference was that each car was double-ended. There was a driving cab at each end and thus corridor connections were fitted at either end also. Across the corridor from the cab at each end was a toilet. This meant that when one looked at a BUT approaching, there was a rather odd 'blank' look to the front, as there was of course no window facing the end in the toilet compartment. The corridor connection itself was an unusual design, a continental design seen nowhere else in the British Isles. It had a hard rubber surround moulded into a convex shape – when coupling up this simply pressed hard against another similar type and made a tight seal. One result of this was that

BUT vehicles were not compatible with any other stock so the trailers (unlike the AEC ones) could not be marshalled in steam trains.

There were doors at either end and the seating was arranged in bays of four in a single compartment with 56 seats in all. The seats themselves were a new design, lower backed than traditional types, though much more comfortable than bus-type seats, for these were mainline railcars – though tables would have been useful.

Primary heating was by means of engine cooling water via two pipes down the car, but in practice this had to be supplemented by steam-heating boilers, as provision was needed for any trailer cars which were to be included in a train. These were placed in the guard's van of a brake/first or second. This meant that every train had to have a trailer with a large guard's van, although a single power car could form a train on its own, using only the heat from the engine cooling system. The other reason that a trailer would be needed in most trains was that neither of the two types of BUT car had a guard's or luggage compartment – although on a light single-car train the guard could use the rear driver's cab.

By May 1958 the last of the 16 double-ended cars had been completed and in July the first of the single-ended units appeared. These driving

The eight single cab composite railcars (901–08) were completed in 1958. This view at Great Victoria Street on 23 July 1958 shows brand new 902 about to lead the 10.30 Up 'Enterprise'. The set is led by three power cars, with a fourth at the rear.

EM Patterson 38N

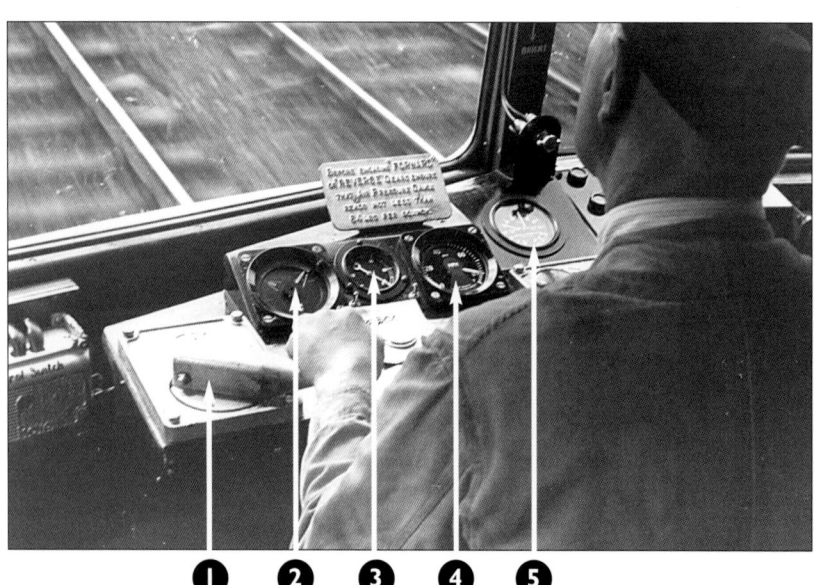

Cab view of BUT railcar 902, taken on the same occasion. Note the speedometer needle touching 80 mph. The BUTs, as they were known, had a good turn of speed.

EM Patterson 38T

1 Deadman's/throttle control.
2 Engine RPM
3 Air pressure gauge.
4 Speedometer.
5 VAC/train pipe gauge.

The right hand side of a BUT '900' series cab. On the left of the shot is the gear selector, centre is the bank of engine start stop lights and switching, and in the foreground the hand brake. This picture was taken from the rear cab passing through Drogheda on a Dublin bound 'Enterprise' working.

DJA Young

motor composites (901–08) were the same length as the double ended units – 65 feet – and were mechanically identical, with the exception that they had of course only one cab. From the front they resembled the AEC cars very closely, with two large windows and a headlight centrally mounted. However, in the BUT cars this was somewhat larger and was mounted higher.

Seating in the eight driving motor composites was 12 first and 44 second class. The first class seats were stepped, with each row a few inches higher than that in front, thus giving all passengers a good view forward. They were very comfortable, as befitted their intended use. Weight remained the same at 38¼ tons, partly as a result of new construction techniques.

A number of existing coaches were converted to run with the BUT railcars, in addition to those

already operating with the AEC types. As BUT railcars continued to use standard vacuum brakes, conversions were straight forward. The trailers were mostly corridor firsts, brake/firsts or composites to provide the facilities the railcars lacked on more important trains, and of course some more buffet trailers were provided.

The BUT railcars proved very successful. As they were produced, they went into traffic. In June 1957 they entered service on the Belfast based Enterprise, working initially as a six-car set with power cars 701–703, a trailer buffet, an all first and a brake/first. Two more power cars were ready in July and one was used to introduce a new morning express service from Enniskillen to Belfast via Omagh hauling an older brake/first. As the Enniskillen line had a trailing connection with the the Omagh–Belfast line, the car had to run round its trailer for the run to Belfast. This was a short-lived service, as the Fermanagh lines closed on 30 September 1957, but it was an example of how the GNR regarded the diesel railcars as a way of providing new and attractive services to the travelling public. However, the government was unimpressed and the closures went ahead. At the end of 1957 ten cars were available, sufficient to also turn the Dublin-based Enterprise over to a BUT set and commence dieselisation of the Londonderry route.

On the break-up of the GNR Board in 1958 all the GNR railcars were initially split equally between CIÉ and the UTA. However, the UTA exchanged some GNR cement wagons for two extra BUT cars, one of each type. The UTA ones remained on the old GNR section of railway on the 'Enterprise' and between Belfast, Portadown and Londonderry until that line closed in early 1965.

The UTA used the best of their BUTs on 'Enterprise' services on which they performed well. In fact, during 1966 the UTA, having increasing troubles with its own designs, was considering buying from CIÉ the nine BUT

BUT railcar 134 (formerly 905) at Omagh in August 1962 on a Londonderry-Belfast working.

EM Patterson 101G

Another Derry Road working, with double ended car 125 leading, near Pomeroy. These railcars worked most passenger trains on this line up to the time of closure in 1965.

EM Patterson 111R

railcars it still had. But the idea was not pursued. The BUTs continued to run the UTA Belfast-based Enterprise set (the CIÉ one had gone over to GM haulage) until 1969 when they were displaced by the new '70' class diesel electric railcars introduced originally to the NCC section in 1966.

Those on CIÉ worked the Dublin based 'Enterprise' for a time and it was while on one such run that car 908 caught fire and was completely destroyed near Lisburn. After that they mainly worked suburban and outer suburban services on the old GNR routes north of Dublin to Howth and Dundalk.

Though technically less advanced than the later UTA railcars, these BUTs were, in the author's opinion, quick and comfortable machines – they were much superior in performance to the AEC cars. They were in fact very similar mechanically to the BR Swindon Inter-City Class 126 railcars which worked just a few miles away on the Stranraer–Glasgow section of the Scottish Region.

The last set of BUT railcars on CIÉ was rostered in the early 1970s on one run which took it from Malahide, north of Dublin, to Connolly Station in 12 minutes non-stop – a timing never bettered. However, as a single remaining set it increasingly failed to appear on rostered turns, being non-standard, and so by the

mid-1970s these final CIÉ BUT railcars were withdrawn and sent to Mullingar where they were ultimately scrapped. At this time the northern composites were disposed of, one having already been withdrawn following bomb damage at Great Victoria Street.

When they entered service the BUT railcars carried the GNR's standard diesel livery of Oxford blue and cream, except for the final single-ended car, No 908. By the time it emerged from the shops, the GNR had ceased to exist and 908 was painted in CIÉ's green livery. Those which went south were repainted in due course either in green or the new black, white and tan livery which was introduced in late 1961. CIÉ was content to just add a small 'n' as a suffix to the GNR number.

The UTA machines retained their GNR livery at first but with the addition of UTA numbers and roundels. The '700' series were renumbered 121–29 and the '900' series 131–35. From late 1960, yellow and black striped warning panels were added to power cars. By 1963 all had been repainted UTA Brunswick green. The first GNR BUT to be repainted was 121, which got the green UTA livery in autumn 1960. Ultimately all the fleet survived to be repainted in the standard maroon and grey livery of NIR.

The BUT railcars were a design which was basically 'right', though they were considered to

If they did venture off ex-GNR, metals, the AEC and BUT railcars usually went south and east from Amiens Street. Presumably recovery to 'home' territory would be easier if anything went wrong. A three car CIÉ BUT set, in final livery, at Wexford makes up the 3.00 pm boat train from Rosslare Harbour, in December 1964. It is running on the quay between Wexford South and Wexford North stations. The set is made up of two double ended units and a brake first trailer.

DJA Young

Single unit workings by the BUT railcars under the UTA were not common. One turn where they appeared regularly for a time was the 10.10 Belfast Great Victoria Street to Lisburn. No.124, a double ended unit in ex-works condition, passes Finaghy on 13 April 1963.

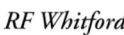

RF Whitford

have some shortcomings. Ride could be bouncy and, with mechanical gearboxes, engine revving and vibration, this could become annoying on stopping services, especially compared with the torque-converted MPDs. However, they had no major design flaws lurking, as befitted a design which had evolved steadily since the 1940s. As a result, most enjoyed long lives in their original

form, many turning in very high mileages, and ultimately engines and transmissions were bound to wear out.

There was no desire (or need) to do major rebuilding, as happened to some first-generation BR types. Only one, No 129, was extensively rebuilt and this was as a result of fire at Castlebellingham, south of Dundalk, in May

BUT No 129 was badly damaged in a fire at Lisburn in May 1960. It returned to traffic in 1962 after rebuilding by the UTA in Duncrue Street. Its styling then rather resembled the last three MPD double cab units. However, it was scrapped in 1980 along with all the rest.

DJA Young

1960, which destroyed its bodywork. The resulting unit was rebuilt at Duncrue Street in a similar style to the last three MPD units which also had two cabs. When it re-entered traffic in July 1962 it had a slightly more rounded look than the angular GNR style due to the windows being in MPD style. The continental type corridor connections were retained, as 129 would continue to work with other BUT railcars.

The last single ended UTA car was withdrawn in July 1974 but the nine double-ended cars found further employment on NIR in de-engined form as hauled stock, even on occasions being added to the end of a '70' or '80' class train when extra accommodation was needed. However, as the 1970s progressed the need for this sort of excursion stock diminished. They were finally disposed of at Crosshill Quarry in County Antrim in 1980. None has survived to be preserved.

While the GNR engineers opted for steady evolution, the fertile minds of the UTA diesel engineering team at Duncrue Street had decided to produce a new type of diesel railcar altogether, and to push the boundaries of this type of traction even further.

BUT car No 132 in NIR livery at Great Victoria Street. The single cab BUTs were similar to the AEC from the front, the most obvious difference being in the position of the headlight – higher up on the BUT cars.

CP Friel

BUT cars Nos 122, 126 and 127 at Crumlin in May 1980, before final disposal. They are in the NIR maroon livery adopted for some de-engined units, used as hauled trailers for a few years. Unlike CIÉ, NIR never contemplated turning any ex-GNR type railcars into locomotive-hauled push-pull units for regular traffic.

CP Friel 8016J

12 The UTA MPD (multi-purpose diesel) railcar fleet

The ex-LMS(NCC) main line of the UTA which ran from Belfast's York Road to Londonderry Waterside was a fast main line, double track for its first 31 miles, but with a fearsome climb out of Belfast at 1 in 75 over the Bleach Green viaduct. In 1956 this line had heavy express trains travelling the length of its 92¼ miles and there was still a substantial amount of goods traffic. This section of the UTA had a relatively modern 'stud' of steam locomotives, the Mogul tender engines and the 2-6-4 tanks, similar to LMS types, the last of which had been built as recently as 1950.

So, when in 1956 it was decided to dieselise the NCC services, a two-pronged approach was adopted – complete dieselisation of all passenger services and the pruning away of goods traffic so that what remained could also be hauled by diesel traction. Steam was to disappear completely.

When this was decided, the engineering and operating departments were looking for something rather different in motive power from previous types. Diesel locomotives on the sort of scale then being considered south of the border had been ruled out on grounds of cost, so what could be done?

On the GNR, the forthcoming BUT railcars would handle the passenger traffic and the remaining steam locomotives the goods, but on the UTA line to Derry the policy was to be complete dieselisation – so that meant railcars of some kind. It is interesting to note that the UTA and the GNR each pursued their own line of development in diesel traction, even though there must have been plenty of coming and going between Dundalk works and York Road/ Duncrue Street, where the UTA team worked.

The GNR BUT type previously described was a powerful railcar, but was seen very much as a development of the older AEC type which the UTA had already developed in a different direction with the MED types. It still used two

With MPD Brake/2nd No 36 in the lead, a four car set passes through Cookstown Junction in May 1958. At the time of their introduction, these 275 bhp 'Multi Purpose' railcars were hailed as a technological marvel. They had a most sophisticated transmission system combining torque converter and automatic gearbox, the only railcars in the British Isles to be so fitted until the BR Class 150s nearly twenty years later.

Kelland collection 24256

relatively small engines. James Courtney and the UTA engineers, with their by now extensive knowledge of using underfloor bus engines in railway applications, were extremely interested in a new type of underfloor mounted diesel engine which was being produced by Leyland – a single six-cylinder 15.2 litre engine that could develop 230 bhp in normally aspirated form. This was more than a 50% increase in power over the BUT type, and 40% more than the new engines being fitted to the MEDs. Torque (pulling power) was also increased significantly. British Railways had recently experimented with this engine in a twin-unit railcar and the results were encouraging (Chapter 9, page 108).

With much greater power and torque available, might not such an engine, fitted in a railcar, be capable of hauling some freight also? The existing designs might be fine for a few trailers or vans, but not a real freight train. Despite the success of the MEDs on suburban-type services, bus seats and a lack of toilets would not do. The passenger ambience of any railcars for the ex-NCC main line had to be more on a par with the 'Enterprise' service, or even the famed 'North Atlantic Express', the NCC's pre-war flyer. Here was a challenge indeed.

Development of the new railcars was once again to be caught between the enthusiastic engineering teams, keen to develop something new and different, and the other main boundary – government indifference. The UTA, as a public body, was of course dependent on government subsidy to keep the railways running and the government of Northern Ireland believed the future for transport lay in the roads. Television programmes of 1956 make this view plain – it wasn't just the government who thought railways generally a bit out of date. There was a public perception that the car was better. So any dieselisation plan had to be cheap, as the government of Northern Ireland persisted in its attempt to find the Holy Grail of profitable public transport – something which today is accepted as being unrealistic.

So this new Leyland 0/900 engine being

developed, attracted keen attention from the UTA railcar engineers – 230 bhp at 1800 rpm was a big improvement but they decided that yet more power and torque would be needed. The way to get it was agreed to be by turbo-charging the engines. (In contemporary documents there are references to both 'turbo-charging' and 'supercharging' – the terms seem to have been used rather loosely, although the actual processes are somewhat different – see Appendix 3.)

The turbo-charging process was to boost output from the engine from 230 bhp by a further 20% to 275 bhp. Here was an engine with serious power. Since it was basically another bus design, it could still be mounted underfloor – unlike the older unit of comparable power in vehicles like the Ganz where the engine had to be mounted in a separate compartment – therefore, capacity would not be

In some of the MPD power cars and trailers the driver did not have a 'cab' as such – the driving area was in the vestibule and separated from it only by a token rope. In such cars, a roll top cover (rather like that on an organ console) was used to lock the controls away from the public. The supports for it can be seen here just above the driver's hands. **DJA Young**

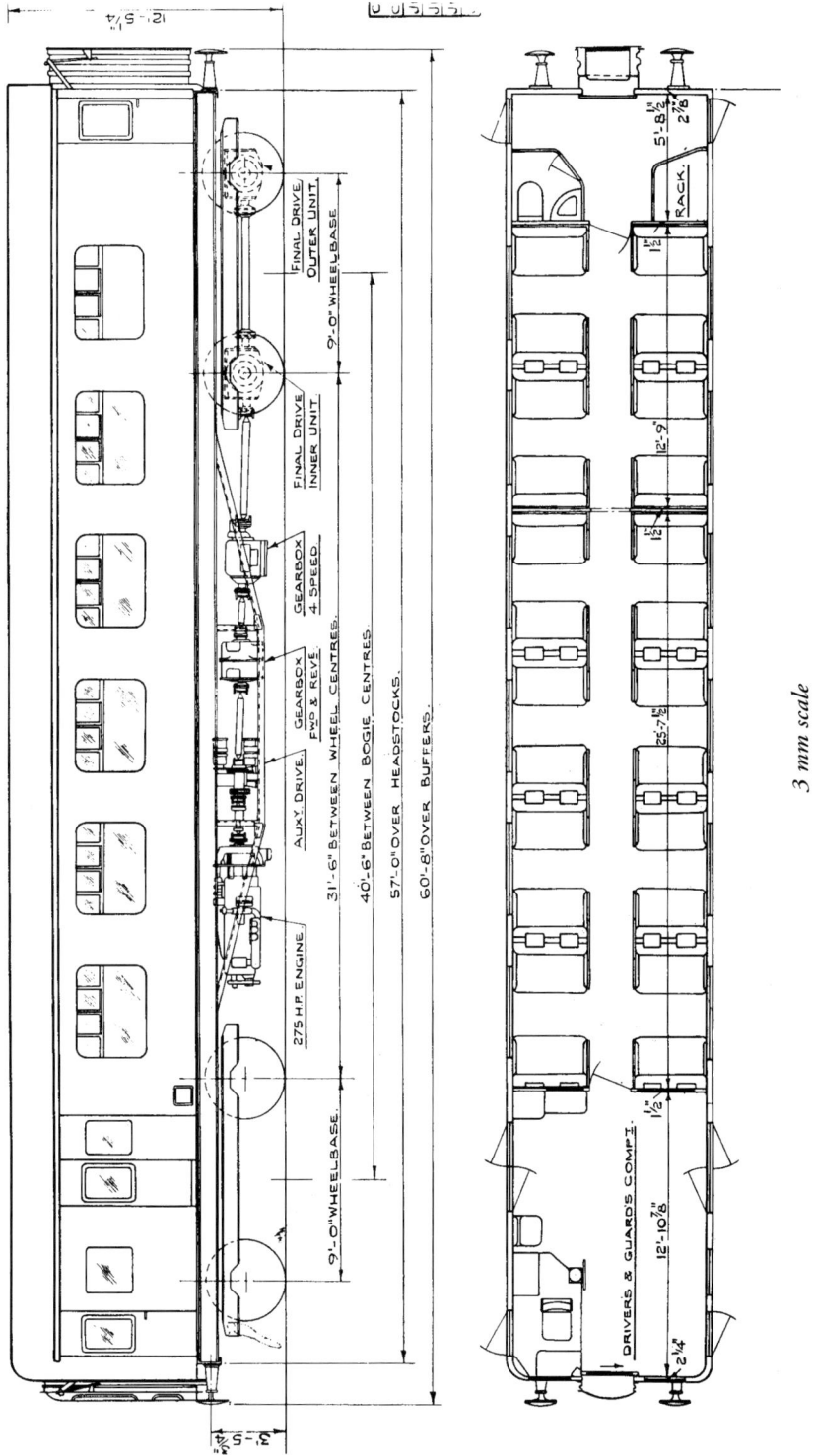

3 mm scale

MPD railcars 36–39.

affected. At a time when 500 bhp was considered sufficient for many applications, power cars of 275 bhp each would give acceptable acceleration and top speed, even when trailers were added, compared to the average steam engine of the time (not exactly a hard job as many such Irish locomotives were upwards of 50 years old anyway.).

The jump in power and torque output can be even more clearly seen when compared with the MEDs' 0/600 engines of some five to six years previously. These developed 125 bhp at 1800 rpm and with maximum torque of 410lb/ft at 900 rpm. The 0/900 turbo-charged equivalent figures were 275 bhp at 1800 rpm, with maximum torque of 840lb/ft at 1200 rpm. Note that the maximum power and torque also occurred within a narrower revolution range.

Coupled with the very much greater power of the new engines was a further development in transmission that was very significant.

To move any train, great starting torque is desirable, even more so on a heavy goods, maybe on an uphill gradient. But as engine speed rises, so torque usually diminishes. Then, if the engine has to be disengaged (however briefly) for a gear change, power drops away and the torque available in a higher gear is of course much less.

This style of transmission, used in AEC and BUT railcars on the GNR and by BR on most of its own DMUs, would not have the haulage capability that was estimated to be needed – no one ever dreamed that any railcar design could be expected to handle freight trains up 1 in 75 gradients! The torque converter system described earlier with the MEDs held more promise, but even here, with direct drive being engaged at a relatively low speed, there was little likelihood that it would be capable of moving a train at the speeds required on such gradients without the risk of stalling or throwing passenger service timetables into chaos. Some diesel hydraulic locomotives had used multiple torque converters, each specifically set to operate over different speed ranges. Such a system worked well but was going to be much too expensive, not to mention heavy, for successful underfloor mounting.

The firm of Self Changing Gears, part of the BUT group by now, had been working on a new form of transmission to combine the best of both

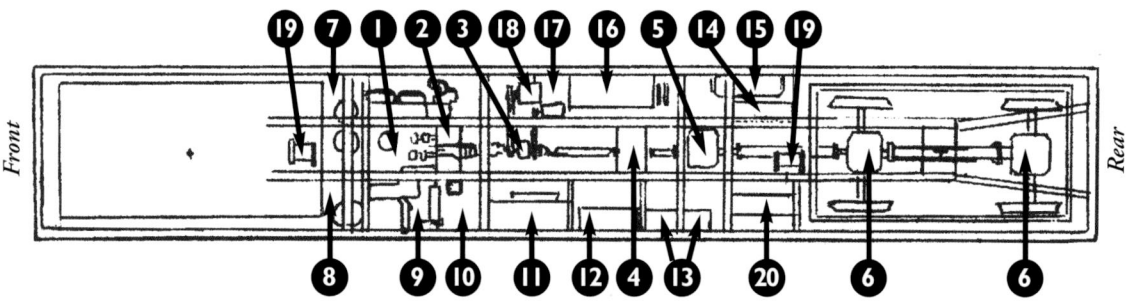

1	Leyland 0/900 engine horizontally mounted	11	Serck Radiator and fan
2	Torque converter	12	Electrical control cabinet
3	Auxiliary drive	13	Torque converter fluid tank
4	Forward and reverse gearbox	14	Main air reservoir
5	Four speed automatic gearbox	15	Auxiliary air reservoir
6	Final drives	16	Fuel tank - 100 gallons capacity
7	Air Cleaners	17	Dynamo
8	Oil Tank	18	Compressor
9	Thermostatic controller	19	Brake cylinders (linkages not shown)
10	Heat Exchanger	20	Battery Box

Ulster Transport Authority Multi Purpose Diesel Railcar underside details plan view. For clarity only major components are shown.

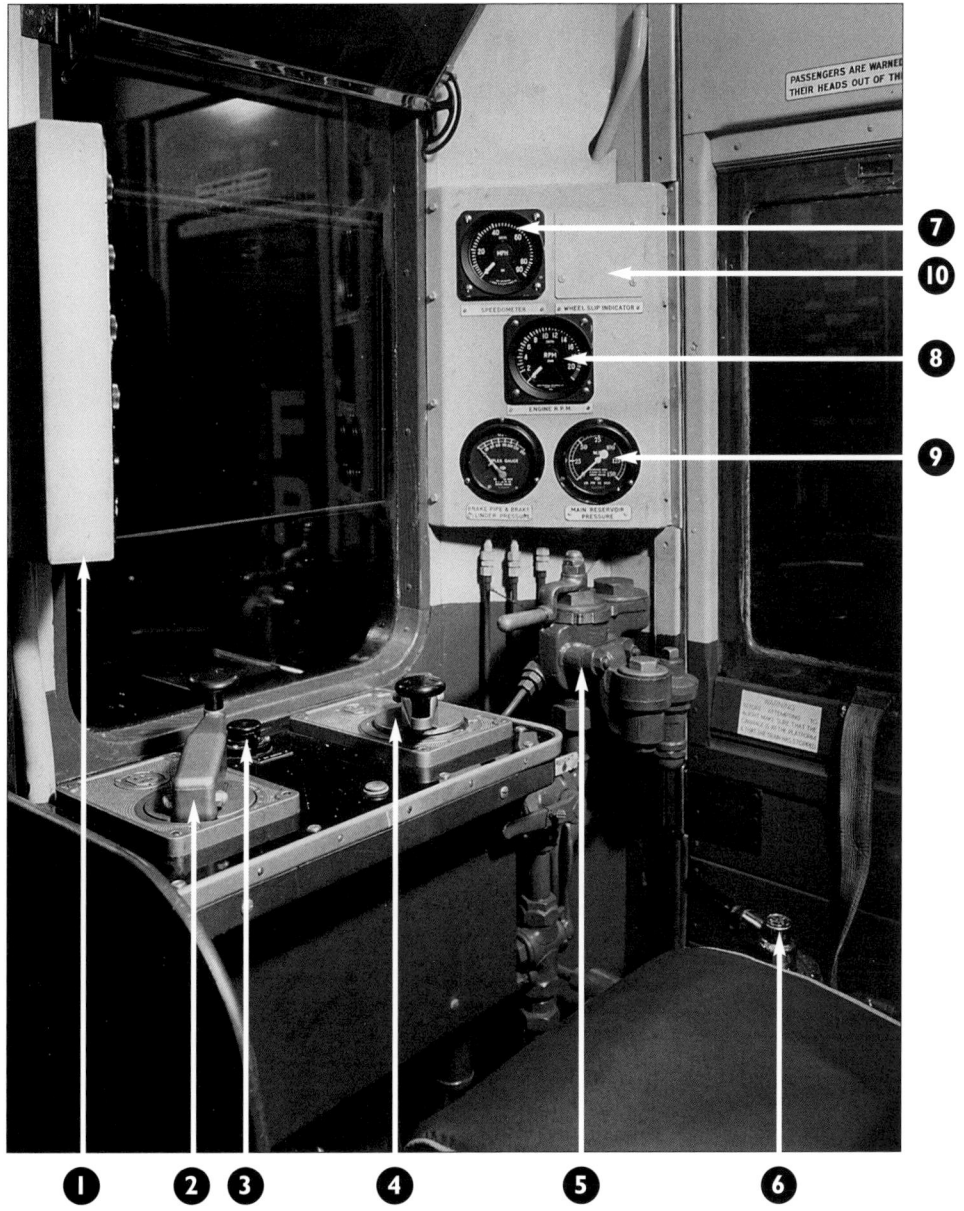

1 Engine start/stop switches. 2 Deadman's handle/throttle (4 speed). 3 Headlight switch. 4 Forward/neutral/reverse lever. 5 Shunting brake. 6 Train brake lever. 7 Speedometer. 8 Engine rev counter. 9. Air reservoir and brake pipe gauges. 10 Wheelslip indicator, fitted later. The Vacuum gauge was also fitted later to the right of the rev counter (see photo on page 134).

Cab of an MPD. cramped compared with that of their MED predecessors, and still showing signs from it's previous life as a corridor carriage end vestibule.

Official UTA photo, courtesy W McCormick

gearbox and torque converter technology. The system they developed was both elegant in engineering terms and effective. The engine output would go to a single stage torque converter and then to an automatic four-speed gearbox, allowing the peak efficiency of the torque converter to be available to four separate gears, which, theoretically, would produce 80% efficiency throughout the operating speed range, and all this at virtually constant engine speed and power to the rails.

James Courtney realised that if this transmission system could be harnessed to the uprated Leyland engine, then the vehicle to which it was fitted should have a far superior performance to anything so far achieved. In discussions with Leyland and Self Changing Gears Ltd, a specification was agreed. The engine should be capable of hauling a load of 100 tons (other than the power car itself) and of starting with that load from rest on a 1 in 75 gradient (that on the Bleach Green viaduct, some four miles out from York Road on the ex-NCC main line). Thus the UTA Dual Purpose Diesel Railcar concept was born.

It was decided initially to produce two complete trains for a high-speed service to Londonderry. The railwaymen of the NCC section in UTA days were determined to try and work the new technologies to the advantage of the railway, whatever the prevailing political opinion. The new trains would provide an improved service, not just a cheaper one – or so was the sentiment.

Each train would have four power cars and a dining car, piped through as a trailer. It was planned to run to Londonderry in less than two hours, so the specification called for high-speed capability. But that wasn't all. Given their high power and sophisticated transmission arrangements, these railcars would be capable of handling freight trains on the NCC section, as well as parcels and stopping trains – and even shunting along the way. They would in effect be usable as small locomotives as well. So, very soon the term 'Multi Purpose' came into common

usage and that was their designation from then on.

The first units appeared in September 1957 and the mechanical arrangements were tested on various turns as new units appeared until a five-car set (four power cars and a buffet trailer) was ready to start serious running tests.

The 275-bhp engines were harnessed to the new design of transmission, with the torque converter itself a new and improved type – a Schneider unit with a 'stall' ratio of 3.05:1. Once again, the engines and it were mounted to the frames with flexible pads. Unlike the earlier MED units, the torque converter did not incorporate a free wheel. A separate free wheel connected the engine to the auxiliary drive. There was a bi-directional gearbox fitted, air operated with a ratio of 2:1. From this, drive was taken to another air-operated automatic four-speed gearbox, with ratios between 2.33:1 and 1:1.87, which was an overdrive position. As this four-speed gearbox was fitted after the bi-directional one in the transmission chain, it had to be capable of rotation in either direction.

On the output end were two DC generators which provided current for the automatic gear control. This was a unique feature for railcars at this time. The driver had control only of forward and reverse, throttle and brakes. The electrical circuits determined which gear each car should be in. The nerve centre of this system was an automatic panel comprising relays, which controlled electro-pneumatic valves operating the air cylinders and throttle motors.

The most noticeable result of these innovations was that driving techniques were quite different from other railcars. No gear changing was done by the driver and the engines ran at a virtually constant speed, with a difference of only about 200 rpm between fastest and slowest in each gear. There was no need to close the throttle between gear changes and so acceleration could be very rapid – the engine developed maximum torque at a speed of approximately 12–15 mph in first gear, so the automatic system changed up at 17 mph (first to second). Then a second torque 'peak' was reached at 20–22 mph, the next change taking place at 27mph (second to third) and then the final change at 41mph (third to top), with a final peak at 60–65 mph. This system was designed to be both speed and throttle conscious. It also meant that in a train, the engines in different cars could be in different gears at the same time. It was thought that this condition would only ever be of short duration, although some anecdotal evidence would suggest that, in practice, it did go on for quite long periods, especially during freight operations. Interestingly, no 'official' maximum speed was ever stated for the Multi Purpose railcars as far as I can determine – their maximum was actually determined by the line speed-limits. But speeds in the 80s were not unusual, although the maximum line-speed on the NCC route was 70 mph, or less, in UTA days.

Brakes were once again air type, though with a safety interlock to prevent damage to the gearboxes through slipping of brake bands – something which needed further attention quite early on in the cars' careers. Both axles of the trailing bogie only of each power car were driven. In addition to the air brakes, the MPDs had equipment to operate vacuum brakes on non-air braked stock such as parcels vans. This allowed the driver to create a vacuum and thereby release

their brakes. If he braked, an air sensitive vacuum reader detected the change in air pressure and applied the brakes on the vans.

And these cars, like the MEDs before them, were to be truly flexible in operation – any car could be coupled to any other (provided there was a driving cab at the ends of the train! Naturally the patented wiring looms used for the MEDs were used for the new cars also.

The mechanical innovation of these MPD railcars has so far taken precedence over the other obvious important aspect – how many passengers did they carry and in what sort of accommodation? The answer here is not a simple one because unlike their near contemporaries on the GNR, the MPDs were converted from existing coaching stock of varying age and type.

Ultimately there were even more bodyshell variants than with any other type of railcar – single-cab power cars and trailers with and without corridor connections; double-cab power cars and trailer cars with corridor connections; open and side corridor cars; standard, composite and brake combinations of most types and buffet trailers – three of them, but all different. It was a train-spotter's delight and an operating department's headache. We now move on to look at the fleet.

An MPD brake/2nd power car (series Nos 36–39) under construction at Duncrue Street in 1957.

CP Friel collection

The MPD fleet

So much for the mechanical aspects of the Multi Purpose Diesels, but what about the passenger accommodation? For many of the MEDs, new bodies had been built. However, a cheaper alternative was adopted for the first MPDs.

In 1951 the UTA had built 19 new coaches. One was a buffet car, 16 were corridor stock (both open and side corridor) and two were non-corridor compartment stock. It may seem odd that this was so, when all the emphasis was apparently on cost cutting and diesel development. However, the explanation relates to events some ten years earlier, when a large quantity of NCC stock was destroyed in the blitz on Belfast. Compensation was due to the successor of the LMS for these and this money came to the UTA, which had of course taken over the LMS assets in Northern Ireland in 1949.

The year 1951 was that of the 'Festival of Britain' and these 57-foot coaches, built to very similar design as LMS pre-war stock (BR Mk1 coaches had not yet appeared), became known as the 'Festivals'. These relatively new corridor coaches were selected for the first MPD conversions and the first units were completed in September 1957.

The initial four power cars, Nos 36–39, were open saloon-type coaches seating 48, with a driver's cab and guard's compartment formed at one end only. There were corridor connections at

Almost complete, MPD brake/2nd power car 37 will soon be rolled out. At this time no-one had thought to put electric rear red lights on diesel railcars! Old practices died hard.

CP Friel collection

A brand new MPD train poses for the official photographer near Whitehead in November 1957. The set is composed of the first four power cars completed – 42 and 41 at the front with 37 and 36 at the rear. The centre vehicle is an ordinary hauled coach. All power cars up to No 45 were converted from modern hauled coaches introduced in 1951.

Official UTA photo, courtesy W McCormick

each end so they could be coupled in any order. In fact a rather neat design of Perspex-fronted gangway cover was provided, though these seem to have fallen out of use as the years passed. Two more cars, 40 and 41, were similar but without the guard's compartment. These six had previously been 321-26 (not in the same order). To run with these on the first train was buffet car No 90 (renumbered 549 in 1959) – this was one of the famous 'North Atlantic' express coaches, built in 1934 with its distinctive high windows. It was joined later by 87, which had also been built new in 1951. It was later renumbered 550 and its seating capacity was increased for the new services. This was to be a high-speed train, made up of just one buffet trailer and four power cars.

Then followed four more power units, all side corridor, with a small cab at one end only. These were composites. Nos 42–3 (formerly 341–2)

seated 18/24 in the two classes, whilst Nos 44–5 (formerly 331–2) were brake composites seating 12/24. Oddly, Nos 44–5 had two first class 'half compartments' seating three.

These units were all turned out in the then standard dark Brunswick green. but unlike the earlier MED units they were unlined, with only a small pale green warning panel at the cab ends and the UTA Red Hand symbol on the sides. Clearly the ingenuity put into the mechanical outfitting did not extend to the livery.

Early in 1959 six side-corridor driving trailers numbered 529–534 (known oddly in official parlance as 'mules') were produced from Nos 301–06 (again not in order) and in 1960 a further buffet trailer (No 548, ex-88) was converted, as a spare for the two cars already running. One trailer per two power cars provided the appropriate power/weight ratio for the express

Another view of the test train posed at Whitehead in 1957 (see also page 141). The set is 42-41-305-37-36. The leading car is a composite side corridor. No 305 is a UTA 'Festival' side corridor second. In 1959 it would be rebuilt as MPD driving trailer 533. The horizontal straw line below window level was carried only on hauled stock.

Official UTA photo, courtesy W McCormick

services envisaged, one to one on local stopping services. Each open coach had tables and there was originally intended to be at-seat meal service for first class passengers, though how this would have been achieved in side-corridor coaches was never made clear. In the event the idea was not pursued.

After some months in service the original cars were joined by others, as the intention was, of course, to dieselise the whole ex-NCC network including the Larne line, which was a much more suburban operation. These new cars were conversions of various classes of non-corridor coaches – some of the coaches thus altered were known as 'Larne Steels'. The power cars were numbered 46–53 and non-powered driving trailers 535–539 and 543. The latter was produced from the last 1951 coach. It was a

composite and had the distinction of being the first trailer to be cut up, in 1974, when it was converted (again) to a conflat wagon.

They appeared during late 1958 and into mid-1959 and some had a new livery. This was a pale blue/green colour sometimes referred to as 'eau de nil' and alternatively as 'Catherwood blue'; by this time new UTA buses were appearing in this colour with a cream window surround. The inspiration for this came from the old HMS Catherwood bus company which had operated in the 1930s – one of the UTA's senior bus managers had worked for and greatly respected this company.

Unfortunately the UTA version omitted the dark blue band and gold lining which had really set the more bland colours off. Certainly the UTA variant wasn't impressive on the buses and

Non-corridor MPD brake/1st/2nd power car No 48 at York Road on 4 July 1959. It would seem that the first batch of these cars appeared in the original dark green livery similar to the 1957 cars opposite. These non-corridor types were a real anachronism – modern under the frames, ancient style passenger accommodation above. The Bangor line had power doors in 1952.

RH Whitford

From April 1959 new MPD cars appeared in the 'Catherwood blue' livery. Here brand new non-corridor trailer 535 and power car No 60 sit outside Duncrue Street Works on the same date. Neither car has had the UTA crest or number decals added as yet. Note how No 535 even retains the quarter lights and drop light slam door in the driving cab – a very basic conversion.

RH Whitford

was even less so on the trains which had no relieving colour but were painted over all with the light blue, no lining or even cream, with the roofs a silvery grey colour.

Photographic evidence suggests that the original green was applied up to about car 53 and the new one applied from April 1959 to cars 54–62 and 530–43. Some of the earlier cars were repainted to match but the colour did not weather well on trains and was abandoned by late 1960.

These new MPDs were basically LMS standard suburban non-corridor coaches, principally intended for working short-distance suburban trains on the Larne line. But as the years passed they were to be found all over the system. As a schoolboy I used to travel regularly from Belfast to Coleraine, a distance of 62 miles lasting approximately an hour and a half. The lack of corridor, drab green upholstery, dim lighting, and no toilets made the journey seem long, especially on winter evenings. A notebook I have from these days refers to this type (both power car and trailers) as 'grotties'. Naturally we did not appreciate these when we found them. However, the lack of a corridor and hence no supervision by a guard also meant that antics

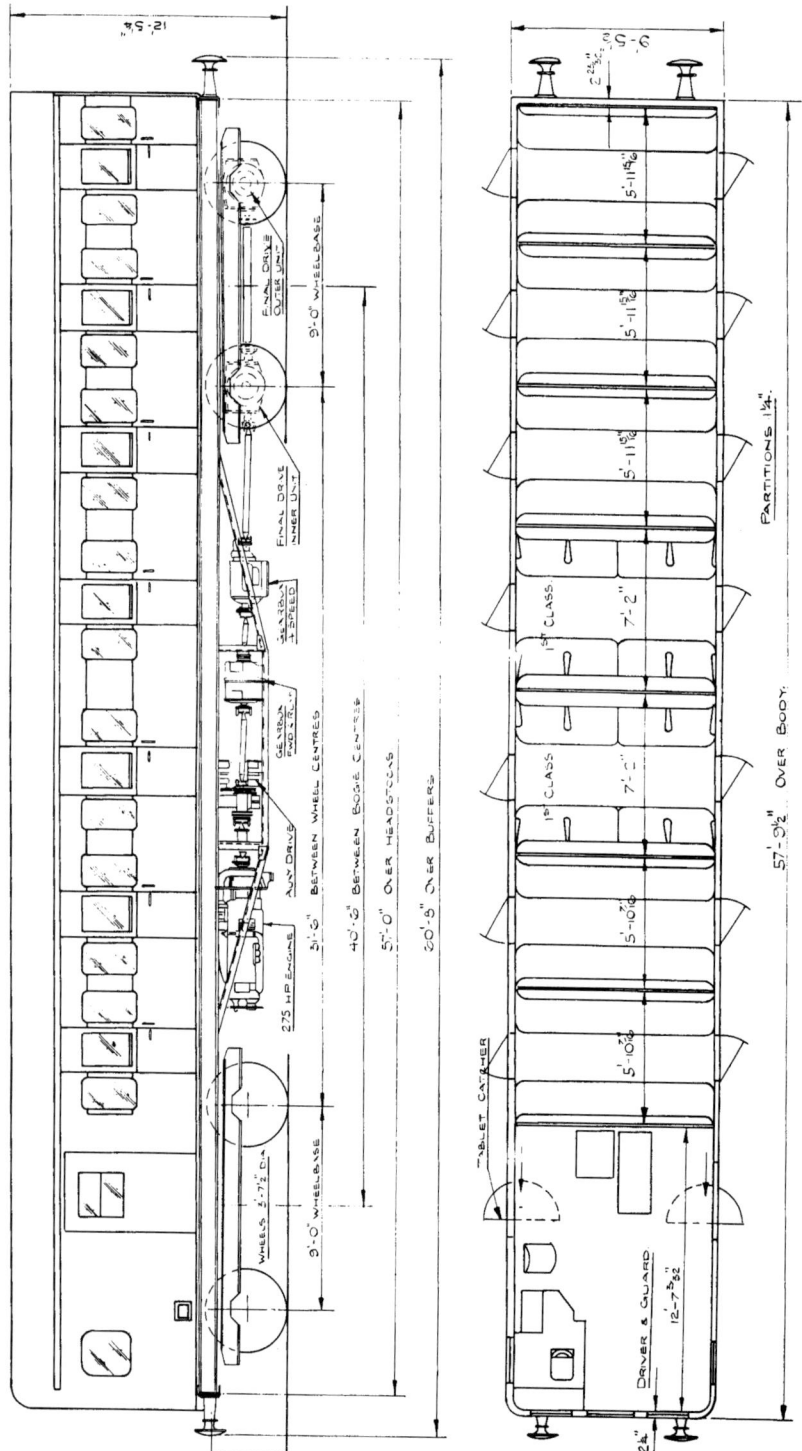

3 mm scale

MPD railcars 46–48.

such as removing the light bulbs could be indulged in!

The third main type of single-ended car to be produced had a new body similar to those on many of the more familiar BR railcars. These had bus-type seats fitted, although some had first class sections, as usual towards the front of the car. But there was no view forward – in all of them the guard's compartment was immediately behind the drivers cab. These vehicles also had corridor connections. The power cars were numbered 54–62 and were turned out in the new livery. Similar style trailers were also built in late 1959 and carried the numbers 540–542.

Among this group was a unique 60-foot vehicle, No 56, which had started life as the NCC Chairman's saloon, built in 1944 at the same time as two LMS saloons. It already had a modern body and this was adapted for railcar use.

In July 1959 No 58 of this series was destroyed in an accident at Umbra crossing near Magilligan, 25 miles from Londonderry. It was completely wrecked and was cut up the following month, though two other MPDs that were damaged, 45 and 36, were able to be repaired.

No 56 also had a relatively short life. It caught fire at Brookmount (on the Lisburn–Antrim line)

Left: Brand new MPD power car No 55 at York Road in May 1959. Nos 54 and 55 were brake composites with bus type seating. They seated 12/60 and curiously first class passengers had to pass through the second class compartment to access the toilet!

Behind No 55 is a new side corridor second class trailer coach, possibly 534.

RH Whitford

Right: MPD brake composite No 56 heads a train out of Portrush around 1960. This vehicle was rebuilt from the 1944 NCC Chairman's saloon. As a railcar it seated 12 first and 60 second. It was destroyed by fire in 1966. The second and third vehicles in this five car set are non-corridor.

Martin Baumann collection

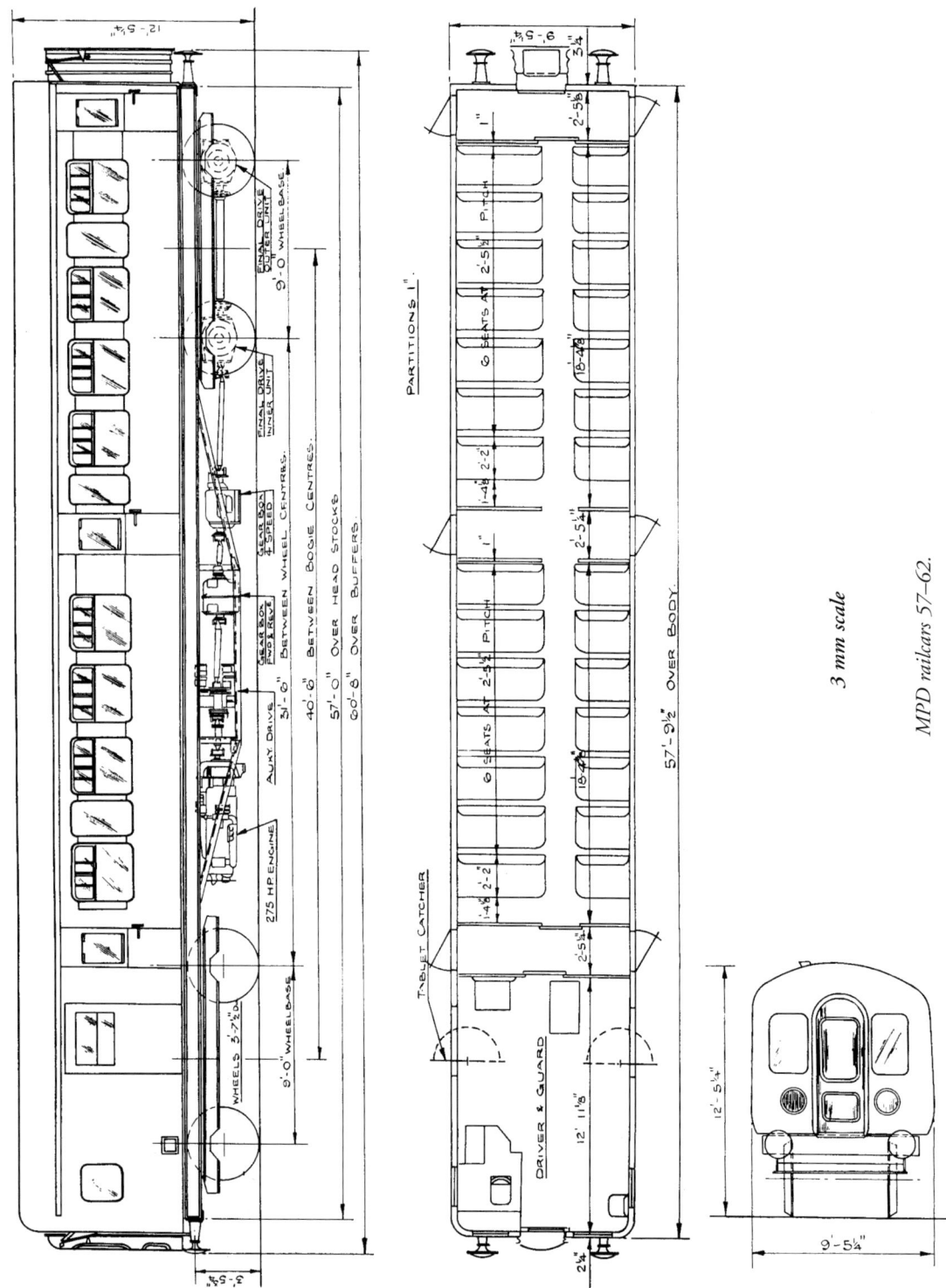

3 mm scale

MPD railcars 57–62.

Left: A Belfast-Londonderry express at Limavady Junction. The last car and the first three are in the pale blue/green livery. The paint on leading car, No 54 is already showing signs of wear, specially on the glazed corridor connection. The fourth vehicle in the eight coach train is diner 549, from the NCC 'North Atlantic' rake of 1934.

EM Patterson 62D

Right: Newly completed double-ended MPD power car No 63 under trials at York Road in November 1961. It is sporting the then recently introduced railcar livery of Brunswick green, grey roof and 'wasp' pattern warning panel which remained standard for all UTA railcars until 1965.

RH Whitford

while hauling a goods train in 1966 and became a total loss.

From the end of 1960, yellow and black warning panels were added to driving ends as on other types of UTA railcar and around the same time cars began to be repainted into a brighter Brunswick green livery than the original 1957 scheme. This was relieved only by decals, the yellow and black warning panel and a rather fine crest introduced by the UTA to replace the older 'Red Hand'.

As a result of the loss of No 58 and the fire on

BUT 129, it was decided to build three more MPD vehicles, numbered 63–65, and these appeared in 1961–2, wearing the lighter Brunswick green. They were each 60 feet long, having been converted from ex-NCC coaches of the I4 class, and different from all the other MPD cars in being double-ended. For some reason the cabs were placed on the left rather than the right, and they had half cabs as they retained corridor connections. They seated 70 in bus-style seats which were reversible, and had a guard's compartment as well, making them very

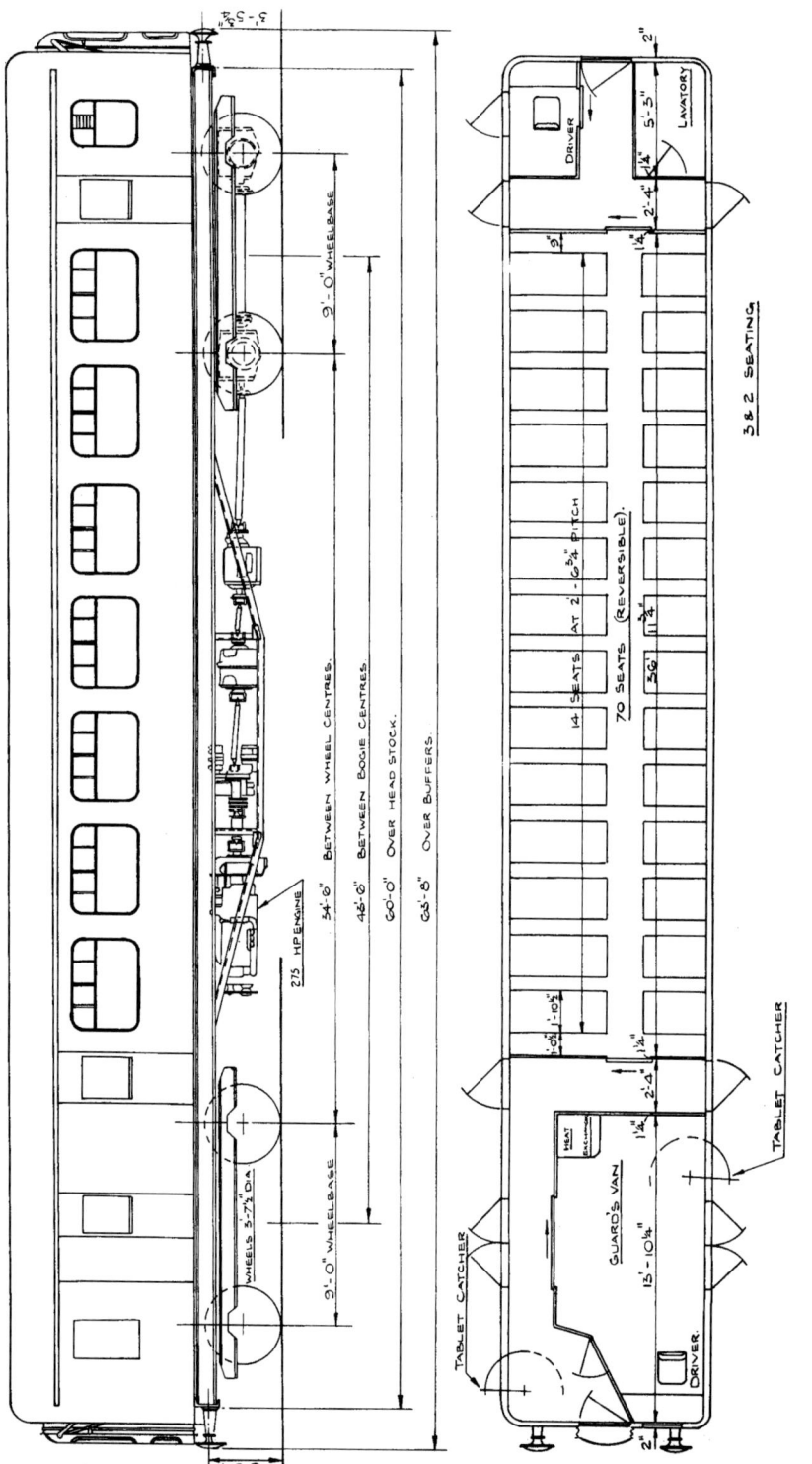

3 mm scale

MPD railcars 63–65.

versatile units indeed. These were to be among the last MPDs to survive in working order.

The MPD power cars, as might be expected, had varying weights, from 39 tons up to 44 tons. Weight naturally fluctuated as they were converted or altered, many losing two or three seats when heat-exchanging apparatus was fitted in the early 1960s.

With the introduction of the 'regional' colours in mid-1965 many MPDs were repainted into the then new NCC area red and grey livery, which certainly improved their appearance externally. There was a slight variation in this livery as on the units designated as 'suburban', the white band was only two feet deep, rather than the full height of the windows. This variation was applied to only a few cars as it was abandoned in 1966 and most of the 'suburban' cars were still in green until the NIR era. Deep red and oyster grey became the standard NIR livery after 1967.

In 1968–72 the non-corridor cars were rebuilt with corridors and toilets. Their internal seating arrangements were altered, and new wider windows in each 'bay' gave the interiors a much-needed 'lift'. Red moquette coverings replaced the older green in many cars around this time.

By 1968 buffet car No 549 was out of service and was eventually scrapped, never having carried the new red and grey livery. The other two (548 and 550) were modified in 1966 to work with the then new Diesel Electric sets coming into service on the line.

Originally, Manson-type automatic tablet catchers were fitted to all the power cars to allow fast non-stop running through block posts. The apparatus (there were two sets, one on each side) was mounted on the floor of the guard's compartment and pivoted about a vertical axis so that the catcher head could be swung in to position through the door opening. Long after the apparatus was removed from the cars it was still possible to see the marks on the floor where it had been. Newspapers could be exchanged too. They were wrapped in cardboard to protect them from damage by the jaws of the tablet receiver. Magheramorne Loop on the Larne line was apparently a common place for this activity, but it took place at other locations as well.

In all, 30 power cars and 15 driving trailers were produced and three buffet cars converted. Nos 63–65 were to be the last of their kind, although the UTA had plans to build more.

After rebuilding by NIR, the non corridor MPDs looked completely different. Compare this view of No 52, rebuilt in 1970, with MPD 48 on page 143. The main features still recognisable are the passenger entry doors which retain small windows either side. The rear car on this train arriving at York Road is 65.

JM Allen

Tablet snatching apparatus was fitted to MPD brake cars. This sequence at Ballycarry shows the operation. In the first view, the signalman fits the tablet into the lineside apparatus.

The second view shows the train about to pick up the tablet. The leading vehicle in this train, No 539, had no guard's section and was not fitted for tablet catching. This would have been done from one of the brake cars further back.

Below we see the apparatus inside the brake van, before the exchange and after receiving the tablet. After the exchange, the apparatus could be revolved on its axis and brought inboard, and the door closed. The special slots cut in the doors were not necessarily used.

EM Patterson 82L, 110Q, 82A, 82B

Double cab MPD 65 was the last MPD car to be built, entering service in 1962. It is seen here operating as a single unit at Niblock crossing, near Antrim, in the summer of 1975, wearing NIR livery.

JM Allen

The MPDs in service

A new timetable was introduced in 1958 when the first sets of these cars were ready. It was an ambitious schedule of 1 hour and 50 minutes over a 92¼ mile route, with five stops and over 60 miles of single track. A typical train was comprised of up to four power cars and two trailers, including the buffet. A ratio of two power cars for each trailer for high-speed services was planned. Stopping and slower ones could manage with 1:1.

There was no doubt that, as conceived and originally executed, the MPD was a step up from anything else. Top speeds of 90+ mph were rumoured and one was certainly timed at 92 mph, while the high 80s were regularly achieved. The smoothness and speed of their running led one publication to enthuse in 1959 that this "lifts the new UTA diesels from the rank and file of commoners into the realm of aristocracy"! The article continued:

. . . we can from personal experience confirm the comfort of these cars which ride smoothly at the high speeds necessary to maintain the schedule and which accelerate rapidly without the feel, however slight, of gear changing to which we have become accustomed in other diesel railcars.

This ambitious schedule called for the running of the 31 miles from Ballymena to Belfast in 31 minutes, start to stop, as well as a further 60+ mph timing between Castlerock and Limavady Junction on the single line section of the line. Indeed, there was also a Saturday morning boat train which is reputed to have run non-stop to Londonderry in an hour and a half – its public timing was 1 hour and 40 minutes non-stop. By 1959 down trains (which had to tackle the fierce grades up past Bleach Green) were being given an extra five minutes, though the 1 hour 50 minutes remained for trains starting in Londonderry. Ultimately these tight

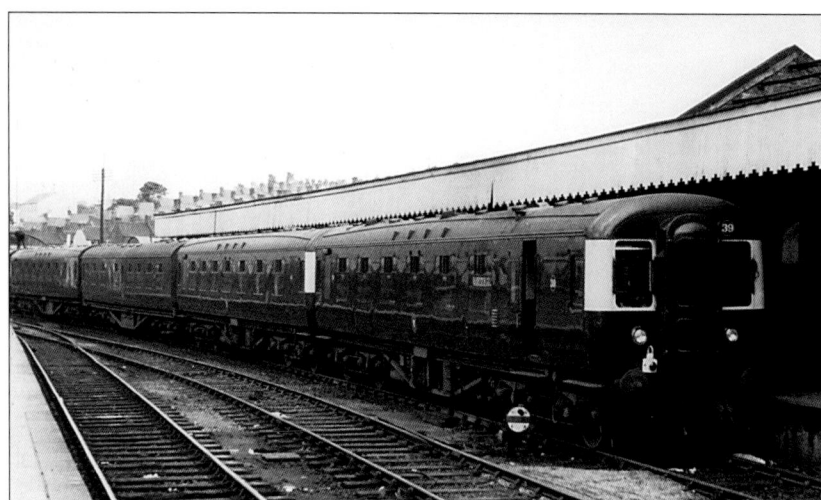

Brake/2nd MPD No 39 heads a five coach train at Londonderry Waterside in May 1958. The third vehicle in the train is buffet car No 87 (soon to be 550). The glazed gangway connections fell out of use after a few years. Most later ones had no windows.

Kelland collection 24258

schedules could not be maintained, especially since the UTA civil engineer had set a maximum speed limit of 70 mph on the ex-NCC lines.

As for their haulage capacities in 'freight' mode, there was a comprehensive test programme. One test train, with five cars (but with only two engines running) and three added coaches (and a respected railway journalist of the time on board) restarted its heavy train, from rest, on the famous Bleach Green gradient of 1 in 75 and was still able to top the gradient at 15 mph.

The engineers were understandably very pleased with their new creation. Later on, trials were carried out using these cars pitted against the GNR's BUT railcars, which by this time were operating the Enterprise services to Dublin, to see which would be superior. Here it was found that the higher gearing of the BUT cars led to economies and slightly higher speeds on the relatively flat route with fewer stops. However, on the NCC main line, with many more regular stops, some at the foot of quite stiff gradients, the MPD's acceleration was superior. So they remained largely on that section. It was, therefore, not surprising that in 1961 a report on the way forward for motive power in Northern Ireland concluded:

> It is recommended that passenger and freight trains are powered by multiple unit diesel cars of the Multi-Purpose type and that shunting is carried out by shunting locomotives powered

with engines and transmissions generally similar to the MP cars.

It was planned that no fewer than 102 MP-type units would be acquired, becoming the standard unit throughout the network, but subject to some current 'minor' problems being sorted out. They would completely replace the GNR AEC and BUT cars, as well as all the older units on the GNR section which would be operated by a total of 56 units. Forty-six new MPDs would be built for the NCC section, making 75 there in all, and all steam would be eliminated. Six steam engines would be converted to diesel shunters and there would be nine new shunters as well.

But it was never to be. The fall from the anticipated high standards of these state-of-the-art diesel trains was rapid. The engine troubles did not go away and reliability for high-speed running was not coming up to expectations. In the report of February 1961 quoted above, amid the enthusiasm, were indications of problems to come when it was stated that "diesel units . . . are much more liable to failure than steam locomotives". Although failures of the other types of railcars had been very considerably reduced, that for the Multi Purpose Diesels remained "embarrassingly high" and an urgent investigation was launched.

Devices to protect equipment had been fitted, as well as one to protect the gearbox due to

"driving with insufficient air". (Presumably this was to prevent overheating and damage due to dragging brakes, though whether this would have been the root cause may be disputed by some engineers.)

The report stated "the 275 bhp supercharged engine has not yet achieved proven reliability". The UTA was working with the engine manufacturers and modifications to piston specifications and engine cooling water systems would, it was hoped, provide a cure. The engine in 230-bhp form had given no trouble before and it seems that the level of supercharging to 275 bhp was putting too much stress on it. Consideration was given to fitting a larger engine with less supercharging but in the end this did not happen and the MPD engine's reliability remained suspect.

Eventually a re-engining project was set in motion and two engines were tested in 1964. The first was an AEC engine, type A1100H, a six-cylinder 17.7 litre normally aspirated engine developing 260 bhp. This was fitted to No 56. This product of the BUT group was considered generally inferior by the UTA's development engineers; yet ultimately it was fitted to a further eleven cars. Possibly it was hoped that the lack of turbo or super-charging would be compensated for by greater reliability. The second new engine type, an experimental Rolls Royce engine fitted to No 38, was the preferred choice. The

production version of this was a turbo-charged six-cylinder engine, type C6/TFHL Type 2677 of 12.2 litres capacity, developing 275 bhp. It was eventually fitted to 17 MPD cars, the prototype being removed and replaced by a production version. There does not appear to have been a great step change in reliability though. Failures were still regular and embarrassing, despite the promise of the then legendary name 'Rolls Royce'. Indeed, British Railways fared little better with their Rolls Royce-engined DMUs.

A recurring problem that the Rolls Royce engine shared with its Leyland predecessor was pitting of the cylinder liners due to overheating. This could cause engine failure in as short a time as four weeks after overhaul. This design flaw was never totally overcome during the MPDs' service life. A further difficulty in later years was with the Self Changing Gears Type R14 automatic gearbox, for which spares became increasingly difficult to acquire.

Indeed, overheating seems to have been the main weakness of the type, exacerbated no doubt by their 'heavy haulage' duties. The AEC engines had a particularly bad record in this regard – of the twelve cars so fitted three ended their careers as a result of fires. They were also generally among the first to be withdrawn, only one surviving until 1979. The Rolls Royce cars did somewhat better with a fire casualty rate of two out of seventeen. Although many of these

MPD 55 had charge of an eight car Londonderry train at Antrim in May 1970. an ex-GNR bogie van brings up the rear.

TJ Edgington

events were far in the future, the writing seems to have been on the wall for the highly stressed underfloor diesel engine as early as mid 1961, when the last few units were still being built. Was it a case of too far too fast? It seems so, because over 25 years later when the BR 'Sprinter' DMUs were being developed, the engines produced a mere 10 bhp more from a 14 litre engine (12.2 for the equivalent Perkins/ Rolls-Royce engine) than Leyland had produced from one of just over 15 litres, more than twenty five years earlier.

And so in 1964, less than three years after the optimistic report referred to above was produced, replacement traction was sought, the MPD type was not considered by the UTA's engineers to provide the best way forward. This change in design philosophy, and its ultimately significant results, is discussed in the next chapter. But one more aspect of these pioneering UTA diesel railcars needs to be considered briefly before that, for it was a matter which concerned the public greatly.

We now come to the vexed question of railcar heat. By 1961, MPD production was coming to an end with the last three double-ended cars. The oldest railcars, 6 and 7, had been in service for ten years. A recurring issue of public dissatisfaction turned out to be that of heating. Northern Ireland has what is officially termed a 'temperate' climate, but it can be, and usually is, damp and

cold in winter. In this year a major report on railcar heating stated, "Inadequate heating of diesel trains during winter is the most frequent and persistent cause for complaint." The then Deputy Chief Engineer NG Russell had been tasked with sorting this matter out.

Heating had been carried out in different ways during the development of the railcars. Four older railcars had steam heating by means of an oil-fired 'spanner' boiler (ex-NCC 1, 4, and Nos 6 and 7). Though efficient in terms of passenger comfort, this was also expensive, costing 4s 0d an hour. This type of system also heated (or supplemented) the heating on the ex-GNR fleet.

A second method of heating was by the use of an oil-fired Smith heater – this was an air heater and was much more cost efficient at 9d per hour for a four-car set such as a MED set. In the case of the MEDs there was also heating supplied by circulating engine cooling water through the car, which was in a sense, free. Air heating from radiators using engine cooling water was the third system in use, but while useful it was only effective in power cars – trailers needed a supplementary system in any case. The fourth system in use, mostly on the Multi Purpose Diesels, was to use the high temperatures generated by engine exhaust to heat water in a device known as a Heat Exchanger, and circulate this hot water throughout the vehicle (See appendix 2).

As regards these systems, it was decided not to produce any further railcars with steam heating from boilers. The only real advantage of this was, it was felt, that the trailers could be used with either steam or diesel. Since the policy by now was that mainline passenger steam would be phased out, this hardly mattered. The expense didn't help.

The Smith's oil heater was useful in that, by blowing air, it did not need any pre-heating. However, on its own it was usually insufficient, so some sort of extra heat would be needed anyway.

The third system considered, engine water circulation, had its advantages. It did not require any extra equipment in the car and was therefore cheap. But it had drawbacks – the water ran a devious route and to achieve adequate circulation, header tanks were needed, mounted quite high up near the doors where there was potential for embarrassing leaks. Also, the actual cooling of the engine could be compromised by this complex routing which led to engine failure. As far as the public was concerned, of course, the only thing worse than a cold train was a cold

one which went nowhere at all! The only future application of this third heating system would be to use boost exhaust gas heat (the fourth type) by fitting small bus-type radiators. These had small air fans behind the radiators, off the direct cooling circuit between the engine and header tank.

In the end the engineers decided that, although the heat exchanger system had its problems – notably air locking and limiting of the surface area of heating pipes because of their location and masking by other equipment – it was the best overall.

Heat was not produced immediately and so pre-heating of vehicles would still be necessary – suggestions were made, and incorporated in official documents, about not running sets with windows open or leaving them standing for long periods with the doors open. So heat exchangers were to be fitted to all MED and MPD power cars, with air radiation from cooling and Smith's heaters. Trailer vehicles would have a more powerful 'Lucas' heater.

The 14 GNR BUT and ten AEC railcars had oil-fired Spanner boilers which still needed pre-

A Larne Harbour bound MPD working waits at Belfast in August 1977. By this time most main line services to Londonderry were in the hands of the '70' class diesel electric units.

JM Allen

Opposite: *Two extra sets of MPDs wait at Larne Harbour for specials as a three car set headed by MPD No 50 leaves for Belfast on 12 July 1977.*

JM Allen

heating but they would be left as they were. Efforts would be made to improve the engine cooling systems of the 28 MED power cars by upgrading radiators and pipe coverings. For the MPD power cars and trailers, the exhaust gas heat exchanger should work but, if necessary, the air heaters could be fitted additionally to the MEDs and MPD trailers.

Work to carry out these improvements went on during 1961 and after, although it has to be said that results were not always totally successful. As the heat exchangers became troublesome, some Multi Purpose units were fitted with a heater known as a 'Dragonair' in the late 1960s. These units could be identified by the prominent exterior grills for this type of heater. Ultimately full air-conditioning would be the answer, and the latest CAF railcars on order for NIR and Irish Rail have an auxiliary diesel generator that provides electric power for this.

The use of the Multi Purpose cars on goods traffic proved to be an unsatisfactory experiment as well – the new stresses on the engines thus engendered quickly began to tell. The original specification was undoubtedly optimistic. The maths may have been sound but the reality of making this type of engine work reliably, day in and day out, to its maximum rating was to prove difficult.

When in 1965 the GNR line to Derry (Foyle Road) was closed, Multi Purpose Diesel railcars had to pull quite long and heavy trains in the late

evening and night from Lisburn, over the steeply graded twisting branch to Antrim and thence to Londonderry Waterside by the old NCC main line. The reason for this was that, though by this time the UTA had decided to cease carrying freight anyway, goods for Donegal came from Dublin through Londonderry and for political reasons this traffic had to continue. However, CIÉ locomotives were not permitted to work through and so the UTA had to do the best with what it had. Obviously it would have been 'politically unacceptable' to use steam regularly – after all, were not the MPDs dual purpose?

However, these trains were not the light freight envisaged in the original plan – freight that by this time had disappeared anyway from Northern Ireland's internal system. They were quite heavy and the Lisburn–Antrim section contained some sharp curves and gradients, which were much more severe than those on the well graded fast NCC main line. The train worked south from Londonderry in the evening and then a loaded train came north in the early hours of the morning. The passenger stock then worked daytime trains.

I can remember these ungainly-looking trains making their way across the River Bann at Coleraine with up to four power cars roaring away as they ground across the lifting bridge, a rake of 30 to 40 wagons rattling behind. They looked like the sort of trains I used to make up on my Hornby Dublo train set just to see how

much an engine could pull! "Flogging the guts out of them," said a railwayman at the time, and one person living by the lineside near Ballymena recalls seeing exhausts glowing red as the straining overheating engines struggled up the steep gradient towards Cullybackey station.

Another friend who managed to ride in the cab on one of these trains recalled watching the engine fail lights come on steadily during the course of the journey until one solitary engine was trying desperately to keep the whole thing on the move! It was while thus employed that power car 56 caught fire and was destroyed.

When in 1966 it was mooted that a second overnight train would operate, there was a realisation that the MPDs could not cope with this and drivers from the UTA went to Inchicore in Dublin to train on CIÉ GM locomotives. However, the drivers there refused to allow their locomotives to run over the UTA to Londonderry and so there was no option but to use MPDs. Ultimately the new DE units took over the work, their stronger engines and traction motors better able to handle this work.

Less than ten years after their introduction, the arrival of the new diesel electric railcars (with engines and transmissions similar to the BR 'Hastings' class 201 DEMUs) brought the MPDs' brief spell as Northern Ireland's premier trains to an end – though on a good day, they were still capable of very fast running. I can still remember one alarming trip with an MPD rake, in the late 1960s, over Bleach Green viaduct, just outside Belfast.

Alas, the practice of sticking a couple of four-wheel vans on the rear of the train stopped this high-speed running. After some derailments, trains hauling vans were restricted to 60 mph.

However, despite their increasing problems, the MPD fleet remained virtually intact until the mid 1970s, apart from losses due to accident or fire. Nevertheless, their use on goods trains was largely passed to the new diesel electric units and their gross trailing load per power unit over the Bleach Green section – scene of their 1958 triumphs – was reduced from 145 tons in 1963 to just 80 tons by 1971.

This was a recognition that highly stressed engines of whatever manufacture were just not capable of this kind of heavy slogging on a regular basis. As time passed, gearbox and final drive units became a constant source of breakdown, with replacements increasingly difficult to obtain (at one point a lead time of 18 months was being quoted). As newer units became available for the main line, MPDs were increasingly used on the outer suburban services to Larne.

The new Belfast Central station was opened in 1976 and, as a result, the Bangor line's isolation came to an end. It was planned to run services to Londonderry from this new station but, in the continuing absence of a bridge across the Lagan to join with York Road station, these would have to operate over the old ex-GNR branch line from Lisburn to Antrim, adding some ten miles to the journey. However, the line was to be upgraded to 70 mph running – it had not been used for regular passenger trains since 1960. The track and signalling work was completed some time before the new through services could start and as a result some MPDs found themselves working shuttle services to Antrim from Lisburn. They were withdrawn once the through services (worked by the then new '80' class railcars) began.

In 1980 an attempt was made to stimulate suburban services on the old NCC main line via Bleach Green to Antrim, which had effectively been useful only for stock transfers to and from the workshops at York Road since the re-routing of Londonderry trains via Lisburn in January 1978. The arrival of the second batch of '80' class DEMUs meant the end for most of the MPD units, which were withdrawn between 1977 and 1980.

Some of the last serviceable MPDs were selected to run the new shuttle service to Antrim which stopped at the old Monkstown station. These included 63, 65 and 541 which had earlier been repainted in the 1970s NIR livery of maroon lower panels with dark blue uppers and white lining, as well as Nos 52 and 64, still in the earlier deep red and grey. Some other trailers and de-engined power cars survived as loco-hauled stock for a time and the body of one trailer (532) eventually went to the RPSI at Whitehead where

it remains at the time of writing.

However, the Antrim service proved short lived and the last two MPD power cars then eked out their final days shunting at York Road, with 65 being the last in regular use. The third double-ended car, 64, did not receive the new livery but remained at York Road in the old livery until the mid 1980s when, like many of its brothers, it was taken to Crumlin for burial. Attempts to consider No 65 for preservation failed due to the presence of blue asbestos and the prohibitive cost of removing it. Truth to tell, nobody loved the MPDs much by then anyway.

The reputation of the MPD railcars for unreliability lived on long after their demise. In the mid-1980s Northern Ireland Railways was considering additional stock to replace the '70' class (the original UTA DE cars). At this time British Rail was developing the Sprinter and Super Sprinter family of DMUs which, on the face of it, might have been the sort of vehicles which NIR could use – they offered improved performance and economy over the 1960s DEMUs they would replace.

However, with memories of his earlier career days at York Road dealing with the engine and gearbox problems mentioned above, the then Chief Engineer of NIR Stan Myers is reported to have said, "No more MPD technology!" It was therefore decided to re-use the original DE power equipment in new bodies. In fact the Class 150 and 156 Sprinters have proved to be one of the more successful designs of underfloor-powered diesel units, with some very high levels of availability being recorded. This performance has not been repeated by some of the more recently introduced types. It is to be hoped that the new 450-bhp DMUs currently on order for NIR will prove to have the success in service which eluded these earlier Northern Irish high-speed railcars.

When virtually all of the MPDs (apart from three mentioned earlier) were withdrawn, their remains were cut up at Magheramorne. Later, regulations concerning blue asbestos meant that the last survivors, along with some MEDs, had

By October 1979 the end was in sight for most MPDs. The Railway Preservation Society of Ireland organized a 'Farewell to the MPDs' tour from York Road to Bangor, via Antrim and Lisburn. It was made up of No 51 (leading), and two double enders, 63 and 64, hauling the RPSI dining car 552. This was only the second known time an MPD set had worked to Bangor. The train is seen at Helen's Bay. In the event the short lived Antrim service kept a few MPDs running in passenger service for another year.   *JM Allen*

to be buried in a quarry near Crumlin, along with other vehicles from both NIR and CIÉ. This was the only solution to the problem of safe disposal as neither company possessed the specialised equipment needed (see Chapter 8). None of the power cars survived, though any of the last three would have been a useful enough machine for a preserved line, with its double cabs and reversible seats.

To return to the early 1960s, it was evident by 1963–4 that the sophisticated underfloor-engined diesel railcar had its limitations and in Northern Ireland the UTA was beginning to find out what they were. The years 1964–5 were to show fleet availability at an all-time low – something needed to be done. The railways were once more under threat from a government which commissioned yet another report on the

future of public transport, the Benson Report. However, to save face they were pushed into providing more finance for the ailing UTA.

The UTA was saddled with huge debts, a legacy from the 'make it pay' policy which had failed for both road and rail, compounded by the GNR's accumulated debt which, when added, had made an already severe internal financial crisis worse. This debt was now to be wiped out and finance provided for new rolling stock, as the public perception was that the services were becoming increasingly unreliable. The earlier hopes that steam could have been eliminated entirely by the MPD fleet had proved to be misplaced. A few years earlier, as recounted above, the MPD type had been considered the answer. Would innovation be pursued again – or could there be another approach?

Retreat from innovation: The UTA '70' class diesel electrics

In October 1964 the government of Northern Ireland made a grant to the UTA to purchase more diesel units. It was less than three years since the final MPDs had been turned out and the official reason given was the necessity of eliminating steam entirely from the system. However, the unreliability of the MPDs, and to a lesser extent trouble with the earlier railcars, probably had a part to play. A grant of £475,000 was provided.

However, this time there was a change in engineering philosophy. James Courtney, a keen enthusiast for the bus-type underfloor engine, had retired in 1963. His assistant, Norman Russell, had often been charged with the working out of improvements to heating and reliability, as well as other engineering aspects of the railcars (the report referred to in Chapter 12 bears his name). As a result of his experiences, Russell was less convinced that the high-tech underfloor-engine route was the one to follow.

So a search began for an alternative that would suit Northern Ireland and the watchword was to be reliability – something which broke no new ground but had a proven track record. Underfloor high-speed engines and sophisticated hydraulic transmissions were therefore out – the new units would use a different and tested technology instead.

The Southern Region of British Railways had a design of railcar which was proving very successful. These were diesel electric railcars (DEMUs) in which the diesel engine was in fact a low-speed generator unit, running at less than 1000 rpm compared with the 2000 rpm of the higher-speed units used for mechanical or hydraulic traction. This provided electricity for electric traction motors similar to those found on locomotives. The whole thing was very much 'heavy engineering' and the electric transmission

A six coach '70' class set passing Kilroot on the Larne Line in August 1967. The power car carries the original Northern Ireland crest, used until 1967. The 'spare' set was regularly used on Larne line services as these railcars proved to be exceedingly reliable.

DJA Young

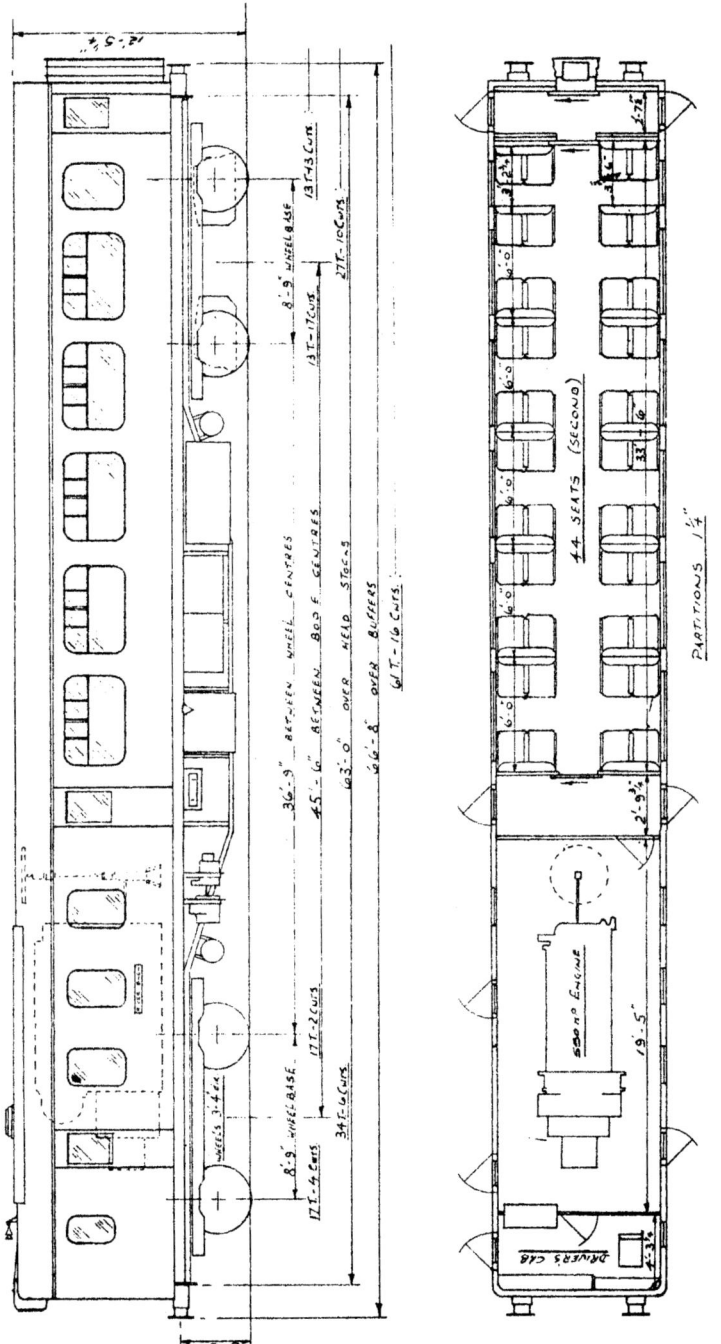

2.5 mm scale

'70' class power cars 71–78.

was in effect that used on EMUs on the Southern Region. The engineers there had wanted nothing to do with mechanical or hydraulic systems, so the DEMU was developed for their unelectrified lines.

The power plant was an English Electric 4-cylinder turbo-charged engine. It developed 600 bhp at 850 rpm and was connected to a 392-kw main generator with a continuous rating of 900 amps at 90 volts. The transmission was electric – each of the two traction motors was rated at 220 bhp giving 440 bhp at the rail for each power unit. Thus each power unit could operate with two trailers of average weight.

English Electric, who built the main generator engines, were prepared to woo the UTA in an effort to get orders for this type and their efforts were successful.

Of course there was a downside – the new power cars were heavy, nearly 50% heavier than existing ones, and this could have implications for the track. The possibility of through corridor connections was excluded as the engine needed its own compartment. It was a massive machine which was situated directly behind the full-width driver's cab. So one of the prime reasons for using underfloor engines – maximising passenger convenience – was sacrificed.

However, the promised high level of reliability from a lower stressed, simpler form of traction proved irresistible and orders were placed with English Electric for the new power units. The only significant deviation from the original plan was that the engines were rated at 550 bhp, not 600 bhp. Did someone at Duncrue Street remember the 40 bhp extra which had proved the downfall of the MPDs?

The new UTA railcars consisted of seven power cars (Nos 71–77, constructed at Duncrue Street – the last to be built there), each containing a main engine/generator set, with the two traction motors mounted in the trailing bogie. A spare engine was provided. The weight of each motor coach was 56 tons and they were 63 feet long – of which almost 20 feet was occupied by the engine/generator. Each had 44

seats in 2+2 layout in a single open saloon.

Two identical sets were provided for Londonderry services. Each had two power cars, a dining car, and three intermediate trailers, one of which had first class accommodation.

The trailer coaches were once again only partly new. As the more modern coaches had already been used for MED and MPD conversions, the UTA had to go further back and use underframes from ex-LMS compartment thirds built in the 1920s and 1930s. However, the conversions produced quite modern-looking coaches, though they were all of side corridor type. Many enthusiasts at the time believed them to be new construction throughout.

There were three four-compartment brake/firsts (701–03), two driving brake composites (711–12) and five seven-compartment standards (721–25). Oddly, only 701 was upholstered as a brake/first, 702 appearing as a brake/composite and 703 as brake/standard. The latter offered first class legroom at standard class fares!

The buffet cars for the Londonderry services in 1966 were simply those used with existing MPD stock, which were given new piping and through wiring to work with the new railcars. Nos 548 and 550 were the regulars. It was planned to convert the 'North Atlantic' buffet trailer 549 but in the event this did not happen.

As well as the two six-car mainline sets, there were also two shorter three-car sets with an intermediate and a driving trailer. The remainder would act as spares. In the event an eighth power car was built using the spare engine and over the next few years more driving trailers were converted as the value of having three-car sets was appreciated.

Belfast–Londonderry services steadily diminished in facilities as the years passed and the six-coach trains with buffet cars were simply no longer needed. (Today some Londonderry trains are composed of a two-car set – a far cry from the 'Festival Express' of 50 years ago.)

As before, air brakes were employed, with provision for working with vacuum-braked stock. Heating was electric – and for once there

A freshly painted 74, pulls into Magheramorne in early 1968. It is without any identifying insignia, but would soon receive the new NIR logo. These 550 bhp diesel electric cars proved to be very successful, and the power units from this first batch are still in service at the time of writing, albeit clothed in BR 1980's style bodywork.

RHG Simpson

were few complaints about this aspect of the trains!

It was planned that two power cars (which would give over 1000 bhp) would be available to work CIÉ goods trains from Lisburn to Londonderry. The new diesel trains entered service in 1966 and their arrival was timely as that summer was a particularly bad one for availability of rolling stock. The DEs and their successors were to be the mainstay of Northern Ireland train services for the next 30 years.

With this type of machine the difference between locomotive-hauled trains and multiple units became blurred – after all, the power cars were really small locomotives and the engine was the 'baby' of a range which powered the English Electric Type 1, 3 and 4 locomotives of BR, as well as the Southern region DEMUs. The power cars had corridor connections at only one end and staff communication through the engine compartment is restricted – rightly so, as clearances were very tight and the noise horrific! Certainly the benefits of flexibility so touted for the MPD/MED type were cheerfully shelved in favour of simplicity.

As regards the passenger, noise in multiple units has always been an issue – the power cars of these trains rapidly became a symphony of rattles and shakes from the heavy vibrations

created (the BR units were known as 'Thumpers', which seems entirely appropriate). In addition, the ride was very harsh in the first batch of power cars and some remedial work was needed on the rear bogie dampers, which helped but didn't ever eliminate the harshness entirely. Later built units of the '80' class are much better in this regard. Naturally, the trailers had a similar ambience to loco-hauled stock.

The DEs (they were called 'Hampshires' by some enthusiasts, though on the NCC section the term DE was more often used) appeared from the first in the then new livery of deep red and oyster grey, which was also being applied to the older NCC section railcars. They had an imposing crest on the front which was really a Northern Ireland coat of arms. However, on closer inspection the crest had no lettering. The reason for this is that by this time the decision had been taken to split up the UTA into three companies, one each for buses, lorries and trains. The interim railway company was known as Ulster Transport Railways. Because the UTA as such no longer existed, the UTR could not carry the latter's crest, yet it had no identity of its own. Once the railways began to trade as 'Northern Ireland Railways' (NIR), on 17 April 1967, the crests disappeared to be replaced by the NIR logo.

Once NIR was formed in 1968, all that was needed was a change of the 'anonymous crest on the front of the DEs for the new NIR logo. Here No 72 pulls into York Road on a train from Londonderry.

RHG Simpson

Despite the manufacturer's reservations, DE units continued to be given very heavy trains. In 1979 this nine coach train consists of a five car '70' class set with two power cars (first and fifth vehicles – No 75 River Maine *leading) with four de-engined MPDs in tow. The train, a special to Portrush, is mostly in the later NIR maroon and blue livery and is seen here near Ballinderry. The UTA DEs in original form were reckoned to be the most powerful of all the type, despite later classes having a nominal extra 50 bhp.*

JM Allen

With the coming of these new trains, there was a pause in the development of diesel railcars in Northern Ireland. The new trains certainly proved their reliability, even when used in ways which the makers frowned upon – for example the practice of shoving three or more extra coaches on the end of a six-car set for use in excursions! One English Electric representative, on seeing this done, threatened to withdraw any guarantee if it continued.

The performance of the new trains was good – they never attained the very high-speeds, or rate of acceleration, of the MPDs but they were entirely adequate for the services they were being asked to undertake. There were no more one hour, 50 minutes schedules to Londonderry by this time! They also performed acceptably on the Enterprise services for a short period until displaced by new locomotives and stock in 1970.

So, in 1974 and again in 1978, when new stock was required, it would be an updated version of the 1966 stock which would become the dominant type on NIR, with a reign which is due to last until 2004 and beyond. Ironically, considering the latter part of this story, the new CAF fleet will have two engines mounted underfloor, though one is a generator for the air conditioning. Have we come full circle after 50 years?

Appendix 1

The torque converter

A torque converter is a hydraulic unit which performs automatically the function of a conventional gearbox. That is to say, it multiplies the output torque from an engine while decreasing the speed. As engine speed increases, the torque multiplication decreases: ie the ratio of engine speed to output rotation decreases.

In a gearbox there are a number of stepped ratios which must be manually selected. A torque converter does this automatically but also provides an infinite number of ratios between about 4:1 and 0.98:1. It consists of three principal internal components:

1 Impeller
2 Turbine
3 Reaction member

It is worth noting that items 1 and 2 on their own are basically a 'fluid coupling'. This is the simplest method of transmitting torque without multiplication.

When the engine starts to turn the impeller, the fluid is thrown outwards towards its outside circumference. The design of the blades then causes the fluid to flow across the turbine blades which then also turn. In the meantime the fluid runs through the hub of the turbine and back into the impeller. Note, however, that the ratio of this coupling will always be 1:1. Fluid couplings were used in the AEC railcars supplied to the GNR and CIÉ, with a more conventional gearbox for selecting speeds. Their big advantage over a mechanical coupling was that they were capable of transmitting much greater torque without undue stress or wear.

The feature which changed this to the more sophisticated torque converter is the addition of a 'reaction member'. The hydraulic fluid circulates in the same manner as the fluid coupling but, whereas in the coupling the impeller blades are straight, in the converter they are curved. Once again, the fluid moves outwards as the impeller turns and causes the turbine blades to turn. However, it then is directed against the fixed reaction member which causes the fluid to return to the impeller, hitting the curved blades of the latter at the optimum angle and increasing the toque. The speed of the impeller is greater than that of the turbine by a ratio of up to 4:1 but this diminishes as train speed rises, until they are both running at exactly the same speed.

The torque multiplication decreases as train speed rises, until it is about 85% at 20 mph. Then it begins to decrease in efficiency more rapidly, but the use of the clutch at this point engages direct drive from the engines and so the converter is no longer in the circuit. Each torque converter had a free-wheel unit built in which would allow the train to safely overrun the engine, for example when 'coasting' on a long downgrade.

All NCC railcars were fitted with torque converter drive, as were the Multi Engined Diesels built in 1952–53. In the UTA MPD railcars of 1957 onwards, the torque converter was harnessed to an automatic four-speed gearbox, a sophisticated arrangement that was the final development of the transmission type to be used in Ireland. It was not replicated anywhere else in the UK in the same form.

Appendix 2

The heat exchanger

The idea behind this device is a simple one. All internal combustion engines produce heat as part of the process, much of which goes to waste. In the earliest forms, the water which was heated by the combustion process, and necessary to keep the engine cool, was piped round the railcar to provide heating for the passengers. Many machines used this system but it did have disadvantages. For example, the amount of heat produced depended on how fast the engine was running and so heat would get less when the engine was stopped or idling. Naturally, producing long lengths of pipework and radiators made the circulation path for engine cooling water more complex.

A second source of waste heat is the exhaust. This does not suffer from the same problems, as once the engine is initially heated the exhaust gas temperature will remain more or less constant. However, the hot gases go to waste – they are simply exhausted to the atmosphere. One use of these exhaust gases is in turbo-charging, which increases engine performance, but another function might be to use it for heating up the vehicle propelled by the engine. The exhaust heat, even from a turbo-charged engine, is going to waste, therefore it makes sense to use it to heat water which can then be circulated round the vehicle to produce heat. The device which makes this possible is called a *heat exchanger*.

In its simplest form this might involve running the exhaust pipe up through a cylinder filled with water – essentially this is a crude form of heat exchanger. However, the more sophisticated form would use multiple pipes, thus increasing the area for exchanging the heat from the hot exhaust into the water surrounding. It is the mirror of a multi-tube boiler.

This 'something for nothing' appealed to the developers of the MPDs, always keen to try new things. And it did work, though there were problems with the plumbing, and airlocking meant that water circulation was not always as steady as predicted.

There are, however, some other problems involved in the heat exchanger. The temperature of the exhaust gases is critical – if an attempt is made to suck too much heat out, this will cause the gases to cool. This may not initially appear to be a problem, except that the heat might be reduced, but as the gases cool so they tend to condense. In the case of a diesel engine, two of the components of exhaust gas are water and sulphur. When combined, these produce sulphuric acid, which is corrosive. Added to this will be the problem of sooty deposits. The diesel engines of the 1960s were not the clean diesels we know today and so the tubes of the heat exchangers tended to soot up, impairing efficiency.

So, all in all, the heat exchanger system of heating diesel trains, while it seemed to promise great things, was actually bedevilled by the combination of problems outlined above. It was a relief to all (including passengers) when spare electrical power became available for use in heating.

Appendix 3

The diesel engine – turbo-charging and supercharging

The diesel engine takes its name from a German engineer, Dr Rudolf Diesel (1858–1913) who is widely credited with its invention and development. It is an internal combustion engine which uses a heavy oil fuel (occasionally the term 'heavy oil' is still used) and differs from a petrol engine in a number of ways. The most significant difference is that in a diesel engine the fuel (mixed with air) is ignited by being greatly compressed. So a diesel is a 'compression-ignition' engine. In a petrol engine, ignition is initiated by spark derived from a high voltage electrical current.

Turbo charging and supercharging are both ways of increasing the power of an internal combustion engine. They have been used in both petrol and diesel engines, though it is in the latter that the main benefits are seen. Not only does it increase the power of the engine but, in the case of a diesel, the more complete combustion means that exhaust gases are also cleaner, since the bulk of diesel emissions are soot, etc – this makes a big difference. Petrol emissions are less affected by the process.

Both systems involve forcing more air into the combustion chamber to mix with the fuel – the more air can be forced in, then the more complete the process. Engines which use neither of these processes are referred to as 'normally aspirated'. Today the majority of diesels used are turbo-charged but in the 1950s it was something quite new.

In supercharging, the air is forced into the cylinders by means of an impeller which is driven from the crankshaft. As speed increases, naturally more air is forced in. The air is unheated, apart from friction effects. The advantage of supercharging is that it progressively boosts power throughout the engine revolution range.

In turbo-charging, the extra air is impelled into the cylinders from an impeller which is driven from the exhaust gases. Thus the air is heated first, causing it to expand and limit the extra amount that may be forced into the cylinders. Turbo-charging relies on engine revolutions being kept relatively high. It does not provide quite as much extra power as supercharging but has advantages of economy, in that the exhaust gas (otherwise lost) is used to generate more power! Many modern engines use an intercooler which cools the air and thus allows more to be forced in – such engines are often referred to as 'charge cooled'. The MPD engines used turbo-charging and were the first Irish railcar engines to be of that type – all the others had been normally aspirated. The diesel engines of the '70' class cars were also turbo-charged.

After the closure of the County Donegal Railway, railcars 19 and 20 (1950–51) were bought by the Isle Of Man Railway. There they usually worked Douglas-Peel services, operating as a pair which eliminated turning. Although this reduced the power/weight ratio of the cars, this was less important on the Peel line as it was not as heavily graded as the lines to Ramsey or Port Erin. Here the two railcars wait at Douglas on a sunny summer day in 1965.

DJA Young

No 16 diesel mechanical shunter at work near York Road in June 1963. This 0-4-0 was the smallest of the diesel locomotives operated by the UTA. It was built by Harland Wolff in 1937 as a works shunter, and finally withdrawn in 1967. Just to the left can be seen the remains of ex-NCC Railcar No 2 withdrawn in 1954. The body was used as a fire training hut!

Colin Boocock

No 28, a 500 bhp diesel-electric, ex-BCDR, ex-NCC, ex-GNR, and now owned by the UTA, working at Belfast's Grosvenor Road yard. Two new CIÉ GM diesel-electrics, using the same principle but built twenty five years later, pass by. No 28 was to enter NIR stock, still with its original number and was finally cut up in 1973. The two GMs are still at work today.   **RH Whitford**

Five of the eight driving motor composite Great Northern BUT railcars passed to the UTA. There was obviously no hurry to repaint them all, as in November 1960 No 132 (formerly GNR 902) leaves Portadown, still retaining its GNR blue and cream livery, albeit with a temporary plain yellow warning panel (the black diagonal lines would be added a few days later). No 132 was withdrawn in 1975.   **JD Fitzgerald, Colour-Rail**

CIÉ inherited seven of the GNR's fleet of double cab BUT railcars. They mainly were employed on the old GNR lines north of Dublin. Most received CIÉ green livery in the early 1960s, as in this picture of a four car set running into Howth station on a suburban working from Dublin Amiens Street in August 1961. **Colour-Rail**

The BUT railcars worked the UTA 'Enterprise' trains during most of the 1960s, until replaced briefly by the English Electric DE units. With a good turn of speed they were well suited to this fast service with few stops. In August 1963 an unidentified single cab unit in UTA green arrives at Dublin's Amiens Street station (now Connolly) at 12.40 on the 10.30 from Belfast. This was just five minutes longer than the same train takes today. **Colour-Rail**

The BUTs were re-painted in blue and cream in the 1965 regional livery exercise. They had a broad cream band around the windows and looked particularly well when in ex-works condition, as seen here on No 134 passing Adavoyle near the Border on an Up 'Enterprise' working in July 1965. **Colour-Rail IR 318**

A train composed of UTA Multi Purpose Diesel cars in their original livery of unlined green with small pale green warning panels, waits at Londonderry Waterside with a train for Belfast in May 1959. The fourth vehicle from camera is the ex-NCC 'North Atlantic' dining car, now numbered 549. Two more power cars are in the train shed. The makeup of two power cars to one trailer (or 'mule' as officially known.) gave a high power/weight ratio and some very high speed runs were made at this time. **JG Dewing, Colour-Rail**

In 1959 new MPDs began to be painted in all over Catherwood Blue or 'eau de nil' livery. It was also applied to a few vehicles which passed through shops at that time, before it was abandoned in favour of dark green again! One such was MPD No.40, seen here at York Road in June 1961, in company with 54 or 55. The 'wasp' warning panels date from early 1961. The gangway cover is in the the post-1960 dark green livery. **Colour-Rail**

Non-corridor trailer 538 is an example of an MPD car built new in Catherwood blue livery. It was not considered a success. though No 538 still retained this livery, now somewhat faded, when photographed at Portrush in April 1962. These non corridor trailers were rebuilt by NIR as corridor opens when conductor/guards were introduced; No 538 was finally withdrawn in 1980. **RH Whitford**

A Multi Purpose Diesel train leaving York Road in June 1966. The leading car is No 50, a non-corridor unit introduced in 1959. Behind it, in red and grey 1965 livery, is a trailer converted in 1959 from one of the 'Festival' coaches, which the UTA built in 1951. All MPDs were converted from earlier coaches although in some later cases all that was used was the underframe. No 50 was rebuilt as an open corridor second in 1969 and withdrawn in 1977.
DJA Young

A rare day-time view of an MPD on a goods train. With the closure of the ex GNR 'Derry Road' in 1965, MPD railcars had the onerous task of providing power for heavy over night cross-border freights on the final part of their journey from Lisburn to Londonderry. No. 46 in UTA green livery, leads 62, and 63, as they provide power for one such train leaving Coleraine for Londonderry at 1.40pm on 13 July 1966. This train had been delayed by a failure.
RH Whitford

The final three MPD power cars (63–65) were double cab units, which at 60 feet long were longer than most of the rest. They appeared in 1961–62 in dark green livery but were among the first to be repainted in the 'regional' deep red and oyster grey in 1965. Here No 63 is just ex-Works when photographed in July 1965 at Portrush. No 63 was one of the last MPDs to remain in service; it was finally scrapped in 1983.   *DJA Young*

On the occasion of the first '70' class test run to Whitehead on 30 May 1966, brand new Driving Trailer 711 waits at the head of a three-car train at York Road's Platform 1 prior to departure. The small square front cab window on these driving trailers gave them a peculiar 'blank' look. Nos 713–4 lacked even the rounded edges to the sides and roof seen here.   *DJA Young*

With the test run to Whitehead completed, the train waits to return, this view showing 550 bhp power car No 71 leading. This car has not yet had final transfers applied to the front. On the left, walking towards the camera, is WG McAfee, the engineer responsible for the introduction of these units to service. **DJA Young**

The 550 bhp DEs quickly took over the principal workings to Londonderry and boat rains to Larne after their service introduction in July 1966. The diesel electric type railcar was to become the standard motive power for railways in Northern Ireland for the next 35 years. Here No 72 passes Kingsbog signal cabin in May 1967 with a nine car Saturday working to Londonderry. **DJA Young**

Appendix 4

Details of the fleets

Compiled by Norman Johnston.
Some dates in *35 Years of NIR* have been
revised in the light of new information

(a) CDRJC narrow gauge cars

On the County Donegal Railways all diesel units, whether locomotives, railcars or trailers were numbered in a separate series from locomotives and ordinary carriages. This list excludes petrol railcars except where they were later converted to trailers.

No	Built	Type	Seats	Remarks	Withdrawn
2	1944	Trailer	17	Converted from a petrol railcar of 1933 (new body and engine on Ex CVBT paraffin railcar of 1925).	1960
3	1944	Trailer	40	Converted from a petrol railcar of 1934 (Ex DBST). Preserved at UFTM, Cultra.	1960
5	1929	Trailer	29	Built as trailer. Sold to Donegal Football Club.	1960
6	1945	Trailer	32	Converted from a petrol railcar of 1930.	1958
7	6/1931	Railcar	32	First diesel railcar in the British Isles.	1949
8	11/1931	Railcar	32		1949
10	1932	Railcar	29	Purchased from CVR in 1942. Preserved at UFTM, Cultra.	1960
11	12/1932	Loco	–	Used frames of CVR Atkinson & Walker steam tractor. Known as Phoenix. Preserved at UFTM, Cultra	1960
12	2/1934	Railcar	41	Preserved in running order at the Foyle Valley Railway Museum, Derry	1960
13	1934	Trailer	16	Originally a DBST petrol railcar	1944
14	2/1935	Railcar	41	Rebuilt with Gardner 5LW engine 3/1953	1960
15	4/1936	Railcar	41	Remains of body at Donegal town (SDRS)	1960
16	12/1936	Railcar	41		1960
17	8/1938	Railcar	43	Destroyed in a crash on Ballyshannon branch 29/8/1949	1949
18	12/1940	Railcar	43	Cab rebuilt 6/1950 following a fire. Restored to original design 1997–8. Preserved in running order at Fintown.	1960
19	1/1950	Railcar	41	Sold to Isle of Man Railway	1960
20	1/1951	Railcar	41	Sold to Isle of Man Railway	1960

Notes:
Nos 10, 12 and 14 had half cabs with bonneted engines.
Nos 7, 8, 15–18 had full width cabs with bonneted engines.
Nos 19 and 20 had full width cabs with 'forward control'.
Nos 7, 8, 10–12 and 14 had 74 bhp Gardner 6L2 engines.
Nos 15–20 had 102 bhp Gardner 6LW engines.

(b) UTA railcars

UTA diesel railcar classification

Class	Nos	Type	Built	Layout	Seats (orig)	Lavs	Remarks
A	1	Leyland	1933	BCO	6/55	–	Twin cab, non-corr
B	2	Leyland	1934	BCO	5/75	–	Twin cab, non-corr
C	3, 4	Leyland	1935–8	BCO	12/60	–	Twin cab, non-corr
D	5	Ganz	1939	BCO	18/38	1	Twin cab, non-corr
E	6, 7	AEC	1951	BCO	8/65	–	
F	8, 10, 12	MED	1952–3	BCO	12/40	–	Air doors
F1	14, 16, 18						
	20, 22	MED	1953–4	BCO	12/40	–	Air doors
G	9, 11, 13	MED	1952–3	CO	12/60	–	Air doors
G1	15, 17, 19						
	21, 23	MED	1953–4	CO	12/59	–	Air doors
H	24, 26, 28, 30	MED	1952–3	BCO	8/50	–	Air doors
I	25, 27, 29, 31	MED	1952–3	CO	8/74	–	Air doors
J	32, 34	MED	1953	BCO	8/50	–	Air doors
K	33, 35	MED	1953	CO	8/74	–	Air doors
L	36–39	MPD	1957–8	BSO	48	1	
M	40, 41	MPD	1957	SO	56	1	54 seats from 12/1960
N	42, 43	MPD	1957–8	CK	18/32	1	15/32 from 12/1960
O	44, 45	MPD	1958	SK	48	1	No 45 altered to CK (12/24), date unknown
P	46–48	MPD	1958–9	BC	16/60	–	Non-corr
Q	49	MPD	1959	BS	84	–	Non-corr
R	50–53	MPD	1959	BS	96	–	Non-corr
S	54, 55	MPD	1959	BCO	12/55	1	High density seating
T	56	MPD	1959	BCO	12/60	1	High density seating
U	57–62	MPD	1959	BSO	70	–	High density seating
V	63–65	MPD	1961–2	BSO	70	1	Twin cab (on left side), high density seating
W	71–78	DE	1966–8	SO	44	–	

Notes:
As demand for first class seating fell on suburban trains, first class in MED sets was declassified at one end (usually in the even numbered cars). In Nov 1964 first class was completely abolished on the Bangor line. Surviving COs and BCOs were declassified to SO and BSO without alteration to the seating. By 1966 only Larne line MED cars 9, 11, 13, 18 and 20–23 retained first class.

Key to layout codes:
B = brake, C = composite, D = driving, F = first, K = side corridor, O = open, S = second.

Ex-NCC railcars

No	Built	Remarks	Last used	Disposed
1	1/1933	Originally petrol engined. Reseated SO (72s) in 1954. Re-engined (diesel) 1947, 1959. Preserved	25/11/1965	12/1968
2	1934	Body survived as shed until 1966	1954	1954
3	1935	Destroyed by a fire at Whitehead	7/1957	1957
4	1938	Burned at York Road 18/11/1969	28/2/1966	12/1969
1	1934	J^9 Trailer, SO, non-corr, 100 seats; ren 544 (1959)	1965?	1967
2	1935	J^9 Trailer, SO, non-corr, 100 seats; ren 545 (1959) Converted to signals van 3109 by NIR in 1970	1965?	1978

Ganz railcars

No	Built	Remarks	Last used	Disposed
5	1939	Built by Metropolitan Cammell. Purchased by UTA To traffic 2/1951	?	5/1965
215	6/1953	K^8 trailer, BSO, non-corr, 80 seats; ren 515 (1959) Smith's heater 10/1961; MED fitted 1963; vestibuled 3/1968; seating reduced to 68 (1972); altered to van 4/1973	11/1977	5/1980

AEC railcars

No	Built	Remarks	Last used	Disposed
6	8/1951	Burned at York Road 18/11/1969	15/7/1966	11/1969
7	8/1951	Burned at York Road 18/11/1969	15/7/1966	11/1969
279	1933	J^7 non-corr 2nd; 10 compts, 120 seats; AEC fitted 1951; ren 528 (1959); used on steam trains 1964–67	1967	1971

MED railcars

No	Built	Ex	Wilson gearbox	Remarks	Last used	Disposed
8	4/1952	206	8/1967		2/1976	2/1978
9	4/1952	201	8/1967		6/1975	2/1978
10	4/1952	207	3/1968		10/1977	9/1980
11	4/1952	202	1/1968		11/1974	5/1980
12	4/1953	204	4/1968	Bomb at Gt Vict St 12/10/1973.	10/1973	late 1974
13	4/1953	203	5/1968		12/1974	5/1980
14	11/1953	248	10/1969		2/1977	by 8/1978
15	11/1953	246	12/1969		2/1977	?
16	12/1953	250	12/1966		1/1975	5/1980
17	12/1953	254	12/1966		11/1974	5/1980
18	10/1953	251	7/1968		10/1977	after 8/1978
19	10/1953	260	3/1968		2/1978	9/1980
20	2/1954	252	10/1967		8/1977	?
21	2/1954	253	10/1967		12/1978	9/1980

No	Built	Ex	Wilson gearbox	Remarks	Last used	Disposed
22	4/1954	257	12/1967		11/1977	?
23	4/1954	259	8/1968		3/1978	5/1980
24	9/1952	–	3/1968	Driving cab in guard's van 3Q/1961	12/1976	5/1980
25	9/1952	–	1/1968		7/1978	5/1980
26	11/1952	–	3/1969	Driving cab in guard's van 3Q/1961	7/1978	5/1980
27	11/1952	–	1/1969	Firebomb at Sydenham 17/9/1976.	8/1977	5/1980
28	3/1952	–	6/1969	Driving cab in guard's van 1Q/1962	4/1978	5/1980
29	3/1952	–	5/1969		1/1978	5/1980
30	3/1953	–	5/1969		4/1978	5/1980
31	3/1953	–	7/1969		12/1976	5/1980
32	6/1953	–	10/1968		12/1978	5/1980
33	6/1953	–	12/1968		4/1978	5/1980
34	7/1953	–	61968		11/1977	5/1980
35	7/1953	–	7/1968		1/1978	5/1980

MED trailers with air doors

No	Built	Class	1959 No	Driving Cab (J^{19})	Smith's heater	Cab remov	Remarks	Last used	Disposed
201	8/1952	J^{18}	501	–	8/1961			12/1977	5/1980
202	10/1952	J^{18}	502	–	10/1961			12/1977	5/1980
203	12/1952	J^{18}	503	–	11/1960			2/1978	5/1980
204	2/1953	J^{18}	504	12/1957	2/1961	–		1/1977	5/1980
205	3/1953	J^{18}	505	1/1958	5/1961	4/1965	(controls 12/1961)	6/1977	5/1980
206	4/1953	J^{18}	506	12/1957	4/1961	4/1964	(controls 12/1961)	10/1973	10/1973
207	6/1953	J^{18}	507	2/1958	12/1960	11/1963	(controls 12/1961)	9/1976	5/1980
208	7/1953	J^{18}	508	5/1958	12/1960	–	Van 631 5/1975	?/1975	10/1983
209	7/1953	J^{18}	509	4/1958	6/1961	–		12/1978	5/1980
210	10/1953	J^{18}	510	–	9/1961			by 7/1975	5/1980
211	10/1953	J^{18}	511	–	1/1961		Van 634 11/1975	?/1975	1/1985
212	12/1953	J^{18}	512	–	7/1961		Van 632 7/1975	?/1975	1/1985
213	2/1954	J^{18}	513	–	9/1961		Van 633 10/1975	?/1975	1/1985
214	4/1954	J^{18}	514	–	8/1961			by 7/1977	5/1980

(Seating orig 91; with Smith's heaters 93; J^{19} 87; 89 with Smith's heaters)

MED trailers with slam doors Vehicles marked 'w' had wooden panelling

No	Built	Class	Conv	1959 No	LMS No	Remarks	Last used	Disposed
169	1938	J^{11}	6/1956	516	12952	All J^{11} had 108 seats	by 6/1970	?
173	1927	J^{11} w	12/1956	517	11013		by 6/1973	?
174	1928	J^{11} w	11/1956	518	11057	MPD fitted 1968	by 12/1970	?
176	1928	J^{11} w	5/1956	519	11211	Reb open 6/1968 (72 seats)	4/1978	5/1980
177	1930	J^{11}	5/1956	520	11386		by 9/1970	9/1970
181	1932	J^{11}	5/1956	521	11539		by 6/1970	?

No	Built	Class	Conv	1959 No	LMS No	Remarks	Last used	Disposed
186	1936	J¹¹	6/1956	522	11767		by 9/1970	9/1970
187	1936	J¹¹	6/1956	523	11847	Reb SO 10/1968 (64 seats, 2T)	10/1977	5/1980
189	1936	J¹¹	12/1956	524	11956		by 6/1973	?
191	1929	J¹¹ w	6/1956	525	10878		by 9/1970	?
255	1929	J⁵ w	3/1957	526	–	} 80 seats, 2 lavs,	6/1976	1982
261	1930	J⁵ w	11/1956	527	–	} Dual MED/MPD fitted 8/1962	5/1977	2/1978

MPD railcars

No	Built	Orig (Date) No	Conv Corr	Re-engined		Remarks	Last used	Disposed
36	9/1957	321 (1951)	–	5/1966	AEC		4/1978	6/1978
37	9/1957	322 (1951)	–	6/1966	AEC	Fire damage, 7/1968	7/1968	3/1970
38	12/1957	323 (1951)	–	9/1964	RR		8/1976	?/1978
39	1/1958	326 (1951)	–	12/1965	AEC		7/1978	9/1980
40	12/1957	324 (1951)	–	11/1966	AEC	Withdrawn after collision damage with a lorry at Larne Town, 12/1973	12/1973	2/1978
41	11/1957	325 (1951)	–	1970	AEC		7/1975	?/1978
42	11/1957	341 (1951)	–	1970	AEC		?/1975	9/1980
43	1/1958	342 (1951)	–	1969	AEC	Fire damage 10/1973	10/1973	2/1978
44	10/1958	331 (1951)	–	11/1967	RR		7/1975	?/1978
45	11/1959	332 (1951)	–	4/1968	RR		4/1977	10/1978
46	12/1958	280 (1933)	7/1969	7/1969	RR		4/1978	?
47	2/1959	281 (1933)	3/1970	3/1970	AEC	Carrick crash 7/5/1977	5/1977	?/1978
48	2/1959	282 (1933)	11/1970	11/1970	AEC		6/1976	?/1978
49	1/1959	351 (1951)	12/1970	12/1970	AEC		8/1977	9/1983
50	3/1959	274 (1933)	10/1969	10/1969	RR	Fire damage, 9/1977	9/1977	2/1978
51	3/1959	275 (1933)	3/1969	3/1969	RR		2/1980	?
52	3/1959	276 (1933)	4/1969	4/1969	RR		9/1980	?
53	4/1959	277 (1933)	12/1968	12/1968	RR	Scr at York Road	7/1974	7/1974
54	4/1959	54 (1931)	–	8/1969	RR		4/1977	1978
55	5/1959	55 (1931)	–	10/1965	AEC		12/1977	7/1978
56	8/1959	5 (1944)	–	4/1964	AEC	Fire damage 30/6/1966	7/1966	?
57	5/1959	265 (1932)	–	6/1968	RR	Carrick crash 7/5/1977	5/1977	2/1978
58	6/1959	266 (1933)	–	–	–	Umbra crash 18/7/1959	7/1959	?
59	6/1959	267 (1933)	–	10/1968	RR		5/1980	9/1980
60	7/1959	268 (1933)	–	12/1967	RR		2/1978	10/1978
61	7/1959	269 (1933)	–	3/1968	RR		12/1978	9/1983
62	7/1959	270 (1935)	–	1/1968	RR		7/1977	9/1980
63	11/1961	*252 (frame only)	–	2/1969	RR		4/1981	10/1983
64	11/1961	*254 (frame only)	–	5/1968	RR		5/1983	8/1985
65	2/1962	*256 (frame only)	–	6/1968	RR		4/1981	10/1983

MPD trailers

No	Conv	Orig (Date) No	Type	Class	Seats	Lavs	Remarks	Last used	Disposed
529	2/1959	303 (1951)	DSK	J^{20}	56	1		1977	7/1978
530	4/1959	301 (1951)	DSK	J^{20}	56	1		?1977	?1979
531	6/1959	302 (1951)	DSK	J^{20}	56	1		?1976	?
532	4/1959	304 (1951)	DSK	J^{20}	56	1	Body to RPSI	?1978	4/1978
533	4/1959	305 (1951)	DSK	J^{20}	56	1	Body to RPSI for parts	11/1977	4/1978
534	5/1959	306 (1951)	DSK	J^{20}	56	1	Conv to DE 728 (10/1976)	1976	–
535	6/1959	188 (1937)	DS	J^{21}	96	–	Reb DSO (3/1971)	4/1981	9/1983
536	7/1959	195 (1939)	DS	J^{21}	96	–	Reb DSO (6/1971)	4/1981	9/1983
537	7/1959	271 (1933)	DS	J^{22}	102	–	Reb DSO (4/1970)	4/1975	2/1978
538	8/1959	272 (1933)	DS	J^{22}	102	–	Reb DSO (3/1969)	4/1981	9/1983
539	9/1959	273 (1933)	DS	J^{22}	102	–	Reb DSO (8/1971)	4/1981	9/1983
540	10/1959	229 (1935)	DSO	J^{23}	85	–		4/1981	9/1983
541	10/1959	231 (1935)	DSO	J^{23}	85	–		4/1981	9/1983
542	10/1959	57 (1931)	DCO	F^{9}	12/65	1		4/1981	9/1983
543	5/1959	361 (1951)	DC	F^{10}	32/36	–	Reb DSO (7/1972)	1974	10/1974
548	5/1960	88 (1924) (Ran as 160 1959–60)	Buffet	B^{2}	32	–	Modernised 1964 DE fitted 8/1966	7/1970	10/1972
549	11/1957	90 (1934)	Buffet	B^{4}	24	–	NAE diner	7/1966	6/1970
550	10/1957	87 (1950)	Buffet	B^{5}	30	–	DE fitted 5/1966. (34 from 4/1964) To RPSI as 87, 1978.	?1973	1978

'70' class diesel electric railcars DMSO, 44 seats, no toilets; reseated 55

No	Built	Name	Reseated	Remarks	Last used	Disposed
71	5/1966	River Bush	?		5/1984	8/1985
72	7/1966	River Foyle	1977	Painted in Sealink livery 4/1983.	10/1985	8/1986
73	9/1966	River Roe	1/1977		5/1985	8/1985
74	9/1966	River Lagan	9/1976		5/1983	1/1985
75	11/1966	River Maine	3/1978	Vandalised 1/4/1986.	4/1986	8/1986
76	1/1967	River Inver	4/1977		4/1984	1/1985
77	4/1967	River Braid	11/1976	Vandalised 1/4/1986.	4/1986	8/1986
78	9/1968	River Bann	1977	Firebomb damage 25/5/1979.	5/1979	5/1980

'70' class trailers

No	Built	Type	Class	Seats	Lavs	Reb	Remarks	Last used	Disposed
701	1966	BFK	D^{3}	24	2	12/1977	Rebuilt DBSO (40 seats?)	10/1985	8/1986
702	1966	BCK	D^{3}	12/16	2	–		1979	1/1985
703	1967	BSK.	D^{3}	32	2	11/1977	Rebuilt DBSO (40 seats?)	?	1/1985
711	1966	DBCK	E^{3}	12/24	1	1976	Rebuilt DBSO (50 seats?)	5/1985	8/1985
712	1966	DBCK	E^{3}	12/24	1	12/1976	Rebuilt DBSO (50 seats?)	3/1983	10/1983
713	1968	DBSK	–	40	1	7/1977	Rebuilt DBSO (50 seats?) (Orig 278 (1924), conv 12/1968; To DAR, but burnt 26/12/2002)	4/1984	9/1991

No	Built	Type	Class	Seats	Lavs	Reb	Remarks	Last used	Disposed
714	1969	DBSK	–	40	1	6/1979	Rebuilt DBSO (50 seats?)		
							(orig 280 (1924), conv 12/1069; wrecked in Dunloy accident)	7/1979	7/1980
721	1966	SK	J^{24}	56	2	?	Withdrawn after vandalism.	4/1986	8/1986
722	1966	SK	J^{24}	56	2	–	Fire bombed 25/5/1979	5/1979	5/1980
723	1966	SK	J^{24}	56	2	?		3/1984	8/1985
724	1966	SK	J^{24}	56	2	–	Withdrawn after vandalism.	4/1986	8/1986
725	1966	SK	J^{24}	56	2	?		4/1986	8/1986
726	1969	SK	J^{6}	64	2	7/1976	Rebuilt SO, new body (70 seats)	3/1983	?10/1983
							(orig 362 (1932), conv 4/1069; wrecked in Hilden accident)		
727	1969	SO	K^{23}	72	1	–	Ex BUT 556 (b 1943), conv 5/1969	1980	1982
							(Last GNR coach to operate; to RPSI 1982, but destroyed 11/1994)		
728	1976	BSK	J^{20}	56	1	–	Ex MPD 534, conv 10/1976 Preserved at Downpatrick Railway Museum	4/1986	9/1991

UTA diesel locomotives All Harland and Wolff two-stroke

No	Built	Type	BHP	Remarks	Last used	Disposed
16	1944	0-4-0	225	H&W works shunter; hired to NCC as No 20 1/1945–4/1946; bought by UTA 1951 as 16.	1/2/1966	1967
17	3/1937	0-6-0	330	Hired to NCC 1937–41; purchased 1941	16/3/1966	mid 1970
22	7/1934	0-6-0	175	LMS 7057; to traffic 2/1935; operated Chester & Heysham; wdn 1/1944; sold to H&W 1/1945; re-engined 225 bhp & regauged; hired to NCC 1/1946; purchased by UTA 10/1949	4/1965	12/1965
28	1937	1A-A1	500	Built for BCDR as D2 (hired); ren 28 1937; returned to H&W 12/1944; hired to NCC/UTA 7/1947–9/1952; at H&W 1952–57; hired by GNR/UTA 1957–62; bought by UTA 1962; to NIR 1967, running throughout as 28.	1973	1974
202	1933	1B	270	Built for BCDR as D1; ren 2 1937; to UTA 1948 as 202; returned to H&W 1/1952 as works shunter	10/1967	6/1969

(c) GNR railcars

Pre-war GNR railcars All Gardner engined unless otherwise stated.

No	Built	Seats	BHP	1958	Remarks	Wdn
A	7/1932	32	130	UTA 101	AEC engine; later Gardner 6LW (102 bhp) Seating increased to 50 (48 from 1940)	5/1964
B	1932	32	120	–	Gleniffer engine, diesel electric; seating increased to 40 (38 from 1940). Engine remov 10/1946 and ran as coach No 500 from 1948.	?1956
C1	11/1934	50	96	CIÉ	Initially 'C'	9/1961
C2	6/1935	52	102	CIÉ		9/1961
C3	6/1935	6/8/32	102	UTA 102		12/1961
D	5/1936	8/50/101	153	UTA 103		9/1963
E	6/1936	8/50/101	153	CIÉ	Sold to UTA 10/1961 for spares	10/1961
F	3/1938	8/51/105	204	UTA 104	Sold to a contractor	11/1965
G	4/1938	8/51/105	204	CIÉ	Sold to UTA 10/1961 (105); last used 1/1965	1968

GNR AEC railcars CIÉ cars retained their GNR numbers rendered c600ℕ, etc

No	Built	1958	Remarks	Last used	Disposed
600	6/1950	CIÉ			1975
601	6/1950	CIÉ			1975
602	7/1950	UTA 112		11/1970	5/1975
603	7/1950	UTA 111		9/1969	?
604	8/1950	CIÉ			1975
605	8/1950	CIÉ			1975
606	9/1950	UTA 114	Became parcel van 622 in 1973	9/1972	1983
607	9/1950	UTA 113	Sold to CIÉ for parts	after 7/1971	?1977
608	10/1950	CIÉ			1975
609	10/1950	CIÉ			1975
610	11/1950	UTA 116	Sold to CIÉ for parts	after 7/1971	?1977
611	11/1950	UTA 115		9/1972	5/1975
612	12/1950	CIÉ			1975
613	12/1950	CIÉ			1975
614	12/1950	UTA 118	Destroyed by fire 9/1952; replaced Autumn 1953	7/1972	5/1975
615	12/1950	UTA 117		after 7/1971	5/1975
616	1/1951	CIÉ			1975
617	1/1951	CIÉ			1975
618	4/1951	UTA 120	Became parcel van 621in 1973	8/1972	1983
619	4/1951	UTA 119		7/1971	?1975

AEC trailers CIÉ cars retained their GNR numbers rendered c401ɴ, etc.

No	Built	Class	Type	Seats	Lavs	AEC fitted	1958	Remarks	Disposed
401	1916	B1	Diner	18/22	–	?1959	CIÉ	Fitted by CIÉ	9/1964
403	1951	B4	Restaur	24	–	1953	UTA 554	'70' class fitted 1969	6/1973
399	1940	B7	Kitchen	–	–	1967	UTA 166	Fitted by UTA/NIR	4/1971
93	1939	K15	SO	70	1	1951	CIÉ		1/1972
98	1941	K15	SO	70	1	1951	UTA 581	Last used after 7/1971	?/1972
129	1943	K15	SO	70	1	1951	CIÉ		6/1969
134	1943	K15	SO	70	1	1951	CIÉ		7/1972
140	1942	K15	SO	70	1	?1951	CIÉ		1/1969
145	1942	K15	SO	70	1	2/1962	UTA 580	Ex 416 1962, L/U 7/1971	?/1972
181	1943	K15	SO	70	1	?1958	CIÉ		8/1968
186	1943	K15	SO	70	1	8/1958	UTA 582	Last used 6/1970	6/1973
97	1941	K23	Buffet	48	1	1/1951	–	Altered to BUT 7/1958	–
127	1943	K23	Buffet	48	1	7/1951	–	Altered to BUT ?/1958	–
170	1942	K23	Buffet	48	1	9/1950	CIÉ		1/1972
188	1943	K23	Buffet	48	1	6/1950	UTA 555	SO 1967 (72 seats), L/U 1970	6/1973
8	1954	K31	DSO	72	1	new	UTA 585	Stopped by 3/1971	6/1971
9	1954	K31	DSO	72	1	new	UTA 586	L/U 9/1972, Preserved by RPSI	6/1973
95	1939	L12	BSO	39	1	9/1950	CIÉ		9/1972
115	1940	L13	BSO	39	1	11/1950	UTA 593	Last used 1970	6/1973

Note: No 98 (581) was also preserved by the RPSI but subsequently lost to rot. See also page 189.

GNR BUT railcars CIÉ cars retained their GNR numbers rendered c704ɴ, etc

No	Built	1958	Remarks	Last used	Disposed
701	6/1957	UTA 121	Conv to hauled coach 1975	9/1972	5/1980
702	6/1957	UTA 122	Conv to hauled coach 1975	11/1974	5/1980
703	6/1957	UTA 123	Conv to hauled coach 1975	8/1972	5/1980
704	6/1957	CIÉ		?1975	?
705	7/1957	UTA 124	Conv to hauled coach 1975	7/1972	5/1980
706	7/1957	CIÉ		?1975	?
707	9/1957	UTA 125	Conv to hauled coach 1975	7/1972	5/1980
708	9/1957	CIÉ		?1975	?
709	10/1957	UTA 126	Conv to hauled coach 1975	8/1972	5/1980
710	10/1957	CIÉ		?1975	?
711	1/1958	UTA 127	Conv to hauled coach 1975	8/1972	5/1980
712	1/1958	CIÉ	Refurbished 1974	1976	?
713	3/1958	UTA 128	Conv to hauled coach 1975	8/1972	5/1980
714	3/1958	CIÉ	Refurbished 1974	1976	?
715	5/1958	UTA 129	Destroyed by fire 5/1960; rebuilt 1962 Conv to hauled coach 1975	11/1974	5/1980
716	5/1958	CIÉ		?1975	

No	Built	1958	Remarks	Last used	Disposed
901	7/1958	UTA 131		7/1974	5/1975
902	7/1958	UTA 132		7/1972	3/1975
903	8/1958	UTA 133	Withdrawn due to bomb damage	3/1972	?
904	7/1958	CIÉ		1975	?
905	9/1958	UTA 134		7/1972	3/1975
906	9/1958	CIÉ		1975	?
907	10/1958	UTA 135		9/1972	3/1975
908	10/1958	CIÉ	Fire damage 1/1960	1/1960	scr 5/1969

BUT trailers CIÉ cars retained their GNR numbers rendered c268ℕ, etc.

No	Built	Class	Type	Seats	Lavs	BUT Fitted	1958	Remarks	Disposed
144	1927	B5	Diner	14/22	–	10/1958	CIÉ	Fitted by CIÉ	9/1964
88	1938	B6	Diner	30	–	12/1957	UTA 552	Preserved by RPSI as No 88	1973
266	1936	B8	Buffet	27	–	5/1958	UTA 551	Last used 1970	6/1973
267	1936	B8	Buffet	27	–	9/1957	CIÉ		7/1961
124	1942	B9	Buffet	24	–	6/1957	UTA 553	Last used 2/1965	4/1971
268	1951	B10	Buffet	26	–	?	CIÉ	Later AEC fitted by CIÉ	1/1973
227	1949	C2	FK	36	2	9/1957	UTA 561	Alt to CK 3/1961, L/U 6/1971	9/1975
396	1923	D3	BSK	40	1	8/1958	CIÉ	BUT fitted to operate on 'Enniskillen express'. Now at Belturbet	9/1965
231	1948	D5	BFK	18	1	12/1957	UTA 562	Last used 11/1974	2/1975
232	1948	D5	BFK	18	1	?1958	CIÉ	Later ran as BSK	7/1972
20	1935	F16	CK	24/24	2	12/1957	UTA 571	Alt to SK by UTA, L/U 6/1971	3/1973
24	1935	F16	BFK	18	1	3/1961	CIÉ	Fitted by CIÉ	6/1969
29	1935	F16	BFK	18	1	9/1958	UTA 572	Last used 6/1971	7/1973
79	1944	F16	CK	24/24	2	?	CIÉ		1/1972
89	1939	F16	CK	24/24	2	1/1958	UTA 573	Last used 4/1971	5/1975
197	1946	F17	CK	24/24	2	?	CIÉ		1/1972
135	1942	K15	SO	70	1	1957	CIÉ		7/1972
176	1942	K15	SO	70	1	6/1957	UTA 583	Last used 8/1972	6/1975
177	1942	K15	SO	70	1	7/1957	UTA 584	Last used 6/1971	5/1975
97	1941	K23	Buffet	47	1	7/1958	CIÉ		1/1969
127	1941	K23	Buffet	47	1	10/1958	UTA 556	Bar removed 1966 (72 seats) '70' class fitted 5/1969 as 727	–
53	1937	L12	BSO	21	1	4/1958	UTA 591	Last used 9/1972	1974
94	1937	L12	BSO	21	1	1/1958	UTA 592	Last used 7/1974	1974
114	1940	L13	BSO	21	1	?	CIÉ	Preserved by RPSI	3/1973
175	1942	L14	BSO	21	1	6/1958	UTA 594	L/U 4/1974, later PWD brake	7/1980
189	1943	L14	BSO	21	1	7/1958	UTA 595	L/U 8/1972, later PWD brake	1982
192	1943	L14	BSO	21	1	?	CIÉ		3/1964

Note: Nos 176 (583), 189 (595), 227 (561), 231 (562) were also preserved by the RPSI but subsequently lost to fire or rot.

(d) CIÉ railcars

AEC Park Royal railcars 12/32 seats, 1 lav; similar to GNR cars but tables at seats and wired for MU operation. Nos 2648–57 had no tables or lavatories and 12/36 seats for suburban work. Nos 2658/9 were built for the W&T section with high density seating of 80 and 96 respectively.

No	Built	Reseated	Converted push-pull	No	Type	Remarks	Withdrawn
2600	3/1952	1970 (70)	12/1973	6109	DSO		9/1981
2601	3/1952	1971 (91)	–	–	–		1975
2602	3/1952	1970 (70)	6/1973	6203	CSO		9/1987
2603	3/1952	1971 (91)	–	–	–		1975
2604	1/1953	1972 (70)	10/1973	6108	DSO		7/1982
2605	1/1953	1971 (83)	12/1972	6302	SO		1985
2606	1/1953	1971 (70)	12/1972	6201	CSO		11/1983
2607	1/1953	1970? (70)	4/1973	6309	SO		11/1983
2608	1/1953	1970? (70)	4/1973	6104	DSO		10/1976
2609	1/1953	1971 (91)	12/1973	6327	SO		9/1981
2610	2/1953	1970? (70)	2/1973	6204	CSO		10/1976
2611	2/1953	1970 (70)	4/1974	6325	SO		11/1983
2612	2/1953	–	–	–	–	Destroyed in Multyfarnham fire	8/1957
2613	2/1953	1970 (70)	12/1973	6323	SO		10/1983
2614	2/1953	1960 (78)	–	–	–	Damaged Hazelhatch1/1955; rebuilt 1960 Conv to MS 2666 (1961)	–
2615	2/1953	1971 (83)	6/1973	6318	SO		11/1982
2616	3/1953	1971 (70)	–	–	–	Not 6212 as recorded elsewhere	1975
2617	3/1953	1960 (94)	–	–	–	Burned 6/1957; rebuilt 1960 Conv to MS 2667 (9/1961)	–
2618	3/1953	1972 (70)	2/1973	6103	DSO		11/1983
2619	3/1953	1970? (90)	4/1973	6306	SO		11/1983
2620	3/1953	1970 (70)	3/1974	6112	DSO		5/1980
2621	4/1953	1971 (83)	12/1972	6304	SO		10/1983
2622	4/1953	1971 (78)	2/1974	6110	DSO		4/1985
2623	4/1953	1970 (91)	1973	6331	SO		1984
2624	5/1953	1971 (78)	4/1974	6111	DSO		9/1987
2625	5/1953	1971 (91)	2/1974	6326	SO		2/1982
2626	5/1953	1970? (70)	12/1972	6102	DSO		10/1976
2627	5/1953	1970? (90)	8/1973	6313	SO		4/1985
2628	6/1953	1971 (78)	2/1974	6210	CSO		11/1983
2629	6/1953	1972 (90)	4/1973	6328	SO		1985
2630	6/1953	1970 (78)	5/1973	6206	CSO		9/1987
2631	6/1953	1970? (90)	–	–	–		1972
2632	7/1953	1971 (70)	12/1972	6202	CSO		1985
2633	7/1953	1970 (70)	6/1974	6212	CSO	See 2616 above	5/1980
2634	8/1953	1972 (70)	6/1973	6106	DSO		4/1985
2635	8/1953	1971 (87)	12/1973	6330	SO		9/1981

No	Built	Reseated	Converted push-pull	No	Type	Remarks	Withdrawn
2636	9/1953	1970? (70)	–	–	–		1972
2637	9/1953	1970 (91)	6/1973	6314	SO		1985
2638	10/1953	1972 (70)	5/1973	6105	DSO		4/1983
2639	10/1953	1970? (90)	10/1973	6310	SO		1985
2640	11/1953	1972 (70)	8/1973	6107	DSO		9/1987
2641	11/1953	1971 (91)	12/1973	6317	SO		11/1983
2642	12/1953	1970 (70)	–	–	–		1975
2643	12/1953	1970 (70)	4/1974	6211	CSO		11/1983
2644	1/1954	1971 (78)	12/1973	6209	CSO		10/1983
2645	1/1954	1971 (83)	12/1972	6303	SO		7/1982
2646	2/1954	1971 (70)	12/1972	6101	DSO		10/1976
2647	2/1954	1957 (80)	12/1972	6301	SO	Reseated 94 (1962–3)	1985
2648	3/1954	1957 (80)	–	–	–	Seating reduced to 78	1975
2649	3/1954	1957 (80)	1974	6332	SO	Reseated 94 (1962–3)	1984
2650	4/1954	1957 (80)	12/1973	6208	CSO	Seating reduced to 78	4/1985
2651	4/1954	1970 (80)	–	–	–	Reseated 94 (1962–3)	1975
2652	5/1954	1957 (80)	8/1973	6207	CSO	Seating reduced to 78 Reseated 83 (1970)	10/1983
2653	5/1954	1957 (80)	1973	6322	SO	Reseated 94 (1962–3)	1984
2654	6/1954	1957 (80)	–	–	–	Seating reduced to 78	1975
2655	6/1954	1957 (80)	8/1973	6324	SO	Reseated 94 (1962–3)	8/1982
2656	7/1954	1957 (80)	–	–	–	Burnt near Tullamore 6/1958 Conv to MS 2668 (1961)	–
2657	7/1954	1955 (96)	10/1973	6311	SO	Reseated for W&T section Reseated 70 (1970)	9/1987
2658	9/1954	1971 (83)	4/1973	6205	CSO	Built for W&T section	11/1983
2659	9/1954		6/1974	6329	SO	Built for W&T section	1985

Bulleid AEC railcars 12/32 seats, 1 toilet, as built; taller than 2600–59 with a flatter front. Rebuilt in 1961 as SO powered intermediates, as cars 2666–8 below. Odd numbered cars had no van.

No	Built	Rebuilt PI	Converted push-pull	No	Type	Remarks	Withdrawn
2660	1957	1961 (52)	5/1973	6312	SO		1985
2661	1957	1961 (64)	5/1974	6320	SO		11/1983
2662	1957	1961 (52)	4/1974	6319	SO		4/1985
2663	1957	1961 (64)	2/1973	6305	SO		10/1976
2664	1957	1961 (52)	2/1974	6316	SO		9/1987
2665	1957	1961 (64)	2/1973	6307	SO		10/1976

AEC powered intermediates Rebuilt from 2600 series cars which had been damaged in accidents.

No	Built orig	Rebuilt	Converted push-pull	No	Type	Remarks	Withdrawn
2666	1953	1961 (52s)	5/1974	6321	SO	Orig No 2614	11/1983
2667	1953	1961 (64s)	6/1974	6315	SO	Orig No 2617	1985
2668	1954	1961 (52s)	5/1973	6308	SO	Orig No 2656	11/1983

CIÉ AEC trailers This list has been compiled from information researched by Colin Holliday. The dates of wiring for railcar use are unknown, though those built in 1953–5 were probably wired from new. AEC-fitted carriages could run in hauled formations as well.

No	Built	Type	Seats	Lavs	Remarks	Wdn
74D	1906	Tea Car	28	–	Ex DSER, orig 1st class, Became tool van 462A, 11/1963	?
351	1902	Saloon	26	2	President's saloon, preserved	–
353	1906	Diner	22	–	Rosslare diner – clerestory roof	7/1968
838	1905	SO	24	–	Tea Car by 1924, steel panelled 1957	10/1965
1130	1914	Kitchen	–	–	Originally 3rd class, conv by 1955	2/1969
1145	1963	FO	42	2	Destroyed at Buttevant	8/1980
1146	1963	FO	42	2	Destroyed at Botanic NIR	10/1978
1300	1916	SK	64	2	Ren 4019 (1969)	5/1971
1301	1916	SK	64	2	Ren 4020 (1969)	?1972
1308	1923	SK	64	2	Ren 4026 (1969)	?1972
1331	1936	SO	72	–	76 before gangways added	1973
1332	1936	SO	72	–	76 before gangways added	1973
1333	1936	SO	72	–	76 before gangways added Sold to RPSI	1973
1334	1936	SO	72	–	76 before gangways added	1973
1350	1952	SK	56	2	Conv to GSV 3203, 1977	by 10/1984
1351	1952	SK	56	2	Conv to GSV 3210, 1977	11/1992
1352	1953	SK	56	2	Conv to GSV 3211, 1977	2/1983
1353	1953	SK	56	2	Conv to GSV 3212, 1977	8/1989
1354	1953	SK	56	2	Conv to GSV 3208, 1977	11/1992
1355	1953	SK	56	2	Conv to GSV 3209, 1977	8/1989
1356	1953	SK	56	2		1984?
1357	1953	SK	56	2		by 6/1985
1358	1953	SK	56	2		by 6/1985
1359	1953	SK	56	2		by 6/1985
1360	1953	SK	56	2		6/1983
1361	1953	SK	56	2		6/1985
1362	1953	SK	56	2		6/1985
1363	1953	SK	56	2		6/1984
1364	1953	SK	56	2	GNR AEC fitted	by 6/1985
1365	1953	SK	56	2		6/1984
1366	1953	SK	56	2		1984
1367	1953	SK	56	2	GNR AEC fitted	by 6/1985

No	Built	Type	Seats	Lavs	Remarks	Wdn
1368	1953	SK	56	2		by 6/1985
1369	1953	SK	56	2		1984
1370	1953	SK	56	2		1984
1371	1953	SK	56	2		1984
1397	1955	SO	82	–		2/1977
1398	1955	SO	82	–	Toilet added later	11/1993
1399	1955	SO	82	–	Toilet added later	10/1992
1400	1955	SO	82	–	Preserved Clonakilty	5/1994
1402	1955	SO	82	–	Toilet added later	1/1995
1403	1955	SO	82	–		1/1995
1407	1955	SO	82	–	W&T driving trailer	10/1992
1409	1955	SO	82	–		12/1992
1410	1955	SO	82	–		11/1993
1411	1955	SO	82	–		12/1992
1414	1955	SO	82	–	Collision Dalkey, scr NI	11/1979
1418	1955	SO	82	–		10/1992
1514	1964	SO	64	2		–
1515	1964	SO	64	2		–
1517	1964	SO	64	2		–
1519	1964	SO	64	2	Damaged at Tralee 11/1993	12/1996
1520	1964	SO	64	2		–
1522	1964	SO	64	2		–
1906	1953	BSO	40	2	Driving trailer	8/1987
2092	1915	Diner	24	–	Refurbished 1969	1973
2093	1915	Diner	24	–	Refurbished 1969	1973
2111	1928	C	50/48	–	Later 40/48, ren 542A, 5/1967	3/1973
2112	1928	C	50/48	–	Later 40/48	7/1969
2113	1928	C	50/48	–	Later 40/48	7/1966
2128	1951	CK	18/32	2	Ren 1620 (1972), conv to van 2580 (1974)	?
2129	1951	CK	18/32	2	Ren 1616 (1972), conv to van 2581 (1974)	?
2163	1957	CO	40/36	–	Ren 1605 (1971)	7/1988
2165	1957	CO	40/36	–	Ren 1602 (1971), ren 1915, to RPSI scr	1985
2166	1957	CO	40/36	–	Ren 1606 (1971), ren 1919	10/1985
2169	1957	CO	40/36	–	Ren 1608 (1971), ren 1921	12/1987
2172	1961	CKO	18/28	2	Ren 1931 (1975)	by 1985
2400	1931	Diner	18	–	Rebuilt 7/1957	2/1973
2401	1931	Diner	24	–		2/1973
2402	1961	Buffet	18	–		by 1985
2405	1953	Buffet	39	1		by 1985
2406	1953	Buffet	39	1		1984
2407	1953	Buffet	39	1	Altered to Kitchen car (1969)	7/1987
2408	1953	Buffet	39	1	Destroyed at Buttevant	8/1980
2409	1953	Buffet	39	1	Sold to GSRPS	1984
2410	1954	Buffet	39	1	Damaged shunting Charleville	2/1971
2411	1954	Buffet	39	1	Destroyed by fire Limerick	5/1969

No	Built	Type	Seats	Lavs	Remarks	Wdn
2412	1954	Buffet	39	1	Conv to Cafeteria, 1976; destroyed at Buttevant	8/1980
2413	1954	Buffet	39	1		7/1987
2414	1954	Buffet	39	1		8/1989
2415	1954	Buffet	39	1		11/1989
2416	1954	Buffet	39	1	Converted to Cafeteria Car, 1976	1990
2417	1954	Buffet	39	1	Fire bombed Enterprise 10/1978	10 1978
2418	1954	Buffet	39	1	Sold to SGPS, 1985, scr 11/1992	1985
2419	1956	Buffet	39	1	Preserved at Downpatrick Railway Museum	12/1987
2420	1956	Buffet	39	1	Converted to Snack Car; sold to RPSI, scr 1995	7/1987
2421	1956	Buffet	39	1	Preserved by RPSI	1988
2422	1956	Buffet	39	1	Preserved by RPSI	by 1985

Ex-SLNCR railcar 59 seats, Gardner 102 bhp engine.

No	Built	Orig	Remarks	Wdn
2509	7/1947	B	Wdn 10/1957, sold to CIÉ 10/1958, reinstated 7/1959 Stored for possible preservation	9/1971

West Clare section 3'0"g railcars Similar to CDRJC Nos 19, 20; 41 seats, Gardner 6LW engine.

No	Built	Orig	Then	Remarks	Wdn
3386	3/1952	286	386	To Bord na Mona, Oweninny, Co Mayo	1/1961
3387	3/1952	287	387	To Bord na Mona, Oweninny, Co Mayo	1/1961
3388	5/1952	288	388	To Bord na Mona, Derrygreenagh, Co Offaly	1/1961
3389	5/1952	289	389	To Bord na Mona, Blackwater, Co Offaly	1/1961

West Clare section 3'0"g trailers Converted from former bus bodies placed on Tralee and Dingle underframes, 43 seats (except 49c, possibly built on a Cavan and Leitrim underframe).

No	Built	Remarks	Wdn
46c	1952	To Bord na Mona, Boora, Co Offaly; later scrapped	1/1961
47c	1952	To Bord na Mona, Derrygreenagh, Co Offaly Now on Cavan & Leitrim Rly, Dromod	1/1961
48c	1952	To Bord na Mona, Blackwater, Co Offaly; body scrapped 10/1993 Frames and bogies on Cavan & Leitrim Rly, Dromod	1/1961
49c	1952	35 seats	1/1961

Bibliography

Allen, Jonathan M, *35 Years of NIR 1967–2002,* Colourpoint, 2003

Barrie, DSM, *The Dundalk Newry & Greenore Railway,* Oakwood Press, 1957

Boocock, CP, *Irish Railway Album,* Ian Allan, 1968

Boocock, Colin, *Irish railways – 40 years of Change 1956–1996,* Atlantic Publishing, 1997

Coakham, Desmond, *Belfast & County Down Railway,* Midland Publishing, 1998

Clements, RN, and Robbins, JM, *The ABC of Irish Locomotives,* Ian Allan, 1949

Collins, Michael, *Rail Versus Road in Ireland 1900–2000,* Colourpoint, 2000

Currie, JRL, *The Northern Counties Railway, Volume 2,* David & Charles, 1974

Ferris, Tom, *Irish Railways in Colour,* Midland Publishing, 1992

Johnston, Norman, *Locomotives of the GNRI,* Colourpoint, 1999

Jones, Peter, *Irish Railways Traction and Travel (3nd ed),* Metro Enterprises, 1994

Patterson, Dr EM, *The Belfast and County Down Railway (2nd ed),* David and Charles, 1982

Patterson, Dr EM, *The Castlederg and Victoria Bridge Tramway,* Colourpoint, 1998

Patterson, Dr EM, *The County Donegal Railways,* David and Charles, 1962

Patterson, Dr EM, *The Great Northern Railway of Ireland,* Oakwood Press, 1962

Sprinks, Neil, *Sligo, Leitrim and Northern Counties Railway,* IRRS London, 1970